Catiline's Dream

Catiline's Dream

An Essay on Ibsen's Plays

JAMES HURT

University of Illinois Press

URBANA · CHICAGO · LONDON

Library of Congress Catalog Card No. 79–186346

ISBN 0–252–00238–5

Contents

Acknowledgments

ALL QUOTATIONS from Ibsen's plays, except *Catiline* and *Emperor and Galilean,* are from the translations of Michael Meyer (New York, 1960–66). Quotations from *Catiline* and *Emperor and Galilean* are from the translations by James Walter McFarlane and Graham Orton in the *Oxford Ibsen* (London, 1963–70). Quotations from Ibsen's poems are from the translations by F. E. Garrett (New York, 1912) and those from his letters and other nondramatic writings are from the translations by Evert Sprinchorn (New York, 1964). I have also consulted with profit the translations of William Archer and his collaborators, those which have thus far appeared in the *Oxford Ibsen* series under the general editorship of James Walter McFarlane, and those by Eva LeGallienne, Una Ellis-Fermor, Peter Watts, and Rolfe Fjelde.

I should also like to acknowledge my general indebtedness to earlier Ibsen critics, especially Georg Brandes, G. B. Shaw, William Archer, Hermann Weigand, Halvdan Koht, Brian Downs, M. C. Bradbrook, P. F. D. Tennent, Janko Lavrin, Raymond Williams, John Northam, Ludwig Binswanger, Eric Bentley, F. L. Lucas, G. Wilson Knight, Robert Brustein, and Maurice Valency. Among recent studies, essays by Brian Johnston and James E. Kerans have been especially helpful.

The chief sources for the analysis of the schizoid personality in the second chapter are W. R. D. Fairbairn's *Psychoanalytic Studies of the Personality* (London, 1952), D. W. Winnicott's *The Matu-*

rational Processes and the Facilitating Environment (London, 1965), Melanie Klein's *Contributions to Psycho-Analysis, 1921–45* (London, 1948), Harry Guntrip's *Schizoid Phenomena, Object-Relations, and the Self* (London, 1968), R. D. Laing's *The Divided Self* (London, 1960) and *The Self and Others* (London, 1961), and Rollo May's *Love and Will* (New York, 1969).

I owe personal debts to a number of people: to the University of Illinois Research Board, for grants which gave me time for writing; to Beverly Seward, for her careful typing of the manuscript; to Lorena Neumann, for her meticulous editorial work; and to Phyllis Hurt and Christopher, Ross, and Matthew Hurt, for their patience and love. A number of friends in the University of Illinois English Department helped me by reading and criticizing sections of the book: Ed and Agnes Brandabur, Bert Petersen, Charles Shattuck, Leon Waldoff, and David Whisnant. I also owe a great debt to my colleagues in the Depot Theatre, where I have had an opportunity over the past several years to work in a theatrical environment of great freedom and congeniality. Among these last, I owe most to Elizabeth Hiller, who followed the progress of the book at every stage and made a number of important contributions to it.

Catiline's Dream

1. The Dream I

Ibsen's plays do not depend for their interest on the action, or on the incidents. Even the characters, faultlessly drawn though they be, are not the first thing in his plays. But the naked drama—either the perception of a great truth, or the opening up of a great question, or a great conflict which is almost independent of the conflicting actors—this is what primarily rivets our attention.

JAMES JOYCE (1900)

IN 1898 Ibsen wrote, in a note of "Advice to the Reader" in the collected edition of his works,

> Simultaneously with the production of my works another generation of readers has grown up, and I have often noticed with regret that their knowledge of my more recent works was considerably more detailed than of my earlier ones. Consequently these readers lack an awareness of the mutual connections between the plays, and I attribute a not insignificant part of the strange, imperfect, and misleading interpretations that my later works have been subjected to in so many quarters to this lack of awareness. Only by grasping and comprehending my entire production as a continuous and coherent whole will the reader be able to receive the precise impression I sought to convey in the individual parts of it.

If we are to follow Ibsen's advice and try to understand all his plays as "a continuous and coherent whole," we must begin at the beginning—with *Catiline,* the fascinating and neglected play with which Ibsen, at the age of twenty, started his career as a playwright. Ibsen himself pointed out how accurately *Catiline* foreshadowed his later work. When he published a second, "jubilee," edition of the play in 1875, a quarter of a century after he had written it and after he had written *Brand, Peer Gynt, The League of Youth,* and *Emperor and Galilean,* he wrote in the preface: "The contents of the book as regards details I had almost forgotten; but by reading it through anew I found that it nevertheless contained a great deal which I could still acknowledge, particularly if it be remembered that it is my first undertaking. Much, around which my later writings center, the contradiction between ability and desire, between will and possibility, the intermingled tragedy and comedy in the individual—appeared already here in vague foreshadowings."

Ibsen wrote *Catiline* when he was an apothecary's apprentice in the isolated little town of Grimstad, and Catiline's ambition to destroy Rome with an "avalanche of fire" was, Ibsen himself admitted, a rather violent expression of his own attitude toward Grimstad. In 1870 he wrote to a correspondent who had requested some notes on the circumstances of the composition of his plays, *"Catiline* was written in a little provincial town, where it was impossible for me to express all that was fermenting in me, except by playing crazy, riotous pranks that brought down upon me the ill will of all the respectable citizens, who could not enter into the world where I fought my battle alone."

He gave a fuller account of the circumstances of the composition of *Catiline* in his preface to the 1875 edition. He had followed the revolutionary activities in Europe during 1848–49 with great excitement and had written "ringing poems of encouragement" to the Magyars and a series of sonnets to King Oscar, calling on him to march into Slesvig at the head of a liberating army. The analogy was not lost on him between those large struggles and his own battles with the pillars of society in Grimstad, where he felt "cramped by conditions and circumstances of life." In this mood, he read, in preparation for his university entrance examinations, Sallust's *Catiline* and Cicero's Catilinarian orations. He "swallowed these documents" and within a few months had completed his play.

Despite its classical sources, there is little of the classical about *Catiline* but much of the nineteenth-century gothic. Ibsen makes Rome an archetypal gothic setting, murky, sinister, and full of crumbling ruins. Catiline himself becomes a thoroughly Byronic hero, a gloomy fallen angel racked by secret guilt, morbid passions, and megalomaniacal dreams. The plot seems to have been Ibsen's own invention; apparently he had read none of the earlier Catiline plays. He opens the play just before Cicero's denunciation of Catiline in the senate. Catiline is a tormented, restless soul, torn by

4

conflicts between his hatred of the corrupt senate, his ambition to restore the glory of Rome, and his guilt over his own licentious life. He goes to the Temple of Vesta to seduce Furia, one of the priestesses. Furia yields to him, but makes him swear to avenge the death of her sister, who drowned herself after she was abandoned by her seducer. When Catiline reveals that he himself was the seducer, Furia's love turns to hate, and in her frenzy she lets the Vestal flame go out. For this crime she is sentenced to be buried alive.

Meanwhile Catiline returns to his wife, Aurelia, and they plan to retire from Rome to Aurelia's family villa in Gaul. His friend Curius has also fallen in love with Furia and rescues her from the tomb. She appears before Catiline and tells him that she will pursue him to his death. Catiline is almost hypnotized by her and he yields to her challenge to win glory by rebelling against Rome. He cancels his plan to retire with Aurelia and announces to his corrupt friends that he will lead them in revolt.

The last act shows the outcome of this decision. Catiline has been betrayed by Curius and Lentulus and his revolt is doomed. He decides to die rather than surrender. The last scene brings together the three central characters: Catiline, Furia, and Aurelia. Catiline enters, the only survivor of the battle with the legions, and Furia summons him to go with her down into the "shadow land of death." Catiline, however, says that he is held in the land of the living by Aurelia's love. Furia tells him to kill her, and the distraught Catiline takes her dagger and stabs Aurelia. Furia then stabs Catiline and they prepare to descend to "gloomy Tartarus." The dying Aurelia, however, appears one last time, repels Furia with the power of her love, and she and Catiline die in each other's arms, rising up to "light and peace" as dawn breaks.

The gothicism of this lurid plot throws into relief the gothic elements in Ibsen's later work. The traditional emphasis upon Ibsen's "realism" has obscured the gothicism in his plays, but it appears throughout his career. Indeed, Ibsen's plays, considered as elaborations of a myth of the romantic self, are special and intensely personal developments of the thinly disguised myths of the self embodied in the gothic novels, with their recurring treatments of a persecuted maiden—the personification of the romantic soul—pursued by degenerate aristocrats, monks and other personifications of traditional authority through dream landscapes of crumbling castles and monasteries. There is something of the guilt-ridden Byronic hero not only in Brand and Peer Gynt, but also in such realistic protagonists as Gregers Werle, John Rosmer, Halvard Solness, and Arnold Rubek. Behind such pairs as Gerd and Agnes, Rebecca and Beata, and Hilde and Aline are the gothic archetypes of the Fatal Woman and the Persecuted Maiden, and behind the Helmer doll's house, Mrs. Alving's Rosenvold, and the gloomy Rosmersholm stand the ruined abbeys and castles of *The Monk* and *The Castle of Otranto*—symbols, like Ibsen's ancestral seats, of a decaying past and crumbling ego-ideals.

The gothicism of *Catiline* is a psychological gothicism, a method and a vocabulary for escaping the restrictions of factual history and surface credibility and for representing the psychological and spiritual progress of the protagonist. *Catiline* makes no pretensions to being a truthful or even a plausible representation of its historical subject; its hero is a mythic embodiment of the rebellious romantic self in quest of realization and its plot contains the basic elements out of which Ibsen was to construct his later, more sophisticated, studies of "the intermingled tragedy and comedy in humanity and in the individual."

These basic elements are encapsulated in a single scene of the play, a scene in the last act in which Catiline, in camp and awaiting the assault of the legions of Rome, reports a dream he has just had to Manlius, the old warrior who has supported him:

> I see a vaulted chamber, black as any grave; . . .
> high the ceiling like the heavens, thick with thunder clouds,
> and the strangest swarm of visions, as some phantom chase,
> whirled around in wild confusion, like a hurricane
> when it sweeps in fury over foam-topped ocean waves.
> But amid the crazy turmoil now and then emerge
> figures from a better home, garlanded with flowers. . . .
> Round about them all the darkness turns to radiant light. . . .
> In the middle of the chamber stands a curious pair;
> both are women, one is tall and dark as night is she,
> and the other fair as evening when the daylight fades.
> Ah, so curiously familiar both did seem to me,

6

one of them was smiling gently, with a look of peace;
from the other's haughty glances savage lightning flashed.
Terrible, and yet with pleasure I observed this sight.
One is standing proudly and the other meanwhile leans
on the table where these women played at some mysterious
    game . . .
all the time the crowding visions floated up and down.
Then at last their game is over and she sinks into the ground,
she who gazes with such radiant gentle eyes of love,
and the fair resplendent figures vanished with her too.
Now the din is growing wild and wilder all the time,
and the darker woman's glances burned like fiery flame.
Then before me all things faded, her alone I saw,
but what else I dreamed of later in my fevered sleep
now lies hidden deep inside me, veiled from memory;
could I but recall what followed; it has gone, alas.

It is not until the concluding lines of the play that Catiline recalls the rest of the dream:

Oh what bliss! Now I remember my forgotten dream,
how that chamber's darkness was dispersed by streaming rays,
how the song of little children hailed the new-born day.
Ah, my eyes are growing dim, my strength is running out,
but my mind is full of light as never yet before,
and my past erratic wanderings lie there clear to see.
Yes, my life has been a storm beneath night's lightning flash,
but my death is morning twilight, tinged with rosy hues.

This dream contains a remarkable concentration of elements that appear throughout *Catiline* and throughout Ibsen's work: the dark, claustrophobic setting, the tone of almost panic-stricken anxiety, the pair of contrasting women, the movement from darkness to dawn, and the ultimate ecstatic death of the central figure. An understanding of these elements, their relationships, and the ways they figure in "the mutual connections between the plays" will take us far toward an understanding of Ibsen's entire work.

The mythic pattern which underlies all of Ibsen's plays may be summarized in the most naked and unqualified form thus: The hero finds himself in a polluted and stifling *primary home* environment, usually represented as a valley by a fjord. Perhaps he recalls a time when this environment was not poisoned, when it was joyful

7

and wholesome, or perhaps the memory of such a time may survive only as a persistent sense of loss. At any rate, the hero leaves his home and reaches a point of detachment and perspective, usually represented as *the heights,* an intermediate point between the valley and the mountain peaks, from which he can achieve a "higher view of things." On the heights, the hero renounces the home environment and adopts a *project of the will,* some goal to which he will devote himself. At this point there occurs a *first child-death,* and a *fascinating woman* and a *gentle woman* appear. The fascinating woman tries to tempt the hero to some fatal action, usually to follow her to the mountain peaks, but the hero, for the moment at least, resists her lure and returns to the valley, where he establishes a *secondary home* and unites himself with the gentle woman. His relationship with the gentle woman usually takes the form of a cooperation in working toward the project of the will. This relationship, however, gradually deteriorates, embittering both the hero and the woman and often terminating in the *death of the gentle woman.* At this point the *project of the will collapses, a second child-death* occurs, and the hero begins an *ascent to the peaks,* where he dies an ecstatic death, often in the company of the fascinating woman.

This myth, thus summarized, is a composite construction; in only a few plays does it appear in its full form and with all the geographic details present. The plot may begin at any point in the myth, and sometimes almost the entire pattern is presented retrospectively. The pattern may be displaced, disguised, or fragmented; sexes may be inverted, characters may be merged, and the pattern may be reduplicated within a single play. But the general sequence of events is remarkably stable, and the geographic imagery, though it may be present only metaphorically, is persistent enough and consistent enough to serve as a guide through the myth's transformations.

The myth appears most explicitly in the early plays and the late plays. In the middle plays it "goes underground" and is displaced by the techniques of realism. Even in the middle plays, however, the shape of the action remains very stable, disguised though it may be by detailed verisimilitude. Ibsen's work as a whole thus assumes a cyclic pattern, beginning in fairly explicit myth, arching out into complex forms of displacement, and then circling back to myth again in the last four plays.

The *primary home* of an Ibsen protagonist is invariably stifling and poisonous, though he may preserve an indistinct memory of a time when it was free and innocent. Almost always in a dark valley, the primary home is fraught with guilt and anxiety. When Brand, for example, in Act I pauses on the mountain path and looks down into the valley, he sees the red roof of his widowed mother's cottage:

> The widow's cottage!
> My childhood home!
> Memories swarm upon me,
> And memories of memories. There, among
> The stones on the shore, I lived my childhood alone.
>
> A heavy weight lies on me, the burden
> Of being tied to another human being
> Whose spirit pointed earthwards. Everything
> That I desired so passionately before
> Trembles and fades. My strength and courage fail me,
> My mind and soul are numbed.
> Now, as I approach my home, I find
> Myself a stranger; I awake bound, shorn,
> And tamed, like Samson in the harlot's lap.

Rome is similarly poisoned for Catiline:

> here soaring pride of spirit is repressed . . .
> here baseness stifles every spark of brilliance
> before it bursts forth into leaping flame.

And for Julian, in *Emperor and Galilean,* Constantinople is a similar lowland of the spirit; he feels that he is "choking" in the palace air. Peer Gynt's attitude toward Aase and her cottage is more complex than Brand's attitude toward his own mother's cottage, but his memories of childhood "numb" him just as effectively. Aase and Peer have escaped from their troubles into "romancing of princes and trolls / And all kinds of beasts." It is not until the closing moments of the play that he fights his way out of these webs of dreams and illusions.

9

In the middle plays, the primary homes have similar associations. In *A Doll's House,* Nora's father has made her into a "doll-child" just as Torvald has made her into a "doll-wife." Nora shares with Brand, Peer Gynt, Ellida Wangel, and Hedda Gabler the circumstance of having been reared by a single parent of the opposite sex, and special situations with the same implications appear in the childhoods of a number of other protagonists. In *Rosmersholm* and *The Lady from the Sea,* Rebecca's relationship with Dr. West and Ellida's childhood with her father in a lonely lighthouse have overtones of the folklore motif of a maiden enthralled by a powerful enchanter.

The protagonist's memories of a polluted primary home may be mingled with memories of another, earlier environment of Edenic innocence. For Catiline it is Aurelia's villa in Gaul:

> Where else, I wonder, was the grass so green?
> Where else such coolness in the forest's shade?
> The little house peeps forth between the trees
> and beckons with its cosy air of peace.

For Julian it is his boyhood home at Macellum, which he contrasts with the stifling environment of Constantinople: "Macellum lies high up. Not another town is as high in the whole of Cappadocia; ah how the fresh wind sweeps over from the Taurus snows . . . !"

The first major action in the myth is the protagonist's struggle up out of the suffocation of the primary home to a position of objectivity which may be called *the heights.* The simplest and most extreme treatment of this phase of the action appears in "On the Fells," the strange poem which Ibsen wrote in 1859–60. The Speaker in "On the Fells" is a young man who sets off at the beginning of the poem for what is intended to be a short hunting trip on the fells (the desolate, rolling upland). He finds it difficult to part from his mother, by whom he has been reared alone, and from his fiancee, but he is drawn to the fells, where "All lawless thoughts, all dark desires / Are driven from my heart." He still intends to return shortly, but he meets a Strange Hunter with cold, bewitching eyes, which rob the Speaker of his "power to will." Months pass, and at Christmas the Speaker notices "a curious light" in his mother's house far below. The house is on fire; the Speaker cries out in agony, but the Strange Hunter is suddenly beside him, laughing a "short dry laugh" and pointing out the beauty of the blaze against the darkness. Strangely, the Speaker quiets his emotions and agrees: " 'Twas a wonderful effect!"

In the ninth and final section of the poem, summer has come; the Speaker has been on the fells for a year. Now he hears wedding bells and sees his fiancee riding to church to be married. He needs no coaching this time: "I held to my eye my hollowed hand / To get the perspective right." Again the Stranger is beside him with his "short dry laugh." He tells the Speaker, "You have no more need of me," and departs. In the concluding lines the Speaker congratulates himself that his veins are "parched" where "a flood-tide ran." He looks into his heart and approvingly finds there "all symbols of petrification." He will remain on the fells: "Up here on the fells must be freedom and God, / Men do but grope, in the valley."

The theme and materials of "On the Fells" are echoed dramatically in *Love's Comedy* (1862), with its final scene in which the poet Falk surrenders his love Svanhild to her businessman suitor Guldstad and climbs the mountain to isolation and poetry:

SVANHILD. And you'll go upward to your goal in poetry!
FALK. In poetry, yes; for every man's a poet
    whether in government, or school, or church,
    whether his calling's glorious or lowly,
    who in his work expresses the ideal.
    Yes, I go upwards; the winged steed is saddled;
    I know you have ennobled my whole life.
    And now, farewell!

Ibsen himself suggested the connection between the two works in an 1870 letter: "Not until I was married did I take life seriously. The fruit of this change was a rather long poem, 'Paa Vidderne' ["On the Fells"]. The desire for freedom which pervades this poem did not, however, receive its full expression until I wrote *Love's Comedy*."

"On the Fells" and *Love's Comedy* are hardly intelligible if read as endorsements of callousness and isolation. Both are, as Ibsen said, poetic and mythic expressions of the "desire for freedom";

11

they present the first stage in the movement out from the stifling home environment to a position of at least temporary freedom. But both have a sinister undercurrent that is to become explicit in Ibsen's later plays in which the latter stages of this movement are presented. Falk's answer to the "call of the ideal" anticipates Gregers Werle's fanaticism in *The Wild Duck,* and the Speaker's pride in his power to view the world "through his hollowed hand" in "On the Fells" contains within it the seeds of Rubek's terrible remorse at having turned Irene into a statue in *When We Dead Awaken.*

On the heights, the protagonist adopts a *project of the will.* The project of the will adopted by the Speaker in "On the Fells" is left unspecified; the Speaker "rallies to the mountain-call" but we are not told what the call is. Falk's project is poetry, though he explicitly includes as poetry any work that "expresses the ideal." Catiline's project is to conquer Rome, Brand's is to remain in the valley and "hallow daily toil to the praise of God," and Peer Gynt's is to leave home and become "emperor of himself."

In the middle plays the decision "on the heights" seldom literally takes place in the mountains, as it does in "On the Fells," *Love's Comedy, Brand,* and *Peer Gynt,* but it has a similar psychological meaning and is usually associated with imagery that connects it with similar decisions in the earlier plays. Nora's rescue of Torvald by means of the forgery is an experience "on the heights" and is marked by the trip to Italy; her project of the will is her decision to preserve her marriage and to withhold the secret of her sacrifice as a means of winning Torvald's respect. Mrs. Alving's midnight flight to Parson Manders and her decision to remain with Captain Alving are similar in their implications, as are Gregers Werle's exile to Hoydal and his mission to present the "claim of the ideal."

The project of the will that appears most often in Ibsen is art, especially in the later plays. Falk, in *Love's Comedy,* is a poet, and it is possible to interpret the Speaker's mission in "On the Fells" as art, and the Strange Hunter, with his advice to aestheticize life, as the "daimon of art." Peer Gynt is a poet who never writes a poem, but Solness and Rubek have sacrificed everything for architecture and sculpture.

Whatever the project of the will is, it is characteristically treated ambiguously and ironically. It may be a laudable goal, but it never represents an absolute good, and it is invariably corrupted by the protagonist's defensive use of it. Catiline's project to restore Rome to its earlier glory, for example, is clearly desirable; the first act is full of examples of the corruption to which Rome has sunk. His motives are lofty:

> they do not know how fast this heart is beating
> for right and freedom, for each noble cause
> which ever stirred in any human breast!

But by the time he begins to pursue his project he seems less motivated by lofty idealism than by a megalomaniacal drive to destroy and thus to imprint his name upon the world:

> All right, if ancient Rome is not to be
> restored to life, then modern Rome shall fall!
> Where stately rows of marble columns stand,
> ah, soon there shall be but a heap of ash!
> The temples shall come tumbling down in ruins,
> and soon the Capitol shall be no more.

Brand's project, to "cure man's sickness of soul," and Peer Gynt's, to be "emperor of himself," are similarly ambiguous; both are apparently commendable, but both are corrupted—Brand's into a sadistic fanaticism and Peer's into a simple selfishness—because they are adopted primarily as defenses against the dangers associated with the valley. Julian's project, to create a Third Empire, suffers the same fate, for the same reason. In the middle, realistic plays the projects are less grandiose, but they have the same kind of ambiguity. Nora Helmer's and Helen Alving's projects of the will, to preserve their marriages by deceit and role-playing, are clearly misguided. Thomas Stockmann's, to help his home town by building the baths, and Gregers Werle's, to bring buried truths to light, sound desirable enough, but they are corrupted by the motives for their adoption. This ambiguity accounts for what sometimes strikes readers as bewildering shifts in Ibsen's values through the middle plays. In one play it seems that the truth should be told at all costs; in the next it seems that it should be concealed. In one it appears that everything should be sacrificed for an "ideal";

in the next it appears that such sacrifice leads to a kind of living death. There is no real inconsistency here: the one wholly consistent element that runs through all the plays is that no "project of the will," however laudable it may appear in the abstract, can ever succeed, since by definition it is a flight from genuine confrontation with reality.

Two recurring elements further mark the experience on the heights: the appearance of a fascinating woman and a gentle woman and a first child-death. In *Catiline,* Furia's appearance coincides with Catiline's adoption of his project of the will; the contrast between her and Aurelia is a typical one. Brand is similarly drawn between Gerd and Agnes, and Peer Gynt's crisis on the heights in the first three acts of that play is marked by the almost simultaneous appearance of the Green Woman and Solveig. A similar antithesis exists between Nora's two lovers, the "diseased" Dr. Rank and Torvald; between the two men in Helen Alving's life, Captain Alving and Parson Manders; and between such pairs as Eilert Loevborg and George Tesman in *Hedda Gabler,* Hilde and Aline in *The Master Builder,* and Irene and Maja in *When We Dead Awaken.*

The other commonly appearing element at this point in the myth is the motif of the death, wounding, or mutilation of a child. This may be called the "first child-death," since a second one often occurs at a later point in the myth. This motif, strikingly enough, appears in some form in every play of Ibsen's after *The Pretenders* and in a number of the earlier ones. In *Brand,* for example, the first child-death appears as the murder of his child by the starving father in Act II, the incident that draws Brand out upon the stormy fjord with Agnes. In *Emperor and Galilean* it appears as the death of the pregnant Helena in Act IV of Part I. This first child-death is often not a death but a wounding, as it is in *Peer Gynt,* in which it appears as the self-mutilation of the boy in Act III; in *The Wild Duck,* in which it appears as Hedvig's congenital defect of the eyes; and in *Little Eyolf,* in which it appears as Eyolf's crippling fall from the table.

The middle section of the myth covers the pursuit of the project of the will and its gradual collapse, often over a period of ten years (as, for example, in *Brand, A Doll's House, An Enemy of the People, The Lady from the Sea, The Master Builder, Little Eyolf,* and possibly *When We Dead Awaken*), although the time may be much shorter (as in *Catiline* and *Hedda Gabler*) or much longer (as in *Peer Gynt* and *Ghosts*). During the pursuit of the project of the will, the protagonist ordinarily returns from "the heights" to the polluted valley and establishes a *secondary home*. These secondary homes have the same characteristics as the primary homes, though the protagonist is now armed against their effects by his project. The guilt and anxiety that torment the protagonist during this stage of the myth are projected in "stifling" environments—narrow, deep, dark, and airless. In *Brand,* for example, the main thing Brand remembers about his primary home, the little red-roofed cottage where he grew up, is its darkness: "At home I never saw the sun / From the leaves' fall to the cuckoo's song." But during his pursuit of his mission, his secondary home becomes equally dark and sunless; the sun falls on the mountain across the valley, but it never reaches his house. As his mission begins to fail and Ulf dies, the house becomes almost literally a tomb—dark, stifling, and choked with snow. The Helmer sitting room, in *A Doll's House,* is similarly dark, sealed up, and overheated, the correlative of the psychological bondage Nora breaks when she walks out into the snow at the end of the play. The underlying action of several Ibsen plays is to open up these stifling interiors and "let in some air" as Lona Hessel declares she intends to do at the end of Act I of *The Pillars of Society*. Similarly, Dr. Stockmann's liberation from his disabling illusions at the end of *An Enemy of the People* is signaled by the breaking of all the windows in his house. Peter Stockmann shivers, but Thomas glories in the fresh air: "Look how beautifully the sun's shining in through the windows today! And smell this glorious, fresh spring sun which is being wafted in to us." In a very different context, John Gabriel Borkman, in the last act of the play by the same name, walks out of the dark, stifling house, in which he has spent the last eight years walking up and down "like a sick wolf," into the winter weather for his ascent to the peaks.

During the second stage of the myth, the protagonist characteristically allies himself with the gentle woman, who joins him in working for the achievement of the project. Thus Aurelia remains with Catiline, renouncing her own hopes of retiring to the villa in Gaul toward which Catiline has such mixed feelings of attraction and repugnance. Thus also, Solveig patiently waits for Peer Gynt, Agnes marries Brand, Nora remains with Helmer, and Ellida marries Dr. Wangel. But in other plays the protagonist joins himself with the fascinating figure: Julian marries Helena rather than Macrina, Helen Alving remains with Captain Alving rather than with Manders, and Alfred Allmers marries Rita. In any case, the gradual failure of the project of the will is accompanied by a parallel deterioration in the relationship between the protagonist and his mate. The reasons for this deterioration are complex. The gentle woman and the fascinating woman are identified with "love" and "will"; the bitterness and impotence of the protagonist's marriage with either indicates, as does the failure of the project of the will itself, the protagonist's dissatisfaction with his divided self and his yearning for integration and wholeness. This stage of the myth is demonstrated in the many sterile and unhappy marriages in Ibsen, from that of Catiline and Aurelia, through those of Helen Alving and Captain Alving, Rosmer and Beata, Hedda Gabler and George Tesman, and Solness and Aline, to the misalliance of Rubek and Maja. Such details as Julian's inability to worship Cybele and Hedda Gabler's disgust at the thought of pregnancy have a similar significance.

The circumstances under which projects of the will deteriorate and the reasons for their collapse vary greatly in Ibsen's plays. Catiline's initial idealism and selflessness rapidly decline into a fanatical bloodlust that clouds his judgment and leads him to trust unreliable confederates. Brand's mission similarly declines into fanaticism and an extremism that alienates all his followers. Julian's dream of a Third Empire leads him to the threshold of insanity until the dream collapses in a tangle of strategic errors in his campaign against the Persians. In the middle plays, such projects of the will as Nora's secret repayment of the forged note and Mrs. Alving's campaign to preserve both her marriage and the reputation of her husband cannot survive such encounters with reality as the revelation of Torvald's selfishness and of Oswald's illness. In all these

16

plays, and in the others as well, the protagonist cannot permanently sustain the renunciation of a part of the self. Whatever the immediate causes of the projects' failures, the underlying cause is always the protagonist's inability to preserve an identity based on will alone.

The last stage of the myth centers around the final collapse of the project of the will and the hero's *ascent to the peaks*. The last act of *Brand* presents this stage in perhaps its fullest and most typical form. Brand's project collapses completely when his parishioners turn against him and stone him on the mountainside. As the parishioners descend into the valley, Brand begins to climb toward the peaks. He again encounters Agnes, now a spirit, and, before the Ice Church, meets Gerd. Brand suddenly becomes "serene and shining" and seems to renounce his whole previous manner of life. Day dawns and Gerd and Brand are swept away by an avalanche as a great voice cries out, "He is the God of love."

This scene presents a cluster of elements that appear again and again in the endings of Ibsen's plays. The dawn that breaks at the end of Catiline's dream is repeated, for example, in the final scene of the play, as Catiline renounces his "past erratic course" and dies on Aurelia's breast and Furia withdraws into the background. The stage direction in *Peer Gynt* also reads "Day breaks," as Peer, whose wandering path has led him high in the mountains to Solveig's hut, buries his face in her lap and the Button Moulder retreats. And in *Emperor and Galilean* Julian dies at daybreak in the company of Macrina, the "pure woman" whose distant presence has been so important in the play, and at the foot of the mountains toward which he has been moving throughout the last act. The mythic elements of the ending of *Brand* are repeated exactly in *When We Dead Awaken,* when Rubek and Irene ascend the mountain "up into the light, where glory shines" and are swept away by an avalanche, as another voice cries out "Pax vobiscum."

In the middle plays the endings are often similar, though the imagery of mountain peaks, dawn, and death is usually muted by the techniques of realism. In *A Doll's House,* for example, Nora's final exit has the same connotations of death and rebirth as do the endings of *Catiline, Brand,* and *Peer Gynt;* it is preceded by the

17

last visit of the dying Dr. Rank and the final confrontation with Torvald, it takes place just before dawn, and the cold winter air and the snow into which she goes recall the environment of the "peaks" in the earlier plays. Mrs. Alving, in *Ghosts,* cannot undergo the spiritual transformation that Brand undergoes in the last scene of his play, but the ending of *Ghosts* uses the same imagery, this time with a bitter irony: "She goes over to the table and puts out the lamp. The sun rises. The glacier and the snow-capped peaks in the background glitter in the morning light." The final tableau of *Ghosts* shows Mrs. Alving, a "woman of the modern age" whose last word in the play is "no," standing in a cramped drawing room over her babbling, syphilitic son, with her back to the sun as it rises. There can be no rebirth for her. Dr. Stockmann's final spiritual liberation in his study with the windows broken, Ellida Wangel's renunciation of the Stranger, Alfred Allmers's final resolution to move with Rita "up towards the mountains, towards the stars, and the great silence," and John Gabriel Borkman's long-delayed escape from the house and his death in the "small clearing high up in the forest"—despite the wide variety of their circumstances—have in common the connotations, direct or ironical, of death and rebirth suggested by Brand's ascent to the peaks. These connotations are frequently, though not always, reinforced by reminiscences of the imagery of dawn and mountain peaks which appears in the un-displaced myth.

The ascent to the peaks is further marked by a *second child-death.* In *Brand,* which here as elsewhere may be taken as a direct and undisguised treatment of the myth, the collapse of Brand's project of the will and his ascent to the peaks is marked by the death of Ulf, deliberately sacrificed by Brand in the pursuit of his project. In *The Wild Duck,* the discovery of Hedvig's congenital weakness of the eyes is followed by a second child-death: her suicide. This sequence of mutilation/death appears also in *Ghosts,* where the first child-death is Oswald's congenital syphilis and the second his final collapse, and in *Little Eyolf,* with Eyolf's fall from the table and later his drowning. The second child-death appears obliquely in *Hedda Gabler* as the death of Hedda's unborn child.

18

It takes the form of muted threats in *The Pillars of Society,* as Olaf's narrowly averted drowning; in *A Doll's House,* as Nora's reluctant abandoning of her children; and in *The Lady from the Sea,* as the psychological threat posed to Hilde by Ellida's remoteness.

Closely related to the second child-death is the *death of either the fascinating woman or the gentle woman* which recurs often enough to be significant. Aurelia dies with Catiline "on the peaks," and Agnes's death from grief is closely associated with Ulf's death, which immediately precedes it. Captain Alving has died ten years before *Ghosts* opens, but Mrs. Alving is not free of his presence until the burning of the orphanage. Dr. Rank's discovery of the imminence of his death, Beata's suicide, the Stranger's departure, and Loevborg's death, all carry implications, to varying degrees, of the death of a part of the protagonist's own self. The same is true of situations, appearing throughout Ibsen's work but becoming dominant in the late plays, in which the characters have undergone a spiritual death. The first, and crudest, instance of this is Furia's ambiguous status after her rescue from the tomb in *Catiline.* Aline Solness has similarly "died" long before *The Master Builder* begins, as have Ella and Gunhild before *John Gabriel Borkman* begins, and the action of Ibsen's last play is the awakening of the spiritually dead.

The experience on the peaks, whether it involves a literal ascent or a metaphorical one, like Nora's exit or Rosmer's and Rebecca's suicidal leap, is a mystical and ecstatic experience. Even in the plays in which the hero is engulfed, the annihilation has overtones not of defeat but of victory, heralded by suggestions of rebirth in the splendor of the rising sun. Catiline's dream ends happily, with the darkness of the cavern "dispersed by streams of light," and his death in the last scene is a rebirth, a mystical transformation:

> Yes, my life was midnight, lurid in the lightning flash,
> but my death is morning twilight, tinged with rosy hues!
> From my soul the gloom you've banished; calm lies in my breast,
> now with you I come to dwell in realms of light and peace!
> Reconciled the gods in heaven smile down from on high . . .
> All the powers of darkness you have vanquished with your love.

Brand, at the point of death, calls upon the same imagery to describe the transformation that has come over him:

> My life was a long darkness.
> Now the sun is shining. It is day.
> Until today I sought to be a tablet
> On which God could write. Now my life
> Shall flow rich and warm. The crust is breaking.
> I can weep! I can kneel! I can pray!

The deaths of Rosmer and Rebecca and of Solness have something of this quality, and those of Rubek and Irene echo Brand's very closely:

> RUBEK. First we must pass through the mists, Irene. And then—
> IRENE. Yes, through the mists. And then up, up to the top of our tower, where it shines in the sunrise.

The protagonists' long progress out of the valley up to the heights, back down into the valley, and finally up to the peaks thus ends with joy, peace, and release.

2. The Dream II

An argument occurred between two patients in the course of a session in an analytic group. Suddenly one of the protagonists broke off the argument to say, "I can't go on. You are arguing in order to have the pleasure of triumphing over me. At best you win an argument. At worst you lose an argument. I am arguing in order to preserve my existence."

R. D. LAING (1960)

"VAGUE FORESHADOWINGS" of Ibsen's later plays are found not only in the separate motifs of Catiline's dream—the tomblike setting, the contrasting women, the death of children, and the ecstatic ending—but also in the character of the dreamer. The dreamer, like Catiline himself and like Ibsen's later protagonists, perceives the world as a threatening place, "a vaulted chamber, black as any grave." He feels that he is weak and helpless and that his very existence is precariously dependent upon chance or the whims of others. His own divided self is projected as a pair of women, one terrifying, the other comforting, toward whom his own feelings are helplessly divided: "Terrible, and yet with pleasure I observed this sight." His entire life is restless and tormented, "midnight, lurid in the lightning flash," but he yearns for peace, the "morning twilight, tinged with rosy hues."

The dreamer's situation is psychologically the situation which underlies Catiline's particular character traits: his preoccupation with his own inner world, his aloofness and detachment from others, his conspiratorial secretiveness, his secret feelings of omnipotence, and his pervasive guilt and anxiety. Such schizoid perceptions not only appear in many of Ibsen's protagonists, but pervade the underlying structure and imagery of his plays.

R. D. Laing has vividly described the schizoid position in *The Divided Self:*

21

The individual in the ordinary circumstances of living may feel more unreal than real; in a literal sense, more dead than alive; precariously differentiated from the rest of the world, so that his identity and autonomy are always in question. He may lack the experience of his own temporal continuity. He may not possess an over-riding sense of personal consistency or cohesiveness. He may feel more insubstantial than substantial, and unable to assume that the stuff he is made of is genuine, good, valuable. And he may feel his self as partially divorced from his body.[1]

The most striking characteristic of the schizoid position is a preoccupation with an "inner world" into which the schizoid retreats from the threat of the external one. Thus withdrawn, the schizoid appears isolated and detached from others. He tends to be secretive and to overvalue mental contents; he tends toward intellectualization and secret feelings of omnipotence. At the same time he is constantly tormented by feelings of anxiety and guilt. The anxiety stems from a fear that his weak ego will collapse and he will be psychically annihilated; it finds expression in obsessive fantasies of being engulfed, emptied, or petrified. The schizoid therefore feels life to be a constant struggle against annihilation. The guilt stems from an unconscious feeling that his own love is dangerous and destructive. This feeling is pervasive and generalized, though it may find a focus from time to time in exaggerated guilt over comparatively minor or even imaginary failings or infractions.

The roots of the schizoid position lie in the deepest levels of the mind and in the earliest experiences of childhood. The newborn infant experiences intense persecution-anxiety; he feels that he is in constant danger from everything that surrounds him. The development of an ego becomes his defense against this formless, all-encompassing threat, and the earliest relationship with his mother is central in this process. The mother is the child's source of security, comfort, and protection, and he introjects her into his own psyche as a source of inner strength. At the same time, however, he experiences inevitable occasional discomfort, frustration, and pain. These, too, are attributed to the mother, and he simultaneously projects onto the mother his own hostility and resentment. The

1. R. D. Laing, *The Divided Self* (Baltimore, 1965), p. 42.

22

resulting bad maternal image is introjected, in turn, along with the good maternal image. Thus the infant gradually builds up an inner world of internalized objects around which his own ego forms. If the mother is loving and supportive, the inner world is dominated by good internalized objects; if she is cold and rejecting, the inner world becomes frightening and threatening. Guilt arises when the infant, unable to differentiate clearly between the external world and his own mind, comes to feel that his own love is the cause of maternal neglect or rejection and is therefore bad in some way. Much generalized, unspecific guilt in adult life is a reminiscence of this kind of infantile guilt.

Everyone undergoes these very early experiences, and the schizoid position is therefore universal, a part of "human nature" itself. In W. R. D. Fairbairn's words, "the basic position in the psyche is invariably a schizoid position."[2] Its fundamental characteristic is a splitting of the ego, and everyone has such a splitting at some level. Even the apparently well-integrated person may experience schizoid episodes, especially in times of stress.

Laing has analyzed three forms of anxiety encountered by the schizoid personality: engulfment, implosion, and petrification. The fear of engulfment is the fear of being swallowed up, of the weak ego being drowned or smothered by a close human relationship. The schizoid fears love or even understanding because they represent the threat of complete absorption into another person. At the same time, however, he fears complete withdrawal from others into his inner world because this represents the threat of ego-loss through ultimate regression. This contradiction leads to a characteristic "in and out" strategy in which the schizoid alternates erratically between entering into relationships and withdrawing from them in something like panic. Fears of engulfment often take the form of fantasies of being enclosed, swallowed up, drowned, smothered, or buried. Fears of implosion are fears that the external world may at any moment rush in and obliterate all identity, as gas rushes into a vacuum. The schizoid feels empty, like the vacuum, and though he longs for the vacuum to be filled, he fears even more the impinge-

2. W. R. D. Fairbairn, *Psychoanalytical Studies of the Personality* (London, 1952), p. 8.

ment of external reality because it will obliterate the fragile ego itself. Fears of petrification and depersonalization are fears of being turned into a dead thing, such as a statue or a robot. The other side of this fear is the fear that one may turn others into stones or robots, as a means of negating the threat they present.

It is often rightly said that in Ibsen the most fundamental and the most important purpose in life is self-realization. But Ibsen's protagonists seek self-realization not only in the ordinary sense of the development of one's potentialities but more basically in the very literal sense of feeling oneself to be real. Tormented by deeply seated fears of ego-loss by engulfment, implosion, and petrification, the Ibsen protagonist experiences life as a constant struggle to maintain his existence. In Laing's words, he is like "a man who is only saving himself from drowning by the most constant, strenuous, desperate activity."

The schizoid *split between an inner world and the outer world* and the introspective turning in upon the inner world is clearly though rather crudely exemplified in Catiline and in his dream surrogate. The play opens with Catiline alone, brooding over the contradictions between his ambitions and his wasteful and self-destructive dissipations. He is haunted by "dreams of night-time":

> . . . figments born of solitude, no more;
> the slightest murmur from the world that's real
> and down they flee to silent depths within! . . .

A major motivation for his revolt against Rome is his longing to escape from his tormented brooding over "the silent depths within" and achieve action in the real world. This preoccupation with inner reality is echoed over and over in the later plays. Brand is similarly given to lonely introspection and feels himself alone even with his beloved Agnes. A major motive for Peer Gynt's impetuous kidnaping of Ingrid is his yearning to escape from the stifling inner world of dreams and fairy tales which he and Aase have created and to implant himself in the real, outer world; the rest of the play traces his attempts to achieve a genuine relationship with others. Like many of his fellow protagonists, he perceives the split between the inner and outer worlds as a split between a "false self" and a "true self." He spends his entire life searching for his true self, only to discover in the closing scene that the "real" Peer Gynt was in Solveig's faith, hope, and love.

The middle and late plays are full of characters as much pre-occupied as Catiline with "the silent depths within." Many of them have lived in lonely places and have occupied their time with intro-spective brooding, as Dr. Stockmann has in his days as a provincial doctor in the north, as Gregers Werle has in the works up at Hoydal, and as John Rosmer has in his gloomy, isolated family home. Even those who appear most sociable and outgoing tend to think of their social selves as "false" and to preserve a secret inner life which they regard as "true." Thus Nora is split between her self as Torvald's little twittering bird and her inner self as a mature, responsible adult, and even the outgoing, impetuous Dr. Stockmann is divided between the idealized picture of the world he has built up in his mind and the real world as it presents itself to him in the course of the play.

The schizoid preoccupation with the inner world and the threat which close external relationships seem to hold leads to a character-istic *aloofness and detachment,* which often expresses itself as a scorn for others. Catiline holds himself apart even from his friend Curius and his wife, Aurelia, and looks upon his fellow conspirators with unmixed scorn. "A mob of good-for-nothings," he calls them, "motivated solely by want and by rapacity." He looks upon himself as mysterious and beyond the understanding of the common herd of men:

> . . . I hide my agony in silence
> and none suspects the fire that glows within . . .
> these worthless men look down on me and scorn me . . .
> they do not know how fast this heart is beating
> for right and freedom, for each noble cause
> which ever stirred in any human breast!

Brand has a similar contempt for his parishioners, which breaks out openly when they refuse to follow him on his mad wanderings into the wilderness, and Peer Gynt hides his longing to be accepted by others under a defensive pose of condescension and contempt for the other wedding guests at Heggestad. Emperor Julian scorns his subjects—Christian and pagan alike—and Dr. Stockmann, Gregers

Werle, John Rosmer, Hedda Gabler, Halvard Solness, Alfred Allmers, John Gabriel Borkman, and Arnold Rubek, for all their differences, are united in despising their neighbors and fellow townspeople. All would agree with Dr. Stockmann's final proud, but
ambiguous, slogan: "The strongest man in the world is he who
stands most alone."

Preoccupied with his inner world and remote from others, the
Ibsen protagonist often takes delight in a *conspiratorial secretiveness.*
It is characteristic of Catiline that his attempt at action in the real
world takes the form of a political conspiracy. His secretiveness is
echoed in Nora's delight in her little secrets ranging from macaroons
to forged notes, in the satisfaction that Gregers Werle and a number
of other protagonists take in expressing themselves riddlingly and
enigmatically, and in Hedda Gabler's pleasure not only in secret
relationships like that with Judge Brack, but also in her delight in
deception, as in her secret indifference to the Falk villa and her pretended misunderstanding about Aunt Juliana's bonnet. Rubek, in
When We Dead Awaken, takes almost gleeful delight in concealing
the faces of animals within the portrait busts he makes for the wealthy
bourgeoisie:

> RUBEK. There is something hidden with those faces. A secret meaning
> which people cannot see.
> MAJA. Oh, really?
> RUBEK. Only I can see it. And I find it intensely amusing. Superficially,
> there are these "striking likenesses" as they call them, at which peo-
> ple gape, entranced. But deep within, I have sculpted the righteous
> and estimable faces of horses, the opinionated muzzles of donkeys,
> the lop ears and shallow brows of dogs, the overgorged chaps of
> swine, and the dull and brutalized fronts of oxen.

This kind of delight in secrets reflects a general overvaluation of
mental contents, an overvaluation that also takes the form of a
sense of omnipotence or megalomania. The Ibsen protagonist may
alternate in his own feelings between an extreme overvaluation of
himself and a withering self-contempt, but he is inclined to feel
secretly that he has been set apart, with the "stamp of God upon his
brow," and that he is capable of almost superhuman achievements.
Thus Catiline feels that he is possessed of "exalted powers" and

26

dreams that he is a god: he imagines himself as Icarus, soaring high above Rome and hurling lightning down upon the city. Brand thinks of himself in messianic terms and identifies himself with both Moses and Christ, and even Peer Gynt says that his self "bore God's stamp upon its brow" and thinks of himself as a "shining button on the waistcoat of the world." Julian literally has himself proclaimed a god and forces his soldiers to sacrifice to him. Gregers Werle, like Brand, identifies himself with Christ (the "thirteenth at table") and Halvard Solness, like a number of other protagonists, fears the power which he fancies he has to compel others to do his will.

A strong *tendency toward intellectualization* also reflects the schizoid difficulty in yielding up the contents of the inner world and a corresponding overvaluation of them. Unable to give or receive love freely and unself-consciously, the Ibsen protagonist turns his love in upon himself, libidinizing the contents of his own mind, and substituting ideas for feelings. The most extreme example of this kind of intellectualization is the pedantry of the Emperor Julian, who in Part II of *Emperor and Galilean* sinks to the level of a stock caricature of a bookworm. He appears in Act III, "wearing a ragged coat, fastened with a piece of rope; hair and beard are unkempt, and his fingers are stained with ink; in both hands, under his arms, and tucked in his belt, he is carrying piles of parchment rolls and papers." He flees from the Dionysian rites, which he theoretically advocates, into niggling and trivial scholarship. John Rosmer and Alfred Allmers use books in the same way. Allmers avoids genuine human responsibility by writing a book on the subject, and Rosmer, when Rebecca West tells him that she has been ennobled by him, responds: "You say you have discovered the true meaning of love. That through me your soul has been ennobled. Is this true? Have you calculated correctly, Rebecca? Shall we check your calculations?" A passionate love is thus turned into a safe mathematical problem.

Despite his secret pride in his inner world, however, the Ibsen protagonist cannot escape a crippling and all-encompassing *sense of guilt*. Fundamentally this guilt stems from the schizoid's infantile fear that the hostile, terrifying world he faces is in some way his own doing, that his own love is destructive because it has been rejected, and that he has in some way deserved to have it rejected. The Ibsen protagonist may feel guilty over particular sins, but the sin is never great enough to explain the amount and intensity of the guilt he feels. Catiline, for example, has ample reason to reproach himself, but the pervasive guilt he feels transcends any specific cause. His offense, he thinks, is in having lived at all: he repents, he tells Furia, of having ever lived. There is a direct connection between Catiline's sense of guilt over the very fact that he has lived and Solness's feeling that a huge stone of guilt is weighing him down and crushing him, and Rubek's torment that leads him to depict himself, in his sculptural group, as a guilty figure beside a spring, forever trying to wash his fingers clean.

Finally, the Ibsen protagonist's sense of guilt is matched by an equally pervasive and inescapable *anxiety* over the omnipresent threat of ultimate regression and the loss of the ego. This generalized anxiety takes a number of characteristic forms, including restlessness and discontent, a feeling of emptiness and futility, and recurring fantasies of engulfment, implosion, and petrification. These fantasies are not always specifically assigned to the perceptions of the protagonist, but pervade the structure of the play itself. The world of an Ibsen play is never a neutral, photographically reproduced world but is rather an affective, emotional projection of the protagonist's inner world.

Perhaps the most important of these schizoid fantasies is the *tomb world,* a perception of the world and oneself as dead. The dividing line between life and death is always precariously thin in an Ibsen play. The uncertainty in *Catiline* as to whether or not Furia died in the tomb is echoed in *Brand* and *Peer Gynt,* in which the protagonists themselves may have died long before the resolution of the action. Solness says that he and Aline have both died long before; Allmers has met death on his walking tour in the mountains; and John Gabriel Borkman, his wife, and his sister-in-law are "one dead man and two shadows." "When we dead awaken," Irene tells Rubek, "we find that we have never lived."

In the middle plays, the tomb world characteristically appears as a dark, stifling environment. Already in *Catiline,* Rome itself is a dark tomb world in which Catiline feels that he is choking. The

28

entire play, until the closing lines, takes place at night, a peculiarity Ibsen offered a whimsical explanation for in his 1875 preface: "My drama was written during the hours of the night. The leisure hours for my study I practically had to steal from my employer, a good and respectable man, occupied however heart and soul with his business, and from these stolen hours I again stole moments for writing verse. There was consequently scarcely anything else to resort to but the night. I believe this is the unconscious reason that almost the entire action of the piece transpires at night." He has Catiline himself offer a somewhat different explanation, however, in Act II. Catiline has just agreed to leave Rome with Aurelia for the villa in Gaul, and he is despondent over the prospect. Aurelia leaves, he is alone, and he immediately puts out the lamp:

> CATILINE. . . . that lamp though is distracting to my dreams . . .
> I must have darkness, dark as in my soul!
> Ah, it is still too light, but never mind!
> The pallid moonlight harmonizes well
> with this dim twilight gloom which now enshrouds,
> which ever has enshrouded all my steps.

The darkness and gloom of Catiline's Rome are, like the darkness and gloom of the stuffy drawing rooms of the middle plays, correlatives of the psychological tomb world in which the protagonist finds himself. The same fantasy is expressed in the gravelike dungeon of Catiline's dream and in the tomb in which Furia is buried alive at the end of Act I.

The "Ibsen drawing room," for all its detailed verisimilitude, is never a mere photograph. The parsonage setting of Act IV of *Brand* recalls Furia's tomb even visually: sealed up against the outside air and lighted only by a flickering lamp—the symbol of the fragile ego. It is choked by drifts of snow outside and Brand in his self-hatred orders Agnes not to open any windows. Mrs. Alving's drawing room, in *Ghosts,* is a fairly detailed model of her mind, with the action of the play going on in the foreground, haunting memories being reenacted in adjoining rooms deeper within the house, a few books with "advanced ideas" lying on the table, a flickering lamp dimly lighting the room, and fog and a steady rain enveloping the house until the terrible white dawn of the final lines.

The multi-room settings of *The Wild Duck* and *Hedda Gabler* are even more complex representations of the protagonists' guilty and anxiety-ridden minds. The first set in *The Wild Duck* sets up a pointed contrast between the brilliantly lighted background where "public" life is going on and the dimly lighted foreground in which the major characters begin to probe into their lives. The Ekdal studio of the other four acts is even more suggestive, with its dimly lighted studio contrasted with the even murkier attic-forest behind it. The Falk villa in *Hedda Gabler* becomes, in the course of the play, a vivid figure for Hedda's cramped character, with the portrait of General Gabler overlooking the action, the curtains drawn against the air and sunlight, and the empty "nursery" within. *Rosmersholm* is named after its setting, and it, too, is a theatrically effective model of Rosmer's mind, with the row of Rosmer portraits a continual sinister presence and the roar of the millrace a constant nagging reminder of "the dead mistress." Solness's new house with its strange tower and its empty nurseries, the Allmer home perched on the edge of a fjord with an eerie "undertow," and Rubek's villa on the Taunitzer See where there is enough room for people to stay out of each other's way, are all houses from the late plays with such vivid affective associations that they become almost expressionistic devices, tomb worlds in a straight line of development from the dungeon of Catiline's dream.

Almost as common as the fear of being buried in a tomb world is the deeply seated fear of falling into *an abyss*. Both *Brand* and *Peer Gynt* open with this image. Brand is climbing a narrow mountain path with thinly covered ice chasms on either side; a single misstep will send him to his death. Peer Gynt is telling his mother a significant lie: of how he rode a giant buck at top speed down the narrow crest of Gjendin Edge with "black and heavy lakes" more than four thousand feet below on either side. Both images encapsulate the psychological positions of the protagonists, in which they are in constant danger of making a misstep and being engulfed in a psychological "abyss." The avalanches that sweep Brand and Rubek into deep mountain chasms are ambiguous fulfillments of this threat, as are also Rosmer's and Rebecca's plunge into the millrace and Solness's fall into the stonepit, the culmination of his long-standing "fear of heights."

Being drowned in *the sea* is similar in its psychological meaning. In Ibsen the sea usually suggests complete regression and is regarded by the protagonists with mingled fear and fascination. Brand's precarious ascent among the chasms is matched by his venturing out upon the stormy fjord with Agnes in Act II, and in Act V of *Peer Gynt,* Peer is literally thrown into the sea and left to struggle for his life. The most extensive use of this fantasy, of course, occurs in *The Lady from the Sea,* in which Ellida's simultaneous fear of the sea and of the Stranger and her fascination with the sea constitute a typical schizoid attitude toward regression, with its threat of annihilation and its promise of release from the struggle for ego-preservation. Hedvig's fascination with "the bottom of the deep blue sea" in *The Wild Duck,* and the sinister undertow in the fjord in *Little Eyolf* have similar meanings.

Fears of *petrification,* of being "frozen" or "turned to stone," are almost equally common. The Speaker in "On the Fells," after he has abandoned his mother and fiancee for a lonely but free life on the heights, looks into his heart and finds there "all symbols of petrification." His attitude includes the mingling of fear and yearning, characteristic of images of regression and ego-loss. Perhaps something of this ambivalence underlies Nora's revolt at having been turned into a "doll." The most characteristic expression of the motif of petrification, however, occurs in connection with art and artists. Ballested, in *The Lady from the Sea,* is working on a painting of "The Death of the Mermaid" and Lyngstrand is doing a sculpture based on the Stranger's return, both of them unconsciously turning Ellida into a work of art. This threat is remote in *The Lady from the Sea,* but it becomes a central image in *When We Dead Awaken,* in which Irene's all-white clothing suggests both a corpse and a statue. Rubek has both killed her and turned her into stone. The fact that in *The Lady from the Sea* the protagonist is being turned into stone and in *When We Dead Awaken* he has turned another into stone illustrates the way petrification operates as both a schizoid fear and a schizoid defense.

There are a number of appearances in Ibsen of the recurring schizoid fantasy of the *citadel,* a place of isolation and security where the ego can retreat and find peace from its ceaseless struggle

31 Go to 35 (A.D.H.)

to preserve itself. The citadel involves regression but it is relatively free of the fears of other images of regression such as the tomb and the sea because it holds out the possibility of partial regression to a secure place rather than complete regression. Aurelia's villa in Gaul, in *Catiline,* is a citadel image of this kind. But the fullest use of the citadel is in Solness's "real castle in the air built on a true foundation," in *The Master Builder.* This imaginary castle has a very high tower with a balcony on top where Hilde and Solness can stand and be safe from everything. Something of the same significance is attached to the tower which Rubek and Irene rather oddly expect to find on the mountain peaks at the end of *When We Dead Awaken.*

The image of *deeply buried precious things* is also characteristic of the regressed ego in Ibsen. It finds an early expression in "The Miner," a poem Ibsen wrote in 1851. The speaker in this poem is obsessed with the thought of the gold, diamonds, and rubies buried deep within the earth and has drilled down to get them. But in the darkness he has "lost the sense of light" and has failed to find the answer to "my life's unending riddle." Nevertheless he will not return to the sunlight above but will remain in the depths:

> Downward, then! the depths are best;
> There is immemorial rest.
> Heavy hammer burst as bidden
> To the heart-nook of the hidden!—
>
> Hammer-blow on hammer-blow
> Till the lamp of life is low.
> Not a ray of hope's fore-warning;
> Not a glimmer of the morning.

The association of "the depths" with "peace and immemorial sleep," the fear of "the glare" in the sunlit world above, and the suggestion that the precious metals and stones hold the answer to "life's unending riddle" all indicate the psychological meaning of the poem as a metaphor for the schizoid inner world with the fragile ego buried deep within. The same imagery appears in *John Gabriel Borkman* in Borkman's mad attraction to buried treasures, to which he cries in Act IV: "But let me whisper this to you now, in the stillness of the night. I love you where you lie like the dead,

32

deep down in the dark. I love you, treasures that crave for life, with your bright retinue of power and glory. I love you, love you, love you."

A closely related image is the small casket full of wealth which Arnold Rubek says he carries deep within his breast: "In here, Maja—in here I keep a small casket, with a lock that cannot be picked. In that casket, all my visions lie. But when she left me, and vanished from my life, the lock of that casket snapped shut. She had the key, and she took it with her. You, my poor Maja, you had no key. So everything in it lies unused. And the years pass—and all that wealth lies there—and I cannot touch it!"

The recurring images of *dead children* and *piercing eyes* are combined, as they sometimes are in Ibsen, in a dream reported by Harry Guntrip from one of his patients: "I opened a steel drawer and inside was a tiny naked baby with wide staring expressionless eyes." [3] Both these motifs appear in Catiline's dream, in the crowd of children who "vanish whence they came" and in the threatening woman's "piercing eye." The death of children, as we have seen, recurs as a motif in almost every Ibsen play, and the piercing eyes reappear almost as frequently. The Strange Hunter, for example, in "On the Fells," has similarly terrifying eyes:

> Cold his eye: my spirit fears
> Depths that it no more has sounded
> Than the blue-black mountain-mere's,
> Glacier-born and glacier-bounded.

Ellida Wangel, in *The Lady from the Sea,* is haunted by the memory of the Stranger's eyes, "like a dead fish's eyes," and of her dead child's eyes, which looked like the Stranger's. And Rita Allmers is obsessed by the sight, merely reported to her, of little Eyolf lying on the bottom of the fjord with his eyes wide open, staring upward. It is significant that all these characters with piercing eyes can be shown on other grounds to be projections of a side of the protagonist's self: the woman in Catiline's dream, the Strange Hunter, the Stranger, and little Eyolf. Dead children and figures with piercing eyes thus seem to be images of the divided self.

3. Harry Guntrip, *Schizoid Phenomena, Object-Relations, and the Self* (London, 1968), p. 88.

The full significance of all these images can be understood only by examining their roles in the most elaborate schizoid fantasy in Ibsen, the myth of the self which, as we have seen, underlies all the plays. The primary home in which the myth begins is always a tomb world. The vague reminiscence of an earlier time of peace and security is a dim memory of a time before the self was divided, but at the point where the myth itself begins, the world presents itself to the protagonist as dark, stifling, and threatening. Catiline's Rome, Brand's mother's red-roofed cottage, Aase's hut, and the parental homes of most of the other protagonists are all places where the protagonists feel constantly threatened by the external world itself. The ascent to the heights is a representation of a schizoid withdrawal "above" the world with which the protagonist cannot cope.

"On the heights" the protagonist makes his crucial choice between "love" and "will." The very fact that he perceives his possibilities in these terms is significant. Love and will are the two major ways by which we establish relationships with the external world, but for the schizoid person these two ways of solving problems of living have become problems in themselves. The Ibsen protagonist sees the two as mutually exclusive. He fears love, despite its overpowering attraction for him, because it seems to involve the threat of being swallowed up, of ceasing to exist as a separate person. The thought of returning to the valley of ordinary life among his fellow country-men, for example, is for Brand like reentering a "stifling pit." The protagonist therefore adopts the project of the will as his defense against love. Even when the project involves service to others, as it does in *Brand,* for example, it is a means of keeping others at a distance and of maintaining one's own isolation and independence. Such a rigid and defensive attitude toward will must inevitably lead to defeat, as it does in the eventual collapse of the project.

The fascinating woman and the gentle woman who appear at the point of the ascent to the heights are projections of the mother figure. The fascinating woman is the side of the mother that has been internalized as threatening and hostile; the gentle woman the side that has been internalized as loving and comforting. This antithesis is preserved even when, as in many of the realistic plays, the sexes are reversed and these two figures appear as men. The

34

compassion ~~at sexist~~ (honest)   Morals

antitheses of Dr. Rank/Torvald Helmer, Captain Alving/Parson Manders, The Stranger/Dr. Wangel, and Eilert Loevborg/George Tesman have the same psychological significance as those between female figures. Whether male or female, these figures are mirror images of each other and are identified with love and will as contrasting strategies of confronting the world. The crisis upon the heights is also marked by the first child-death. The child, like the one in the second child-death, is a projection of the protagonist's own ego; its mutilation or death reflects the protagonist's anxiety about his own existence.

The middle section of the myth shows the protagonist pursuing a typically schizoid strategy of living. By means of the project of the will, the protagonist has tried to keep himself psychologically "on the heights." His alliance with one of the contrasting women indicates that he has not succeeded in integrating his divided self, but has merely suppressed one side of it. Aloof, withdrawn into his inner world, pursuing an impersonal project, he tries to maintain a secure position. As the suppressed side of his nature begins to reassert itself, his faith in the will hardens into fanaticism, but eventually the whole strategy collapses. The death of one woman signals this collapse, as the reappearance of the other woman marks the return of the suppressed side of his nature, and the second child-death marks a second ego-crisis.

The ascent to the peaks is full of implications of a triumphant rebirth of the self. It thus brings the myth to a "comic" conclusion, in the sense that Dante's vision of God brings *The Divine Comedy* to a comic conclusion. The best gloss upon the ascent to the peaks is perhaps the paradox the Button Moulder presents to Peer Gynt: *Good reputation.* So True "To be oneself is to kill oneself." Annihilation upon the peaks is the "killing" of the self in self-transcendence and in the brilliant clarity of the dawn being reborn, whole and undivided. It thus brings to an end the restless quest that dominates the lives of Ibsen's protagonists. ← (To truly find their identity — Like Invisible Man.

The structural pattern and the psychological position implied by Catiline's dream underlie all of Ibsen's plays from *Catiline* to *When We Dead Awaken*. The myth appears in a prophetically full form in *Catiline,* winds its way through the other apprentice plays, and then is stated most openly and completely in *Brand* and *Peer Gynt,* Ibsen's major "mythic" plays. In *Emperor and Galilean,* his long "world-historical" play, the myth not only underlies the life of the Emperor Julian but also provides the basis for a general interpretation of history. It thus constitutes the link between individual and collective experience which forms the subject of that play. In the middle, "realistic" plays, Ibsen continues to build his plays upon the myth, but provides an elaborate superstructure of credible detail which obscures its shape. It is nevertheless actively at work in each play, charging each detail with a resonance that derives from our sense, half-unconscious though it may be, of the detail's place in a large, coherent whole. In the last group of plays, from *The Master Builder* through *When We Dead Awaken,* the myth once more emerges fairly openly, though Ibsen retains many of the devices of realistic displacement of the middle period. These last plays might be called "mythic-realistic" plays, because their most important characteristic is the way they counterpoint a mythic structure against the structure of the realistic plot. The patterns set up in Catiline's dream thus provide a key, as Ibsen said, to the great themes of the later plays: "the contradiction between ability and desire, between will and possibility, the intermingled tragedy and comedy in humanity and in the individual."

3. Brand

Does Brand *stand for revolution or reaction?*
I cannot tell, there is so much of both in it.

GEORG BRANDES (1871)

To MODERN readers of *Brand* and of the commentaries it has inspired, the earliest comment on the play might seem the best. *Brand,*
wrote Johan Vibe in the *Norge* of April 3, 1866, is "brilliant madness." The play was hailed, when it first appeared, as a ringing celebration of individualism, and its protagonist was regarded as a hero
of the individual will. The play made Ibsen, after years of discour-
agement and failure, famous all over Europe as the fiery spokesman
of the liberal movement. "Every receptive and unblunted mind,"
Georg Brandes later recalled, "felt, on closing the book, a penetrat-
ing, nay, an overwhelming impression of having stood face to face
with a great and indignant genius, before whose piercing glance
weakness felt itself compelled to cast down its eyes."

The idea for *Brand* had come to Ibsen on his trip from Norway to
Italy in 1864. He was deeply angered over the failure of Norway
and Sweden to come to the aid of Denmark in the Dano-Prussian
War; in Berlin he saw captured Danish cannons being drawn
through the streets and spat on by the crowds. He seems to have
felt some degree of guilt himself for not having volunteered to fight
against Germany, especially after he met in Rome a young theo-
logical student named Christopher Bruun who had volunteered and
fought at Dybbøl. The idea for *Brand,* he wrote, "began to grow
within me like an embryo." At first he planned an epic poem about
an uncompromising minister, perhaps suggested by his memories
of a revivalist named G. A. Lammers who had converted his family

37

in Skien, by the character of Bruun, and by other models as well, including himself. "Brand," he once wrote, "is myself in my best moments."

After a year's slow work on the poem, he suddenly abandoned all he had done and started afresh. He described the circumstances in a letter to Bjoernson:

> I have been at my wits' end, not only in regard to money, but in regard to my work [on *Brand*] also. I could make no progress on it. Then one day I strolled into St. Peter's—I had gone to Rome on an errand—and there I suddenly saw strongly and clearly the form for what I had to say. I threw to the winds all that I had been unavailingly torturing myself with for a whole year [the epic version of *Brand*] and in the middle of July began something new, which progressed as nothing has ever progressed with me before. . . . It is a dramatic poem, modern in subject, serious in tone, five acts in rhymed verse (not a second *Love's Comedy*). The fourth act is now nearly finished, and the fifth I feel I can write in a week. I work both in the morning and the afternoon, which I have never been able to do before. It is delightfully peaceful here; no acquaintances; I read nothing but the Bible— it has vigor and power.

The final version of the play was written in three months. Ibsen's publisher had at first been reluctant to publish a regular first printing of 1,250 copies and had wanted to print only 625, but the first printing was sold out within two months and two more printings were required before the year was up. It quickly became the textbook of the liberal movement in Norway and maintained this position for twenty years or more; young people committed sections of it to memory and phrases from it entered permanently into Norwegian speech. Koht testifies that no other work, except the Bible, has left such an impact upon the language of Norway. It was the same elsewhere. In Sweden, *Brand* became almost a devotional book to the young liberals who gathered around August Strindberg. Strindberg himself wrote that in *Brand* Ibsen spoke with "the voice of a Savonarola," and one of his disciples wrote, "It would be vain to attempt a description of the unbounded enthusiasm with which the youth of whom I speak, read and discussed the great poet.— Ibsen became a binding tie between friends and lovers; no one could offer anyone a gift more sacred than *Brand;* it was a tribute to intelligence and character."[1]

Even among the first reviewers there were those who protested the simple acceptance of Brand as a hero, and a few ministers spoke out from their pulpits against the book's ethical extremism. Brand, after all, in following his creed of "All or Nothing" leaves a trail of corpses behind him—his mother, his child, his wife—and ends his life in a mad, suicidal mountain ascent. The definitive expression of the reaction against simplistic readings of the play as a celebration of Brand, however, appeared in Shaw's little book on Ibsen, *The Quintessence of Ibsenism* (1891). *Brand,* wrote Shaw, far from being a celebration of idealism, is "an autobiographical anti-idealist extravaganza." To regard Brand as a hero is a Philistine error: "Readers of Ibsen—not playgoers—have sometimes so far misconceived him as to suppose that his villains are examples rather than warnings, and that the mischief and ruin which attend their actions are but the tribulations from which the soul comes out purified as gold from the furnace." Not so, says Shaw. "Brand the priest is an idealist of heroic earnestness, strength, and courage," and in his pursuit of the ideal "he plunges from depth to depth of murderous cruelty." He finally "dies a saint, having caused more intense suffering by his saintliness than the most talented sinner could possibly have done with twice his opportunities."

To Shaw, one might reply that to regard Brand as a "warning" is as crude an oversimplification as to regard him as an "example." Ibsen is very far from being an "anti-idealist," and it is obvious that, throughout much of the play, Ibsen at least partially approves of Brand and presents his course of action as praiseworthy. To regard *Brand* as an "autobiographical anti-idealist extravaganza" is as inadequate as to regard it as a saint's legend in some strange religion of the will.

The fact is that *Brand* is an extraordinarily complex and difficult work, and its early sensational success can only be attributed to the fact that the time was ripe for such a book. A large audience of young liberals was waiting to be told what *Brand* seemed to say:

1. Gustaf af Geijorstam, quoted in Halvdan Koht, *The Life of Ibsen* (New York, 1931), vol. 1, p. 294.

that a person should never compromise but should follow his own will regardless of consequences. They were able to overlook the fact that *Brand* actually says something quite different.

To decide what it actually does say, we must consider some basic problems in the play. One is the mode of the play; the world of *Brand* is wholly unlike the objective, emotionally neutral world of realistic drama. The landscape, the characters, and the action are instead only partially objectified; they are charged with the affective coloring of Brand's mind. Another problem is the exact course of the spiritual progress of the protagonist. Brand is by no means the single-minded idealist he is sometimes taken to be throughout the play. He undergoes a series of spiritual crises, culminating in the ambiguous transformation he experiences in the final scene. These crises and the final transformation can hardly be understood in isolation, but must be seen as part of a large pattern.

Brand opens with Brand high up in the mountains, struggling along a narrow path through mist and snow in the company of a guide and his young son. The guide warns that they are in great danger; they are walking on a thin crust of ice over a deep abyss which the river has hollowed out beneath them. He insists that they turn back, despite the fact that he is going to the bedside of his dying daughter. Brand contemptuously dismisses him and struggles on. He is on his way to the coast to take a steamer and leave Norway in order to carry God's word out into the great world. He changes his mind, however, as a result of three encounters in Act I: with the guide, with Ejnar and Agnes, and with Gerd.

BRAND. Where are you going now?
EJNAR. Over that last mountain peak, westwards down
    To the mouth of the fjord, and then home to the city
    For our wedding feast as fast as ship can sail.
    Then south together, like swans on their first flight—
BRAND. And there?
EJNAR.   A happy life
    Together, like a dream, like a fairy tale.
    For this Sunday morning, out there on the mountain,
    Without a priest, our lives were declared free
    Of sorrow, and consecrated to happiness.

40

Brand rejects them as contemptuously as he has rejected the guide:

> All you want is to flirt,
> And play, and laugh; to do lip service to your faith
> But not to know the truth; to leave your suffering
> To someone who they say died for your sake.
> He died for you, so you are free to dance.
> To dance, yes; but whither?
> Ah, that is another thing, my friend.

Brand's third encounter is with Gerd, the strange, crazed gypsy girl who lives alone in the mountains. She comes running down the path, pursued by a Hawk, and calls Brand to come up to the "Ice Church," a chasm at the top of the mountain covered by a great snowdrift. The Hawk perches over the Ice Church "like an ugly weathercock."

These three encounters inspire Brand to go back down into the valley:

> Which is best? Who gropes most blindly?
> Who strays farthest from home? The light of heart
> Who plays along the edge of the crevasse?
> The dull of heart, plodding and slow because
> His neighbors are so? Or the wild of heart,
> In whose broken mind evil seems beautiful?
> This triple enemy must be fought.
> I see my calling. It shines forth like the sun.
> I know my mission. If these three can be slain,
> Man's sickness will be cured.
> Arm, arm, my soul. Unsheath your sword.
> To battle for the heirs of Heaven!

This decision is extended and confirmed in Act II. In the valley, Brand reproaches the starving villagers, who almost attack him. He wins their admiration, however, by venturing out on the stormy fjord to minister to a dying man who has killed his starving child. The villagers ask Brand to become their priest. At first he refuses, until he has a strange interview with his mother, who asks him to remain nearby so he can "look after her soul" when she dies. Brand agrees to attend his mother when she dies, but only on one condition:

> Everything that binds you to this world
> You must renounce, and go naked to your grave.

After this interview Brand changes his mind and decides to give up his dreams of going out into the world and instead to remain in the valley:

> My Sunday song is over, my winged steed
> Can be unsaddled. My duty lies here.
> There is a higher purpose than the glory of battle:
> To hallow daily toil to the praise of God.

Agnes rejects Ejnar and decides to stay and marry Brand, although she realizes that she is choosing darkness over light and death over life. "Into the night; through death," she tells Brand. "Beyond the morning glows."

The meaning of the sequence of events in Acts I and II and of Brand's crucial decision to remain in the valley is by no means obvious. It is tempting to accept at face value Brand's own idealistic declarations, but these are undercut at almost every point, so that the total effect is highly ambiguous. Brand himself is far from being as sublimely self-confident as he at first appears to be or as his rhetoric would lead us to believe. The opening scene constitutes a vivid dramatic image of Brand's fundamental psychological position: one in which he feels constantly threatened with annihilation of the self. In this scene, as in the rest of the play, the landscape is a barely objectified projection of Brand's state of mind, and his walking upon a thin crust of ice over an abyss through darkness and fog epitomizes his life situation. Similar images of psychic threat are multiplied throughout the play: the precariously balanced roof of the Ice Church, the stormy waters of the fjord, and—most vivid of all—the avalanche, all waiting to engulf him.

The personality pattern which develops from this central, dominating sense of a fragile self under constant threat of annihilation gradually becomes clear during the course of the first two acts. Preoccupied with inner reality, Brand is aloof and detached from others; his situation in the first act, high on the mountain, alone and gazing scornfully down on the people in the valley, is typical of his psychological stance. Ejnar recalls how isolated he was from others even as a child:

EJNAR.   How good to see you!
Look at me! Yes, you're the same old Brand

42

Who always kept to yourself and never played
With us.

BRAND.   No, I was not at home
Among you southerners. I was
Of another race, born by a cold fjord,
In the shadow of a barren mountain.

His feeling of being set apart, of being of "another race" is a characteristic schizoid perception.

Brand's sternness and rigidity in condemning others—the guide, Ejnar and Agnes, the valley dwellers—is a strategy for keeping others at a distance. Despite his declarations of good will and benevolence, he has a really savage contempt for the people in the valley:

Oh, I know you through and through,
Dull souls and slovenly minds. Your prayers
Have not the strength nor the agony to reach
To Heaven—except to cry:
"Give us this day our daily bread!"

Brand combines this scorn for others with secret feelings of personal omnipotence. Early in the play, he makes the first of many identifications of himself with Christ when he hints to the guide that he can walk on water. "I have dared to take upon myself / The salvation of Man," he meditates after ministering to the dying father who killed his child. And in the second act, he confesses to Agnes his secret dreams of glory:

This morning visions flocked to me
Like wild swans, and lifted me on their broad wings.
I looked outwards, thinking my path lay there.
I saw myself as the chastiser of the age,
Striding in greatness above the tumult.
The pomp of processions, hymns
And incense, silken banners, golden cups,
Songs of victory, the acclaim
Of surging crowds, glorified my life's work.

One of Brand's most significant traits, however, is his hatred of "halfness" and his insistence that men be "whole." He tells Ejnar,

You don't understand me.
It isn't love of pleasure that is destroying us.

It would be better if it were.
Enjoy life if you will,
But be consistent, do it all the time,
Not one thing one day and another the next.
Be wholly what you are, not half and half.

Whatever the validity of this ethic, it is significant that Brand conceives of what he hates and fears in terms of halfness, being only part of a man, as it is also significant that he expresses his ideal in the opposite terms:

> [Christ] threw a bridge
> Of human faith from flesh back to the Spirit's source.
> Now it is hawked round piecemeal, but from these stumps
> Of soul, from these severed heads and hands,
> A Whole shall rise which God shall recognize,
> Man, His greatest creation, His chosen heir,
> Adam, young and strong.

Brand's rigidity and his ethical extremism are presented, then, as defenses against his pervasive fear of loss of self. Lonely and aloof, preoccupied with his own inner world, scornful and fearful of others, he defends himself against the threatening outer world by adopting a lofty stance of uncompromising idealism.

The origins of this psychological position are suggested early in the play, in the extraordinary monologue in which Brand meditates upon the sight of his mother's house, far below in the valley:

> The widow's cottage!
> My childhood home!
> Memories swarm upon me,
> And memories of memories. There, among
> The stones on the shore, I lived my childhood alone.
>
> A heavy weight lies on me, the burden
> Of being tied to another human being
> Whose spirit pointed earthwards. Everything
> That I desired so passionately before
> Trembles and fades. My strength and courage fail me,
> My mind and soul are numbed.
> Now, as I approach my home, I find
> Myself a stranger; I awake bound, shorn,
> And tamed, like Samson in the harlot's lap.

Brand experiences this feeling of paralysis and impotence in the

44

presence of his mother again in Act II when she comes to ask him to remain in the valley. She is a sinister, bowed figure who shrinks from the sunlight and hastens to return home to her dark cottage where it is "dark and cold." Brand shudders when he sees her coming: "What icy gust, what cold memory from childhood / Numbs me? Merciful God!" Mother and son are openly hostile; when Brand approaches her she draws back and threatens him with her stick. Brand tells her of a memory from his childhood around which his thoughts often circle. As his father lay on his deathbed, his mother came into the room and frantically groped under the pillows and bedclothes for the dead man's money and finally "slunk out of the room like a damned soul, / Groaning: 'So this was all!' " Brand's mother reminds him that she "paid dearly" for that money. She rejected the boy she loved in favor of Brand's father, although he was old and withered, because he was rich.

Brand's spiritual struggles and his decisions in the first two acts must be seen in the context of his general psychological position and as part of a large pattern that takes in his entire life. The immediate choice he makes is between staying in the valley and leaving it. This choice has obvious biographical significance for Ibsen. It was a choice he had just made, and the character of Ejnar, fleeing the gloomy north for a gay and irresponsible life as an artist in the south, may represent some of Ibsen's feelings about his own behavior, as the character of Brand may represent his thinking about the Reverend Mr. Lammers and Christopher Bruun, each of whom, in his own way, had accepted stern responsibilities in the north. In *Peer Gynt* Ibsen was to explore the implications of leaving home, as in *Brand* he explores those of staying at home.

But the most crucial choice Brand makes is not between staying in the valley or leaving it, but rather the more fundamental one between love and will as the organizing principle of his life. The first two acts of the play constitute a mythic ascent to the heights for Brand, and they contain all the elements of this experience as they appear throughout Ibsen's work. Brand's lonely and loveless childhood has left him emotionally crippled and he looks upon his childhood home as a polluted valley. Not only his mother's house but the valley itself fills him with dread and loathing: "Away from this stifling pit," he tells himself as he looks down into the valley from above. "The air down there is poisoned, as in a mine. Here no breeze can ever stir."

His position on the heights at the beginning of the play suggests his general psychological position at this crucial point in his life. He has struggled up out of the valley to a position of detachment and objectivity and faces the decision of escaping from the threat to his ego which the valley holds or of adopting some defense against that threat. He chooses, as other Ibsen protagonists do, to defend himself against the threats to the self which the everyday world holds by adopting a project of the will: his "mission" to "cure man's sickness." Brand's "heroic" descent into the valley at the end of Act I must be seen, then, as an ominous adoption of a defensive strategy which involves denying a large part of his own nature. It is significant that both stages of the decision take place in direct reaction to his mother. In Act I, he conceives his mission soon after his despairing meditation over his mother's house; in Act II, he decides to stay in the valley immediately after the sinister interview with his mother.

As the landscape in these two acts—the abyss, the heights, the valley—is charged with emotional associations and is partially a projection of Brand's own state of mind, so Agnes and Gerd are presented in terms of their psychological significance for Brand. Although both have lived in the neighborhood all their lives, Brand seems never to have met them before. Mysteriously, they appear almost simultaneously at the point of Brand's crucial spiritual decision. Agnes is a gentle woman figure, Gerd a fascinating woman figure, and they represent the division in Brand's own self at this point. Their partial status as projections of Brand's own character is suggested by the almost mystic empathy each feels with Brand. Agnes is powerfully drawn to Brand at their first meeting and almost casually breaks her engagement to Ejnar to stay with Brand soon after. Gerd almost magically appears at each point in the play where Brand is faced with a fundamental decision; Ibsen's attempt to rationalize this later in the play, by establishing a tie between the two based on the fact that Gerd's father was the boy rejected by Brand's mother, is rather incredible and seems almost a perfunctory attempt to account for a much deeper psychological tie.

46

Brand's decision on the heights is further marked by a first child-death, the murder of his child by the starving father in Act II. This bizarre incident is rather tenuously linked to the rest of the plot; it serves only to provide an emergency great enough to draw Brand out upon the stormy fjord. Thematically, it is integrated into the play by Brand's soliloquy after the father's death, in which he meditates upon the burden of guilt that the father's action will lay upon the other child who watched him kill his brother.

> . . . what chain of sin and crime will not stretch on
> From them, link upon link? Why?
> The hollow answer echoes: "They were their father's
> Sons." Silence cannot erase this,
> Nor mercy. Where does responsibility
> For man's inheritance from man begin?

This motif of the inherited burden of the past is to reappear in the play, but it hardly seems required at this point. The more basic function of the episode is to signal, in mythic terms, the death of the part of Brand's self which he has renounced.

By the end of Act II, then, the cluster of events which makes up a mythic ascent to the heights is complete. Brand has withdrawn from his threatening primary home up to a position of temporary detachment and has adopted a defensive project of the will, thereby renouncing a basic part of his own nature. He has committed himself fully, he thinks, to his mission and to his exaggerated emphasis upon will:

> I see it now.
> It is not by spectacular achievements
> That man can be transformed, but by will.
> It is man's will that acquits or condemns him.

This decision has been further signaled by the appearance of mythic contrasting women, by his choice of the gentle woman, and by the symbolic death of a child.

Acts III and IV cover the period of Brand's pursuit of his project of the will. The action in these acts centers around three decisions by Brand: to let his mother die unblessed, to let his son Ulf die, and to let Agnes die. Each decision demands more strength of will from Brand to resist the temptation to compromise. His mother offers first to give up half her goods, then nine-tenths, but Brand refuses to go to her bedside until she surrenders everything. He sees the choice between taking Ulf to a warm climate and remaining in the valley as a choice between his love for his son and his duty to his parishioners, and he chooses to let his son die rather than compromise his mission. And he demands that Agnes give Ulf's cap, her last remembrance of him, to a gypsy woman in full realization that she will die if she loses this last tie to love.

This progression of events is like the decision on the heights which formed the subject matter of the first two acts, in that it is presented in heroic and idealistic terms. Brand grieves over his mother's death, but he seldom wavers in his conviction that he was right:

> Henceforth I shall fight unflinchingly for the victory
> Of the spirit over the weakness of the flesh.
> The Lord has armed me with the blade of His word;
> He has inflamed me with the fire of His wrath.
> Now I stand strong in my will;
> Now I dare, now I can, crush mountains.

The decision to let Ulf die is agonizing but Brand compares himself to Abraham, whom God similarly tested. He sees his implacable demands upon Agnes as a virtuous attempt to free her from bondage to the claims of earth, and she confirms him in this before she dies:

> Yes, I have conquered now. Conquered death
> And fear. He was born to die. Ulf is in Heaven.
> If I dared, if I could, I would not beg for him back again.
> Giving my child has saved my soul from death.
> Thank you for guiding my hand.

As in the first two acts, however, Brand's idealistic self-justification is undercut sharply by other interpretations of his actions. The most explicit criticism of Brand comes from the first in the long line of doctors in Ibsen's plays who minister to the spirit as well as to the body. The doctor, who is on his way to tend Brand's mother, asks him to go even though she has not sent for him, but Brand refuses.

> BRAND. As her son, I shall pay her debts.
>   They are my inheritance.
> DOCTOR. Pay your own!

48

BRAND. One may pay for the sins of many.
DOCTOR. Not when he himself is a beggar.
BRAND. Whether I am rich or a beggar, I have the will;
    That is enough.
DOCTOR, *looks sternly at him.* Yes, in your ledger your
    credit account
For strength of will is full, but, priest,
Your love account is a white virgin page.

Later, when the doctor tells Brand that he must take Ulf out of the
valley and Brand at first agrees, he points out the inconsistency in
Brand's unwillingness to compromise in his demands upon his
mother and his readiness to compromise when his son's life is at
stake. But he praises Brand for this:

You act as a father should. Don't think I blame you.
I find you bigger now with your wings clipped
Than when you were the Angel of God.

Ironically, however, the doctor's words make Brand decide not to
compromise, but to stay in the valley and let Ulf die.

Brand himself constantly reveals the intolerable pressures which
his renunciation of love puts upon him. He seems to half-realize that
his fear of love and his fanatical emphasis upon the sternness of a
father-God have origins in his childhood experiences. He confides
to Agnes,

With you
Love came like a sunny spring day to warm my heart.
I had never known it before. My father and mother
Never loved me. They quenched any little flame
That faltered from the ashes. It was as though
All the gentleness I carried suppressed within me
Had been saved so that I could give it all to you
And him.

He almost immediately recoils from this uncharacteristic self-
revelation, however, into another renunciation of love:

What the world calls love, I neither know nor want.
I know God's love, which is neither weak nor mild.
It is hard, even unto the terror of death;
Its caress is a scourge.

He also is quick to repress his own partial realization that his idealistic demands upon his mother are only a rationalization for a more deeply seated hostility and fear of her. He wavers momentarily in his self-confidence when word comes that she is dead, but immediately represses his "weakness": "If I weaken now, I am damned tenfold." The relation between his memories of his father and his attitudes toward God are made clear in another revealing exchange with Agnes:

> I see God closer
> Than I ever saw Him before.
> Oh, so near that it seems as though I might touch Him,
> And I thirst to cast myself into His bosom,
> To be sheltered by His strong, loving, fatherly arms.
> AGNES. O Brand, always see Him so,
> As a God you can approach,
> More like a father, less like a master.
> BRAND. I must see Him great and strong,
> As great as Heaven. I must fight
> In the heat of the day, keep watch through the cold night.

Brand's idealistic rationalizations of his project of the will are undercut most decisively, however, by the mythic imagery of Acts III and IV. Brand, on the heights, has renounced the polluted valley of his primary home where he feels the threat of ego-loss and has adopted his mission as a defensive project of the will. Armed with this source of security, he returns to the valley and sets up a secondary home with Agnes, who is made a symbol of his choice on the heights. Ironically, however, his secondary home gradually becomes a duplicate of the polluted primary home from which he fled. Brand's parsonage is as much a tomb world as the red-roofed cottage of his mother, which filled him with such vague dread upon the heights. His childhood home was dark and cold:

> At home I never saw the sun
> From the leaves' fall to the cuckoo's song.

But his parsonage is even darker:

> BRAND. Yes; this place is cold and bitter. The rose
> Has faded from your cheek; your gentle spirit freezes.
> The sun never warms this house.

AGNES. It dances so warmly and mildly on the shoulder
Of the mountain opposite.

BRAND.   For three weeks
In the summer. But it never reaches the valley.

As Brand is progressively tested and as his fanaticism in pursuing his mission becomes more extreme, the setting becomes even darker and more claustrophobic until, in Act IV, the parsonage has almost literally become a tomb. The act opens in darkness, with the snow falling, "binding the church in a tight shroud." Brand's dark drawing room recalls Furia's tomb in *Catiline* and anticipates the dark interiors of the later realistic plays as an image of the protagonist's inner world. A single candle "illumines the room feebly" as an image of Brand's threatened self. His psychological self-mutilation and withdrawal from the outer world into his "mission" are suggested dramatically by his refusal to allow Agnes to light more candles or to open the shutters:

BRAND. Close the shutters.
AGNES. Brand!
BRAND. Shut them! Shut them tightly!
AGNES. Why must you be so hard? It is not right.
BRAND. Close the shutters.

Brand has nearly reached the ultimate point in his pursuit of his project of the will, and the imminent collapse of the project is signaled by a second child-death, the death of Ulf, and by the death of the gentle woman, Agnes. These two events thus serve a double purpose, as episodes in the overt plot and as mythic representations of Brand's psychological state. Ulf's death suggests, as all such child-deaths do in Ibsen, the psychological consequences to Brand of his radical repression of half of his nature, and the death of Agnes suggests the approaching collapse of the "mission" with which she has been identified.

The last stage of the myth is presented in Act V, which has proved to be the most difficult part of the play for most readers. The meaning of Brand's pilgrimage up the mountain, the significance of the scene with Agnes's spirit, the symbolism of Gerd, the Hawk, and the Ice Church, and the meaning of the final line have all offered

51

difficulties of interpretation. But here, as in the rest of the play, the separate elements, ambiguous in themselves, become clearer if they are seen as parts of the overall pattern of the action.

The act opens six months after the death of Agnes. The Sexton and the Schoolmaster are outside the new church, which is ready for the ceremony of consecration. This church is one in a series of church buildings, both real and metaphorical, which like the landscapes have mirrored Brand's spiritual life. In Act I, he had decided to abandon the series of little mission churches, scattered along a winding circuit, and to go out into the world to raise an all-encompassing church that would stretch "from pole to pole." Gerd has tried to taunt him into going with her up into the perilous Ice Church, but he has chosen to descend into the valley to the church Gerd calls "small and ugly." In Act II, after the interview with his mother, he has chosen to remain in this church, but he has quickly become impatient with it, and in Act IV, at the suggestion of Agnes, he has decided to tear down the old village church and build a spacious new one. The Mayor has wanted to build a town hall which, in its design, reflects the Mayor's view of human nature as perfectly as the church reflects Brand's:

> I thought, for example, we might build
> A poorhouse. And while we're at it, we might combine it
> With other amenities under the same roof:
> A gaol, a hall for meetings and banquets,
> With a platform for speeches, and guest rooms
> For distinguished visitors—

Brand has volunteered to devote his inheritance from his mother to building the new church, and he has won out over the Mayor. But the razing of the old church and the building of the new one have had ominous overtones, noted by the Sexton and the Schoolmaster at the beginning of Act V:

> SEXTON. The new church hasn't brought him much happiness.
> SCHOOLMASTER. Or any of us. The day the old church fell
> It seemed to take with it everything
> In which our life had been rooted.
> SEXTON. They shouted: "Down with it, down with it!" But when
> the beams began to fall,

They dropped their eyes guiltily, as though a sacrilege
Had been committed against the old house of God.

SCHOOLMASTER. As long as the new church was unfinished
They still felt they belonged to the old.
But, as the spire climbed upwards, they grew uneasy.
And now, yes, now the day has come.
How quiet everything is. They are afraid,
As though they had been summoned to elect
A new God. Where is the priest?
I feel frightened.

SEXTON. So do I, so do I!

As for Brand, the consequences of his decision to remain in the valley have taken their toll on him. He sits at the organ of the new church, idly playing "as though he were weeping / For his wife and child."

No. I can find no harmony. Only discord.
The walls and roof imprison the music,
As a coffin imprisons a corpse.

In his bitterness he sees the Lord as rejecting the offering of the new church, so petty in contrast to his former vision of "a vault spanning the world's pain." He is lost without Agnes, and feels that he would recover his strength if he could find one person to share his faith. He is surrounded, however, by compromising scoundrels such as the Mayor and the Provost, who counsel him not to give so much individual attention to his parishioners and not to try to be a saint but just be a "good fellow."

At this point, Ejnar, "pale and emaciated and dressed in black," appears. Brand greets him as one who can share his faith: "I have been longing to meet someone whose heart / Was not of wood or stone." But to his dismay, the joyful Ejnar of Act I has become a gloomy, life-hating fanatic. He is a total-abstinence preacher and a missionary to Africa, and on hearing that Agnes is dead he tells Brand that both he and Agnes are damned. When Ejnar leaves, Brand undergoes a radical transformation. Ejnar was his last hope of strength from others and he now determines to stand alone:

BRAND, *stares after him for a moment, then his eyes flame and
he cries:* And that was the man who was to give me strength!

> Now all my bonds are broken. I shall march
> Under my own flag, even if none will follow.

He throws the keys to the new church into the river, fires the villagers with a passionate desire to follow him up into the "Church of Life," and leads them on a mad trek up into the mountains. In scene two, however, the villagers are tired and hungry, and the Provost and the Mayor, with a few casual lies, easily persuade the people to abandon Brand. They turn on Brand, stone him, and return to the valley.

The third scene is the most extraordinary in the play. Brand, weary and bloody from the villagers' stones, has arrived "among the peaks," actually in the Ice Church, though mist hides it until the end of the scene. He hears voices in the mist, counseling despair; his work has been in vain, for man can never aspire to be like God. Now a gap appears in the mist and the Figure of a Woman, the ghost of Agnes, appears. The Figure tells him that everything has been a dream, that he will recover from his sick fantasies if he will renounce his ideal of All or Nothing. Brand calls for Agnes to come, instead, with him; he regrets nothing and would live his life again the same way:

BRAND.   The horror of dreams
  Is past. Now comes the horror of life.
FIGURE. Of life?
BRAND. Come with me, Agnes.
FIGURE. Stop! Brand, what will you do?
BRAND. What I must. Live what till now I have dreamed;
  Make the illusion real.

In the face of Brand's stubborn refusal to repent or alter, the Figure disappears in a clap of thunder, and a scream, "as though from one in flight," is heard: "Die! The world has no use for you."

The intensely subjective mode of *Brand* is very obvious in this scene. It is possible to read the scene as casting doubt upon the literal reality of almost everything that has gone before. Has the entire action taken place instantaneously in Brand's mind, perhaps at the moment of decision to go or stay, early in the play? The Figure tells Brand that "it was all a dream," that he has been sick and that none of his sufferings has actually occurred. Brand does not reject this explanation, but insists that even if "the horror of dreams is past," he will now confront "the horror of life," presumably to work out in fact what he has thus far only dreamed.

Brand may be a dream-play. If so, this helps account for the degree to which the action, the settings, and the characters are charged with emotional associations and the way in which they are presented as projections of Brand's state of mind.

When the Figure disappears, Brand identifies it as the Hawk:

> BRAND, *stands for a moment as though dazed.* It disappeared
> in the mist,
> Flying on great rough wings across the moor
> Like a hawk. It was a deceitful spirit;
> The spirit of compromise.

Gerd appears, armed with a rifle loaded with a silver bullet, with which she hopes to kill the Hawk. She sees Brand's wounds and identifies him with Christ:

> GERD. Let me see your hands.
>
> BRAND. My hands?
>
> GERD. They're scarred with nails. There's blood in your hair.
> The thorn's teeth have cut your forehead.
> You've been on the cross. My father told me
> It happened long ago and far away.
> But now I see he was deceiving me.
> I know you. You are the Saviour Man!

Brand, however, replies that he is "the meanest thing that crawls upon the earth."

The clouds lift and Brand finds that he is in the Ice Church. He cries out in pain:

> BRAND. I wish I were far away. Oh, how I long for light
> And sun, and the still tenderness of peace.
> I long to be where life's summer kingdoms are.
> *Weeps.*
> O Jesus, I have called upon Your name,
> Why did you never receive me into Your bosom?
> You passed close by me, but You never touched me.
> Let me hold one poor corner of Your garment
> And wet it with my tears of true repentance.

His tears begin to melt the Ice Church and Gerd cries out in terror, but Brand suddenly undergoes a complete transformation:

> BRAND, *serene and shining, as though young again.*
> My life was a long darkness.
> Now the sun is shining. It is day.
> Until today I sought to be a tablet
> On which God could write. Now my life
> Shall flow rich and warm. The crust is breaking.
> I can weep! I can kneel! I can pray!

Gerd sees the Hawk above and fires her rifle at him; the report loosens the roof of the Ice Church and an avalanche starts down toward them. Brand's last words are,

> Answer me, God, in the moment of death!
> If not by Will, how can Man be redeemed?

As Brand and Gerd are buried by the avalanche a voice cries out through the thunder, "He is the God of Love."

The strange sequence of events which makes up the last act of *Brand* can best be understood as the last stage in the myth of the self. At the beginning of the act, Brand is approaching the point of the final collapse of his project of the will, his "mission." The collapse itself comes after Ejnar's exit, when Brand renounces any hope of help in the valley and determines to ascend the mountain. At first his motivation is only an intensification of his exaggerated emphasis upon the will which made up his mission. Brand is obviously mad when he leads the villagers up the mountain. His attitude toward the new church indicates that he will never acknowledge any limits at all; no church will ever be big enough for him. Although his madness does not mitigate the villagers' weakness and cowardice, Brand's behavior shows the final bankruptcy of a life built upon will alone.

Brand's ascent to the peaks is accompanied by a gradual stripping away of his ties to the valley as he moves toward a final self-confrontation, heralded by the reappearance of the two women who personify the division in his personality. Brand identifies the Spirit of Agnes and the Hawk as compromise, as he has always rationalized his inability to love as a resistance to compromise. But on the peaks, confronted by the Ice Church, identified throughout

56

the play with will, and by the Hawk, identified throughout with love, he undergoes a mystic transformation as "the crust breaks" and the sun rises on the darkness of his life. He already knows the answer to the question he asks as the avalanche roars down: Man is redeemed not in the Ice Church of will but by a secure love.

It is no accident that *Brand* has inspired diametrically opposing interpretations. The young Norwegian liberals in its first audience were right in seeing it as a celebration of the individual will and a scathing attack on compromise. Ibsen's initial intention seems to have been to attack what he regarded as the cowardice and opportunism that had kept Norway from intervening in the Dano-Prussian war and to celebrate the courage and commitment he recognized in such men as the Reverend Mr. Lammers, Christopher Bruun, and, more remotely, Kierkegaard and Galileo, both of whom he acknowledged as parallels to Brand (provided, of course, that Galileo had not recanted). He was also apparently dramatizing in *Brand* his own sense of courage during his first years in Rome. "Last summer when I was writing my drama [*Brand*]," he wrote to Bjoernson, "I was indescribably happy, even in the midst of all my pain and misery. I felt the exultation of a Crusader; I would have had the courage to face anything on earth."

But Shaw was also right in pointing out the "anti-idealist" elements in *Brand*. Ibsen's study of a saint of the will is less hagiological than psychological, and undercutting the heroic rhetoric of the play is an ironical and skeptical exploration of the psychological roots of Brand's commitment to the creed of "All or Nothing." Emotionally crippled by parental neglect, unable to love, haunted by a pervading fear of loss of self, Brand adopts his creed as a defense against his own anxieties. His creed leads him down from the heights into a progressively more stifling tomb world until it collapses and Brand ascends the peaks and renounces the entire course of his life at the point of death.

Brand is a turbulent and romantic play, full of tensions and conflicts which are never resolved. And the clear implication of the play is that they are irresolvable. Brand's real quarrel is with life itself, with all its limitations and imperfections, which he calls "compromise"; he yearns for a peace and perfection unattainable this side of the grave. Shaw shrewdly recognized the importance in the play of Brand's longing for a prelapsarian perfection: "Brand acts as if he were the perfect Adam in a world where, by resolute rejection of all compromise with imperfection, it was immediately possible to change the rainbow 'bridge between flesh and spirit' into as enduring a structure as the tower of Babel was intended to be, thereby restoring man to the condition in which he walked with God in the garden." Ibsen uses the same Edenic imagery in the last scene, when he has the Spirit of Agnes tell Brand,

> Remember, an angel with a flaming rod
> Drove Man from Paradise.
> He set a gulf before the gate.
> Over that gulf you cannot leap.

Out of his hopelessly divided soul, Brand answers: "The way of longing remains."

4. *Peer Gynt*

Peer Gynt is the antithesis of Brand. Many consider it my best book. I do not know how you will like it. It is wild and formless, written recklessly and without regard to consequences—as I dare to write only when far away from home.

IBSEN TO EDMUND GOSSE (1872)

Brand AND *Peer Gynt* are so closely related in so many ways that they come close to constituting a single, two-part play. "After *Brand* came *Peer Gynt,* as though of itself," Ibsen told a correspondent in 1870. The spectacular success of *Brand* in the spring of 1866 had added to Ibsen's exhilaration and sense of power. "Rome is beautiful, wonderful, magical," he wrote to a friend in May. "I have an extraordinary capacity for work, and I feel as strong as a giant killer." He cast about for new projects for some time, beginning and abandoning a play about Magnus Heinnesson, struggling with the plans for *Emperor and Galilean,* and revising *Love's Comedy* for a new edition. By the end of the year, however, he had settled on the plan for *Peer Gynt,* "a long dramatic poem, having as its chief figure one of those half-mythical, fanciful characters existing in the annals of the Norwegian peasantry of *modern* times," as he described the play to his publisher.

Ibsen took eight months to write *Peer Gynt;* as the work progressed, the play became more and more closely related to *Brand.* "It will have no resemblance to *Brand,*" he had told his publisher when he began the play, but by the time he completed it the two plays had become so intricately and pervasively interrelated that either can stand as a kind of commentary on the other. As the Thin Person tells Peer in Act V,

There are two ways in which a man can be himself.
A right way and a wrong way.

59

You may know that a man in Paris
Has discovered a way of taking portraits
With the help of the sun. Either one can produce
A direct picture, or else what they call a negative.
In the latter, light and dark are reversed;
And the result, to the ordinary eye, is ugly.
But the image of the original is there.
All that's required is to develop it.

Peer Gynt is, in many ways, the "negative" of *Brand*. Brand is the heroic enemy of compromise, Peer almost its personification. Brand will not turn aside for anything, Peer characteristically "goes round about." Brand stays at home in his valley; Peer escapes to the great world Brand renounced. Brand hates his mother and refuses to go to her bedside when she is dying; Peer loves his, and his most generous action in the play is his comforting of his mother during her final moments. Brand marries Agnes and stays close by her; Peer flees from Solveig and makes her wait half a century for his return.

And yet for all these differences, *Brand* and *Peer Gynt* are profoundly similar, as if the two plays were positive and negative prints of the same man. Both characters are haunted by fears of ego-loss and they retreat from the threats that ordinary life holds into secret, inner worlds. Both alternate between secret feelings of omnipotence and of abject self-hatred, and both defend themselves by adopting obsessive "projects of the will" which involve the renunciation of love. Both pursue these projects to a point just before death, when they renounce them in mystical experiences of reintegration and rebirth.

Peer Gynt begins with a lie, appropriately enough, and the lie of the buck of Gjendin announces the central motif of the play, as Brand's initial situation of crossing a thin shell of ice over an abyss announces the central motif of that play. Peer tells his mother that he has ridden a gigantic buck at top speed along Gjendin Edge:

Have you seen the Gjendin Edge?
Three miles long and sharp as a scythe.
Down over glacier, slide and cliff,
Straight down over sheer grey scree,

60

You can see, on either side,
Straight into the lakes that sleep
Black and heavy, more than four thousand
Feet below.

This fantasy, borrowed though it is from the legend of Gudbrand
Glesne, suggests what is to be later confirmed about Peer's character:
that life for him, as for Brand, is a precarious journey in which he
is constantly threatened by annihilation of the self. Peer, like Brand,
has a very fragile sense of self, but whereas Brand seeks security
in a lofty and rigid morality, Peer finds his in compulsive role-
playing, lying, and fantasizing.

The opening scene is "a wooded hillside near Aase's farm."
Peer, like Brand, is an outsider; he has grown up on an isolated
hill farm. His childhood has been strikingly like Brand's; like so
many other Ibsen protagonists, they have both been reared by one
parent. We learn from Aase's conversation with Solveig in Act II
what life was like for Peer during his childhood:

Mind, when times were tough we stuck together,
For my man had a tongue red for drink.
An idler he was with his bragging, wasting our wealth,
While I and my baby sat at home
Trying to forget. What else could we do? . . .
Some take to drink, others to lying,
So we took to romancing of princes and trolls
And all kinds of beasts. And stealing brides
From their white wedding-beds.

Gradually, throughout the play, we learn more about Peer's father,
a vain and extravagant man while his money (inherited from his
father, Rasmus Gynt) lasted. Aase, while she is packing up to
move away from her confiscated house in Act III, tells a characteristic story of her husband's flamboyance:

Oh, Kari, look! It's an old casting-ladle!
With this he played at being a button-moulder;
Melted and shaped and stamped.
One day at a feast, the little lad came
And asked his father for a lump of tin.
"Tin!", said John. "No! Good King Christian's coin!
Silver! Let people know you're John Gynt's son!"

61

God forgive the poor man, he was drunk,
And then he cared neither for tin nor gold.

This casting-ladle, of course, is to turn up again in Act V and provide the starting point for Peer's button-moulder fantasy.

John Gynt, when his inheritance was spent, took to the roads as
a peddler, leaving his wife and child as lonely as before. He died
while Peer was still young, leaving the house inherited from Rasmus
Gynt falling into ruins, "Half the window-panes stuffed with rags, /
Hedge and fence falling down."

Brand's fatherless childhood has left him loathing his mother and
yearning hopelessly for a father; he longs to cast himself into God's
bosom, to be "sheltered by His strong, loving, fatherly arms."
Peer's response to a similar childhood has ostensibly been the
opposite; he shares his mother's resentment of his father and loves
her deeply. For Peer, Aase is part mother, part playmate, and part
lover, and they run the gamut of these relationships in the teasing,
playful first scene of the play. Oedipal feelings are, if anything,
even more overt in *Peer Gynt* than in *Brand,* and they underlie
Peer's entire relationship with Solveig, culminating in the merging
of mother and wife in the final scene.

In scene two of Act I, Peer, on his way to Ingrid's wedding,
pauses on "a small hill with bushes and heather." From this vantage
point he looks down on the valley below, as Brand does in the
second scene of his play. For both, it is a place from which they
can achieve perspective, a "higher view of things." But whereas
Brand fixes his gaze down into the "stifling pit" of the valley, Peer
characteristically quickly dismisses the valley, throws himself down
on his back, and stares up into the sky. He sees pictures in the
clouds: himself, riding at the head of a great procession, receiving
homage from an assembled throng. Brand has had similar fantasies
of himself as "the chastiser of the age, / Striding in greatness above
the tumult." Both dream of assuming the roles of powerful authority
figures to take the place of their absent fathers. But Brand at least
overtly renounces his fantasies to entomb himself in the valley.
Peer pursues his vision to the very end of his life.

Scene three takes Peer down into the valley for Ingrid's wedding,
as Brand descends into the valley in the first scene of the second act

of *Brand*. Brand's descent was a sacrificial act; Peer's a casual search for entertainment. But for both of them the valley represents the world of ordinary life by which they feel so threatened. Peer, stung by the jeering and ridicule of Aslak and his friends, characteristically reacts by exaggerated boasting and lying:

PEER, *with a gesture*. I can ride through the air on horseback!
There's a lot I can do, I'm telling you!
They shout with laughter again.
ONE OF THE CROWD. Peer, ride through the air for us!
SEVERAL. Yes, dear Peer Gynt!
PEER. Oh, there's no need to beg me!
I'll ride over the lot of you like a storm.
The whole parish shall fall at my feet!

The bride-rape which ends the act is an extension of this same spirit of extravagance by which Peer tries to assert himself in the face of the scorn or indifference of others. He meets Solveig, who first appears, like Faust's Gretchen, holding a prayerbook, but she is frightened by his boisterousness, with its hysterical edge. He responds by retreating even further into his extravagant and grotesque lies:

SOLVEIG. Let me go in peace.
PEER. No.
Softly but sharply and menacingly.
I can turn myself into a troll!
I'll come to your bedside tonight at midnight.
If you hear something hissing and spitting
Don't think it's the cat. It's me, my dear!
I'll be drawing your blood in a cup,
And your little sister, I'll gobble her up!
For at night I'm a werewolf. I'll bite you
All over your loins and your pretty back.
Changes his tone suddenly and begs as though in anguish.
Dance with me, Solveig!
SOLVEIG *looks darkly at him*. Now you're ugly.
She goes into the house.

The transition from this lying, desperate and self-destructive as it is, to the action of the bride-rape is crucial, for it leads to outlawry and the confiscation of his mother's property. Peer has blundered across the thin line that separates fantasy from action, almost without knowing it. The act itself occurs at the same point in the play as Brand's feat of crossing the stormy fjord does in *Brand;* Peer's act, in its very pointlessness, is as characteristic of Peer's strategy of self-realization as Brand's act is of his.

Peer, as a consequence of the rape of Ingrid, is driven in Act II "high up in the mountains": for him, as for Brand, the place of self-confrontation and of freedom from entanglements with others. Peer, in the first scene, brutally rejects the weeping Ingrid and sends her back down the mountain. He himself is almost hysterical from the shock of his sudden passage from dreams to action:

> PEER *runs in at full tilt and stops on the hillside.* The
>   whole parish is after me in a mob!
>   They've armed themselves with rifles and sticks.
>   I can hear Ingrid's father hollering at their head.
>   The news has spread quickly: Peer Gynt's on the loose!
>   This is better sport than bashing a smith!
>   This is life! I feel as strong as a bear!
>   *Punches around and jumps in the air.*
>   To smash and overturn! To dam up the waterfall!
>   To strike! To wrench the fir up by the root!
>   This is life. It hardens and elevates.
>   To hell with all bloody lies!

The first fruits of this new determination to act rather than dream are his debaucheries with the three sex-crazed Saeter Girls. With Peer's reentrance in scene four, experiencing "the expense of spirit in a waste of shame," the play modulates into the blend of external and internal action which Ibsen had used before, most recently in the last act of *Brand.* Peer, full of self-disgust, his head aching from the Saeter Girls' mead, throws himself to the ground and falls into his old game of staring at the clouds and losing himself in dreams. His feet in the "mire and filth," he nevertheless dreams of "soaring":

> I shall soar! I'll wash myself pure in
> The gleaming christening-font!
> I'll fly high over the farmhouse,
> I'll ride till my black soul shines,
> Far over the salty sea
> And high over England's prince!

But in the midst of his dreaming he "takes a running leap forward, but strikes his nose against a rock, falls and remains lying on the ground."

The three scenes which follow—those with the Greenclad Woman, the Old Man of the Mountains, and the Boyg—are thus dream scenes. Peer's dream ends only when he awakens in scene eight, yearning for a salted herring. The dream, in its three stages, represents a progressive descent into Peer's mind, climaxed by the crucial confrontation with the Boyg, the formless personification of the chaos of the unconscious. The dream is made up of bits and pieces from Peer's recent waking thoughts and experiences: his lust for the Saeter Girls, his memories of John Gynt's banquets, and his dreams of restoring the family homestead, and even his headache from the Saeter Girls' mead.

The scene with the Old Man of the Mountains and his troll court is full of satirical references to Norwegian chauvinism and provincialism. But the heart of the scene is the Old Man's explanation of the troll creed:

Out there, under the shining vault of heaven,
Men tell each other: "Man, be thyself!"
But in here, among us trolls, we say:
"Troll, be thyself—*and thyself alone!*"

The troll creed is to provide the basis of Peer's lifelong goal to be "emperor of himself." Although the trolls' brutish rationalization of selfishness seems to have little in common with Brand's heroic creed of "All or Nothing," both are justifications, from the protagonists' inner worlds, of isolation and withdrawal from the world of ordinary human relationships.

The grotesque comedy of the troll scene is succeeded by the cold horror of the scene with the Great Boyg, as powerful an image of engulfment as appears in Ibsen's work. Peer is in "pitch darkness"; he is enveloped by the folds of the Boyg:

Forward or back, it's equally far.
Outside or in, I'm still confined.
There he is! And *there!* And round that bend!
As soon as I'm out I'm back in the middle,
Encircled. Name yourself! Let me see you!
What on earth are you?

The encounter with the Boyg is the nightmarish climax of Peer's dream. In the deepest levels of his mind lie the terrors of darkness and formlessness, of ultimate regression and complete loss of ego. Peer is saved by his ties with the outside world, as Aase and Solveig, in the distance, ring the church bells: "He was too strong. / There were women behind him." The sun rises and Peer wakes up, badly hung over and having found his way in his sleep to Aase's mountain saeter.

Act III, like the first two, is full of reminiscences of *Brand*. The act opens with Peer building his outlaw's hut high in the mountains. *Peer Gynt* uses a series of real and metaphorical houses as *Brand* uses a series of churches to represent its protagonist's states of mind. Peer's memories of his childhood spiral around the house his father inherited from Rasmus Gynt, and his favorite dream is of restoring the house to its past glory, when "light poured from every window" and host and guest alike smashed their bottles against the wall. The clouds become castles in the air, and he tells the Greenclad Woman that his home is a prince's castle, though she at first "may think each crystal window-pane / Is just a fistful of socks and rags." Now, as he builds his outlaw's hut, he dreams of making it look like John Gynt's house:

> It'll be a grand sight! A tower with a weathercock
> I'll have on the roof-beam! And I'll carve on the gable
> A mermaid, shaped like a fish from her navel!
> There'll be brass on the weathercock and all the locks.
> And glass! I must have some of that!
> Strangers will stare and wonder at it
> Glittering there high on the hillside—
> > *Laughs angrily.*
> Bloody lies! There they are again!
> You're an outlaw, my lad.

Peer does not achieve the mermaid and the brass locks, but he does put a set of reindeer antlers over the door and a large wooden bolt on the door, to "lock out all nagging goblins." Aase's home by now has narrowed to the single room allowed her in the confiscated house. The home Peer searches for throughout the play he achieves only when Aase's room and Solveig's hut merge emotionally in the last lines of the play.

Solveig comes to Peer in the mountains, freely choosing him as Agnes freely chose Brand: "I ran here on my skis. I asked my way. / They said: 'Where are you going?' I answered: 'Home.'" Peer is overjoyed:

> My princess! Now at last I've found and won her!
> Hey! Now I'll build my palace on firm, true ground!

But as Solveig waits for him inside the new hut which is to be a palace, the Greenclad Woman reappears, leading, as she had promised, an "ugly child," the product of "nothing but thinking." It is clear that the mode of the play has shifted again from external to internal action and that we are back in the dream world of the troll scene. But what is going on in Peer's mind? The Greenclad Woman's visit is shattering. Even after she has left, Peer cannot go in to Solveig:

> PEER, *after a long silence.* Go round, said the Boyg. So
>   I must here.
> There falls my palace in ruins about me. . . .
> They have gone. Gone, yes; but I can't forget them.
> Tiptoeing thoughts will follow me in.
> Ingrid! And those three that danced on the mountain!
> Will they join me too? With cruel laughter
> Demanding like her to be clasped in my arms?
> To be gently lifted and lovingly laid
> At arms' length? Go round, lad.
> If my arm were as long as a pine tree's trunk
> I fear even then I'd hold her too near
> To set her down white and unstained as before.

It would seem, then, that Peer is kept from Solveig by his guilty memories of his debauchery with Ingrid and the Saeter Girls, of which the dream reappearance of the Greenclad Woman is a reminder. But this is too abrupt to be really convincing; the incoherence of Peer's reasoning, the violence of his reaction, and the fact that he retreats immediately to Aase's hut suggest another explanation of Peer's flight. Bound by his oedipal relationship to his mother, Peer separates women into the Ingrids and the Solveigs. The Ingrids can be sexual objects, especially if they are abused and degraded, but the Solveigs must remain on a pedestal, because they are too closely associated emotionally with the mother. Tenderness and sensuality cannot be directed toward the same woman.

This pattern certainly underlies Peer's actions, as it also underlies those of the Speaker in "On the Fells" and those of Brand. But it does not constitute a complete explanation of Peer's retreat from the door of the hut. Peer's behavior is part of a larger pattern; what he basically fears is intimacy, understanding, and love, for he perceives such a relationship as a threatening invasion of the self. He therefore holds other people at a distance, turning them into objects upon which he can look down from the heights of his imaginary eminence. Solveig offers an escape from this pattern; Brand, though hardly an authority on love, is right when he says, "No one can love all until he has first loved one." But Peer is paralyzed by anxiety at this prospect of not "being himself, and himself alone." He must "go round about."

The final scene of Act III, Aase's death, is clearly inspired by Brand's refusal to go to the bedside of his dying mother. Peer summons up the memory of the old stories his mother told him of Soria-Moria Castle and the horse Grane, and eases his mother's dying with a tender fantasy. As usual, Peer's notions of heaven involve a feast like those his father used to give, but in a play that treats fantasizing so harshly, the scene constitutes a kind of tribute to the fictive imagination. With the bed as the sledge and the cat as Grane, he drives his mother up to the gates of Paradise:

> Gee-up now, Grane, my beauty!
> My word, the excitement is great!
> They've spotted Peer Gynt and his mother,
> And they're fighting to get to the gate!
> What's that you're saying, St. Peter?
> You won't let her in? My good sir,
> You can sit on your backside till Doomsday
> And you'll find no-one better than her.

The scene escapes sentimentality by virtue of the dramatic tension that underlies Peer's actions. In the course of the scene he makes his decision to leave Norway. This decision is at least superficially the antithesis of Brand's crucial decision to remain in the valley. Brand decides to work his way to self-realization *through* the mundane elements of existence. But Peer, both spiritually and physically, must "go round about."

This antithesis, however, like the other antitheses between the two plays, masks a deeper, underlying similarity. The first three acts of *Peer Gynt* constitute a mythic ascent to the heights very similar in its psychological meaning to the action of the first two acts of *Brand*. Peer, his precarious sense of self threatened by life in the valley, has ascended the mountains to the crucial self-confrontation represented by the troll dream. His self-division is signaled by the appearance of two women: the "fascinating" Green-clad Woman and the "gentle" Solveig. His renunciation of his potentiality for love is signaled by a first child-death, in this case the self-mutilation of the boy in the beginning of Act III whom Peer sees chop off his finger to evade military service.

Peer's project of the will involves something of a paradox. Superficially, Peer's impulsive, opportunistic behavior seems to imply a fundamental weakness of will; certainly it is very different from the single-minded fanaticism of Brand. But Peer's very commitment to a policy of selfishness and opportunism has a psychological function very much like Brand's commitment to his mission. Peer's unconscious adoption of the troll creed, "Be thyself—and thyself alone," and his conscious project to become "emperor of himself" is like Brand's adoption of his creed of "All or Nothing" in that both are defenses against love.

The impression of *Peer Gynt* as a sprawling fantasia stems primarily from the fourth act, a wild gallimaufry of grotesque comedy, topical satire, and unstageable spectacle. It presents little that is not already implicit in the first three acts, and Ibsen apparently wrote it only because he could afford to be expansive and "capricious" in a "dramatic poem" intended for reading rather than for the stage. It is a working-out of implications that would remain tacit in a stage play, as Ibsen himself acknowledged by the alacrity with which he dropped it when he was preparing the play for theatrical production. He wrote to Grieg,

> Almost the whole of the fourth act will be omitted in performance. In place of it I think there should be a large-scale musical tone picture, suggesting Peer Gynt's wandering all over the world. American, Eng-

lish, and French airs might be used as alternating themes, swelling and fading. The chorus of Anitra and the Girls [scene six] should be heard behind the curtain, jointly with the orchestra. During this music, the curtain will be raised, and the audience will see, like a distant dream picture, Solveig, now a middle-aged woman, sitting in the sunshine singing outside her house [scene ten]. After her song, the curtain will be slowly lowered again while the music continues, but changing into a suggestion of the storm at sea with which the fifth act opens.

The sequence of events in Act IV shows the consequences of Peer's adoption of his project of the will as the sequence of deaths of mother, son, and wife shows the consequences of Brand's adoption of his. He has declined to take up the challenge Solveig offered and has instead "gone round about." In the spiritual vacuum that results from this choice, all that is left Peer is to resume his old strategy of self-delusion and role-playing, now with the world as his stage. In succession, he plays the roles of predatory capitalist, philanthropist, messiah, sensualist, and philosopher. But the more things change, the more they remain the same, and he sees the pattern of his Norwegian experience repeated all around him. His Arabian charger is the Greenclad Woman's pig, the Moroccan monkeys are the troll children, Anitra is another Ingrid, the Statue of Memnon speaks like the Old Man of the Mountains, and the Sphinx echoes the Great Boyg. The deserts of Morocco and Egypt over which the action takes place reflect Peer's spiritual aridity. He has escaped, not into the castles-in-the-air of his childhood imagination, but into a desert and, ultimately, into the nightmare madhouse of self which ends the act.

All this is rather diffuse dramatically, however, and the crucial consequences of Peer's decision are shown not in the fourth act, but in the fifth, which Ibsen told Grieg should be called "the fourth act or the epilogue." Again, the fifth act is full of cross-references to the ending of *Brand;* both are mythic ascents to the peaks. The act opens with a shipwreck. Peer, "a vigorous old man with grizzled hair and beard," has returned to Norway, lonely and embittered by his life of selfishness. When the captain tells him that all the crew have families waiting for them, he angrily withdraws his offer of a tip for the crew:

70

PEER *bangs the gunwale with his fist.* I'll be damned if I will!
   Do you think I'm mad?
   Why should I pay for other men's children?
   I've had to work hard to earn my money.
   There's no one waiting for old Peer Gynt.

The Strange Passenger now appears, an eerie personification of a premonition of death. He expresses delight at the prospect of all the corpses drifting ashore and asks Peer to bequeath him "his valuable body." Peer characteristically goes round about and offers him money, but the Passenger withdraws, promising to return. As death approaches, Peer is about to be faced with something he cannot "go round." His enforced confrontation with death in this epilogue will call into doubt his whole way of life and bring about a transformation in him like that of Brand in the final scenes of his play.

The lowest point in Peer's career is reached when he is thrown into the sea in scene two. When he is stripped of all supports and confronted with a crisis, the extreme implications of his troll creed are made clear in his brutal killing of the cook. Ironically, in the preceding scene Peer has pleaded with the cook to risk the ship in order to save three men struggling in the water after their own shipwreck. But now, when the wreck, like the wreck that opens *The Tempest,* has dissolved the structures of human culture and a naked, unaccommodated Peer confronts a choice between self-preservation and self-sacrifice, the viciousness that lies beneath his easygoing charm becomes explicit.

From this point in the play, Peer's path leads steadily upward, literally and geographically, to the final confrontation with Solveig. The third scene—the funeral scene—picks up the story of the boy who cut off his finger to avoid conscription at the opening of Act III. This boy is presented as a foil not only for Peer, but by extension for Brand as well. He is a man who stayed home:

   His vision was narrow. Beyond the tiny circle
   Of those who stood close to him, he saw nothing.
   Those words that should have resounded in his heart
   To him rang meaningless like tinkling cymbals.
   His race, his country, all we think great and glorious,
   Were from his eyes veiled in perpetual mist. . . .

> But on his mountainside,
> In the narrow circle of home, where his work lay,
> There he was great, because he was himself.

He has devoted his life to the family he loved, his mother, his wife, and three sons, whom he carried across the mountain to school. Brand's aim has been similar—to "hallow daily toil to the praise of God"—but staying at home has been for him what flight has been for Peer, a strategy for avoiding a proper resolution of the conflict between love and will. The boy who cut off his finger, despised though he was by his neighbors, has achieved such a resolution.

Peer's feet are now set upon a path winding upward to the encounter with Solveig and the long-delayed encounter with himself. The stripping away of the shipwreck scene is continued in the onion scene:

> You old fake!
> You're no Emperor. You're just an onion.
> Now then, little Peer, I'm going to peel you,
> And you won't escape by weeping or praying.
> *Takes an onion and peels it layer by layer.*

> . . . .

> What a terrible lot of layers there are!
> Surely I'll soon get down to the heart?
> *Pulls the whole onion to pieces.*
> No—there isn't one! Just a series of shells
> All the way through, getting smaller and smaller!

At the end of this scene Peer sees the hut with the reindeer antlers, Solveig still sitting before it. Peer's sudden insight here governs the rest of the play:

> PEER *gets to his feet silently, pale as death.* One who
> remembered—and one who forgot.
> One who kept what the other has lost.
> And the game can never be played again!
> Oh, here was my Empire and my crown!

The nature of the succeeding scenes—those with the Threadballs, the Button Moulder, the Old Man of the Mountains, and the Thin Person—is ambiguous. As with the troll dreams of the first acts, there is no transition between action that is realistic and external and action that is expressionistic and internal. It has been suggested that Peer actually dies either in the Cairo madhouse or in the shipwreck and that the last scenes present the experiences of "a soul after death." Michael Meyer even suggests that these last scenes occur instantaneously, as "the film of his life, with its failures and errors, unreeling before his eyes in the moment of death." Except for the scenes with Solveig, this seems to be a legitimate interpretation. At the end of the onion scene Peer is standing before Solveig's hut. The shock of the realization that Solveig has been waiting for him triggers the Button Moulder dream as the drunken fall in Act II triggered the troll dream. Ibsen does seem to have intended that the dream be regarded as occurring instantaneously, since at the conclusion of the dream, in the last scene, Peer is still standing before the hut.

The Button Moulder dream, like the troll dream, is made up of fragments from Peer's immediately preceding waking experience, especially the sight of the casting-ladle being auctioned off in scene four. The Button Moulder himself is the last and the most powerful of the images of personal annihilation that pervade the play from the fantasy of the buck of Gjendin through the encounter with the Boyg and the descent into the sea. Peer's desperate attempts to prove that he has been himself in some sense, if not as a virtuous rebel against trollishness then as a great sinner, recapitulate his life of role-playing and self-delusion. His progress during this struggle is, almost in spite of himself, upward, along a narrow path that "winds up towards the mountains" past the three crossroads of the mind.

The last scene of the play is charged with all the characteristic imagery of Ibsen's concluding scenes of spiritual rebirth. Peer is standing in a thick mist, like Brand before the Ice Church, and like Catiline, he sees his life as a shooting star:

> Hail, brother star! A greeting from Peer Gynt!
> We flash for a moment, then our light is quenched,
> And we disappear into the void for ever.

As Brand in his last moments sees his life as "a long darkness" and longs for "life's summer kingdoms," so Peer, at this point, is suddenly calm and sees his life more clearly than ever before:

> How unspeakably poor a soul can be
> When it enters the mist and returns to nothing!
> O beautiful earth, don't be angry with me
> That I trod your sweet grass to no avail.
> O beautiful sun, you have squandered
> Your golden light upon an empty hut.
> There was no one within to warm and comfort.
> The owner, I know now, was never at home.
> Beautiful sun and beautiful earth,
> Why did you bear my mother and give her light?
> The spirit is mean, and Nature is wasteful.
> Life is a terrible price to pay for birth.
> I want to climb, up to the highest peak.
> I want to see the sun rise once again,
> To gaze till I am tired at the promised land.
> Then let the snow pile over me,
> And let them write above: "Here lies no one."
> And afterwards—let the world take its course.

At this point the mist rises and day breaks. It is the morning of Pentecost, the festival that commemorates the descent of the Holy Spirit upon the Apostles, and on the path below, the singing of churchgoers is heard:

> O thrice blest morn, when tongues of fire
> God's spirit did proclaim!

The Button Moulder appears for the third and last time, and in desperation Peer at last approaches the hut: "This time straight through, / However narrow the path may be."

As the sun rises, Solveig first tells Peer, "You have sinned in nothing, my only child," and then answers Peer's riddle:

> PEER. Tell me, then!
> Where was my self, my whole self, my true self?
> The self that bore God's stamp upon its brow?
> SOLVEIG. In my faith, in my hope, and in my love.
> PEER *starts back*. What do you say? Hush! Now you speak in
> riddles!
> Ah! You are the mother to that child?
> SOLVEIG. Yes, I am. But who is its father?
> It is He Who forgives when the mother prays.

PEER *bathed in light, cries.* My mother! My wife! O, thou pure
woman!
O hide me in your love! Hide me! Hide me!
*He clings tightly to her and buries his face in her
lap. A long silence. The sun rises.*

Meanwhile, the Button Moulder, like Furia at the end of *Catiline,*
retreats into the background with a final threat: "We shall meet
at the last crossroads, Peer." But Solveig's cradle song keeps him
at a distance.

In the last act, as in the rest of the play, the superficial antitheses to *Brand* mask a close underlying similarity. Peer, like
Brand, has been reduced at the beginning of the act to the lowest
point in his fortunes, the last stage in the working-out of the
consequences of his project of the will. At this point he begins a
recovery which will lead him to a mystical experience of reintegration upon the peaks. On his slow progress up the mountain, the
mythic elements of the death of one of the paired women and
a second child-death appear. He hears of the recent death of Ingrid
in the auction scene, and he listens to the funeral sermon of the
boy whose self-mutilation in Act III constituted the first child-
death. Like Brand, he ends his journey high up in the mountains
and as dawn breaks he renounces the whole course of his life,
finally acknowledging the claims of love which he had denied upon
the heights.

The years during which Ibsen wrote *Brand* and *Peer Gynt* were
a time of great energy and joy for him, but as we know from
his letters, they were also a time during which he was wrestling
with a number of profound questions about his life: the validity
of his calling as an artist, the wisdom of his leaving Norway and
whether he should not have remained to face responsibilities in
the north. Both plays bear the marks of this self-examination.
"Brand is myself in my best moments," Ibsen wrote, "and it is
equally true that by analyzing myself I brought to light many of
Peer Gynt's characteristics."
Peer Gynt is a portrait of the Ibsen protagonist as artist, as
Catiline is a portrait of the Ibsen protagonist as rebel and *Brand*

is a portrait of him as minister. Peer never writes a poem, but his is the artist's strategy of coping with life by spinning out lies and fantasies. He is brother to Brand, however, in the way his life is organized around a fundamental insecurity about his identity and in the shape his life assumes as a result of this insecurity. Their lives progress from spiritual valleys to heights, back down to valleys and finally up to the peaks, in similar reenactments of what Ibsen saw as "the tragedy and comedy of mankind and of the individual."

5.
Emperor and Galilean

One day I took the liberty of asking Ibsen:
"Which work does the Herr Doktor regard as his
masterpiece, Brand *or* Peer Gynt?" *I supposed, of*
course, in the inexperience of my youth that it
must be one of these works. Then Ibsen looked at
me, and said simply, "What about Emperor and
Galilean? *In any case it is incontrovertibly the one*
that cost me the most work!"

ARNT DEHLI (Ibsen's masseur) (1928)

Emperor and Galilean occupies a very peculiar position in Ibsen's work. Seldom read and almost never produced, it is generally regarded as something of a literary curiosity. A double-drama with a total of ten acts, the action covers the twelve years of the mature life of Julian the Apostate and calls for twenty elaborate sets, a cast of almost fifty principal characters, and numerous crowd scenes of "soldiers, church-goers, pagan spectators, courtiers, priests, students of philosophy, dancing-girls, servants, the quaestor's suite, and Gaulish warriors" (to cite the cast list for only the first half).

The play is in some ways the pivot around which Ibsen's work turns. He regarded it, at least at the time of its composition, as the masterpiece that would at last establish him as a major dramatist. He worked on it sporadically for seven years, intensively for two more. It stands literally at the center of his career, with thirteen plays preceding it and twelve to follow. When it appeared, four years had passed since *The League of Youth* and four more would pass before his next play, *The Pillars of Society.* The nine years of its gestation had coincided, furthermore, with the crucial period of intellectual and emotional ferment that had begun with the move to Italy in 1864.

In the letters the first reference to the project appears in a letter to Bjoernson on September 16, 1864: "I have also in preparation a tragedy, *Julianus Apostata,* a work which fills me with irrepressible joy." He was also working on the epic version of *Brand* at this time,

77

and he told Bjoernson that he expected to have both *Brand* and the Julian play finished "in the spring or at any rate in the course of the summer." *Brand* was to be finished in 1865, but as a play, not as an epic poem; he was to continue to wrestle with the Julian material for almost a decade and to lay it aside many times, twice to write *Peer Gynt* and *The League of Youth.*

Even after he actually began the writing, in June of 1871, progress was slow. He was determined from the beginning to make the play his masterpiece; he wrote his publisher soon after he began writing: "And now the reason for my long silence: I am hard at work on *Emperor Julian.* This book will be my chief work, and it is taking up all my thoughts and all my time. That positive philosophy of life which the critics have demanded of me will finally be given to them." At first he expected the play to be completed by Christmas, but by December 27 he had finished only the first part. By January 19, 1872, he was thinking in terms of delivering the complete manuscript to his publisher, Hegel, in June, but on July 23 he wrote to Brandes that "that monster *Julian* still has such a grip on me that I cannot escape." At this stage, he still planned the work as a trilogy. On August 8 he wrote to Hegel, "I am glad to be able to tell you that I have finished the second part of the trilogy. Part One, *Julian and the Philosophers,* a play in three acts, will come to about one hundred printed pages. Part Two (of which I am now making a fair copy), *Julian's Apostasy,* a play in three acts, is about the same length. The third play, *Julian on the Imperial Throne,* will be in five acts."

In September he wrote to his brother-in-law that his play would be finished by Christmas, 1872, but now came a radical change in the design. The first two parts were recast as a single five-act play, *Caesar's Apostasy,* and Part Three now became Part Two, *Emperor Julian.* He began writing this second part on November 12, 1872. As he had predicted, this went comparatively quickly, and the play was finished on February 13, 1873. The nine-year project finally completed, he was still confident that it would be his supreme accomplishment: "The work that I am now bringing out will be my chief work," he wrote to Ludwig Daae, soon after the play was done. The book was published on October 16, 1873, in an edition of 4,000 copies. These were quickly exhausted and a second edition of 2,000 copies was almost immediately ordered. From his home in Dresden, Ibsen anxiously followed the work through the printing and impatiently awaited critical reaction, especially from Brandes.

As he had hoped, the play was well received, not with the wild enthusiasm that had greeted *Brand,* but with a kind of respectful awe. He noted with satisfaction, in a letter to Hegel, that "none of my earlier books has caused such a stir up there as this one. It has made its mark in circles that otherwise never concern themselves with literature." He seemed to continue to regard it as his masterpiece for the rest of his life. In 1888, he wrote to Julius Hoffory,

> *Emperor and Galilean* is not the first play I wrote in Germany but it is the first work which I wrote under the influence of German intellectual thought. . . . During my four years' stay in Rome I had occupied myself with all kinds of historical studies with a view to writing *Emperor and Galilean*. I had made notes for it, but I had evolved no distinct plan or plot, much less written any part of the drama. My point of view was still that of the Scandinavian nationalist, and I could not accommodate myself properly to the alien subject. Then came the experience of Germany's great era. I was in Germany during the war and the events following it. In many ways all this acted on me with a force that transformed me. My view of history and of human life had until then been a national one. Now it expanded into a racial view, and with that change I could write *Emperor and Galilean.*

Ibsen considered *Emperor and Galilean* as his chief claim to be regarded not merely as a Norwegian local-colorist, but as a truly European writer, a dramatist-philosopher capable of interpreting, from the lofty heights of a "world-historical" view, the tangled confusion of the present age. "The trend of affairs in Europe," he wrote to Brandes on the day of publication of *Emperor and Galilean,* "is making this work more timely than I myself had thought possible."

The sources of the "positive philosophy of life" in *Emperor and Galilean* have been traced to Hegel, Hebbel, and perhaps Lessing and Goethe. But perhaps more of the play than is generally acknowledged came from Ibsen's own imagination. Fundamentally,

Emperor and Galilean is less a dramatization of Hegelian philosophy than an attempt to construct a theory of world history based on the projection of personal forces upon a world canvas. Ibsen seems to have regarded Julian as one of those rare individuals whose characters epitomize centuries of human development. The philosophy of the Third Empire in *Emperor and Galilean* is a translation into world-historical terms of the psychology of Julian himself. And Julian is the prototypical Ibsen protagonist, close kin to Catiline, Brand, and Peer Gynt, and perhaps to Ibsen himself. "It is a part of my own spiritual life that I am putting into this book," Ibsen wrote to Edmund Gosse in 1872, and as he was finishing the play he wrote to Daae, "In the character of Julian, as in most of what I have written in my riper years, there is more of what I have lived through in spirit than I care to acknowledge to the public."

The philosophy of *Emperor and Galilean* centers, as Ibsen explained to Daae, around the "struggle between two irreconcilable powers in the history of the world—a struggle that will always repeat itself." The two powers are, most immediately, paganism and Christianity, though they are also identified on a number of other levels during the course of the play, and the action of the play centers around the progress of Julian's religious allegiances.

At the point where *Caesar's Apostasy* begins, Julian is nineteen years old and deeply committed to a rigorous and ascetic Christianity, tinged with mysticism. He is suffering intensely, however, amid the corruption of the nominally Christian court at Constantinople. On the throne sits his cousin Constantius, who has climbed to power over the bodies of eleven of Julian's family, including his father and mother. Constantius's guilt has led him to paranoia and to an exaggerated and agonized religiosity. He sees enemies everywhere around him and fears retribution even in the sacraments of the church:

> CONSTANTIUS. That I—I—must enter in before the sight of the Lord! Oh pray for me, Julian. They will offer me the consecrated wine. I can see it! It sparkles like a serpent's eyes in the golden chalice. . . . *Screams.* Bloody eyes. . . . ! Oh, Jesus Christ, pray for me!

80

The poison of such an environment has infected Julian, too. Constantius suspects him and his half-brother Gallus of conspiring to seize his throne and has set them against each other by keeping them in suspense over who is to be named his heir and by enveloping them in a net of vague accusations and veiled threats. Julian has responded by retreating into an almost fanatical asceticism: "Here the anguish of my soul grows worse every day. Evil thoughts crowd in on me. For nine whole days I have worn a hair shirt, and it has not protected me; for nine nights I have whipped myself with scourges, but that does not drive my thoughts away." Despite this piety, he feels his faith constantly threatened. Under the tutelage of Hecebolius he has become a brilliant scholar, but the Emperor has jealously kept him from the classroom, and he himself sees his learning as a temptation to vanity. He has an almost pathological fear of the brilliant philosopher Libanius whose teachings are spreading through Constantinople.

In the course of the first act a series of events alters this pattern, however, and sends Julian out of Constantinople to Athens in search of the wisdom of philosophy. First is an encounter with Libanius himself, who confesses that he came to Constantinople only to seek the friendship of Julian, who has it within him to be an "Achilles of the spirit." He also is instructed by a vision experienced by his childhood friend Agathon, in which an angel said, "Arise, Agathon; seek him who shall inherit the empire; bid him go into the den and wrestle with the lions." When Constantius unexpectedly proclaims Gallus his heir, it at last becomes possible for Julian to leave Constantinople and he wins permission to go to Athens to study philosophy, so that he can "wrestle with the lions" of paganism on the pagans' own terms.

Julian is far along the road to apostasy by Act III. In Athens he has seemingly been leading the pagan life of his companions; the act opens with Julian demonstrating his virtuosity in eloquence and tricks of reasoning to the cheers of his drunken fellow students. But when they leave and he is left alone with his friends Basil of Caesarea and Gregory of Nazianzus, he confides his disillusion. The emperor's power hangs over him even in Athens, though nothing but an ominous silence has greeted his flight from Constantinople, and he hears news from time to time of Gallus's savage and corrupt rule in Antioch. But Athens is hardly more attractive to him now. The admired Libanius he has discovered to be a hypocritical flatterer, who is now engaged in currying favor with Gallus, the future emperor. His disillusion extends beyond individuals, however, to pagan beauty and to learning itself. The beauty of Socrates and Plato and "all the other gay revellers" has degenerated among his companions to drunken debauchery, and pagan learning has become a bag of empty tricks. He yearns for something more: "Books, . . . Always books! When I went to Libanius the answer was: books, books! When I come to you, . . . books, books, books.! Stones for bread! Books are no good to me, . . . it is life I am hungry for, communion with the spirit, face to face. Did a book teach Saul to see? Was it not an overwhelming flood of light, a vision, a voice. . . ?" He tells Basil, "I've learnt only one thing in Athens. The old beauty is no longer beautiful, and the new truth is no longer true."

The hope of a new "communion with the spirit" beyond the possibilities of either Christian faith or pagan learning appears with word of the teachings of Maximus, who has announced in Ephesus that he has power over spirits and shades. Libanius ridicules his claims, but Julian is transformed by the possibilities Maximus holds out, and at the end of the act he rushes off to Ephesus, "where torches ignite and statues smile."

In Ephesus all Julian's hopes are apparently realized. As the third act begins, Julian has been with Maximus for some time, and when Gregory and Basil arrive he tells them that "Maximus is the greatest man who ever lived." "In him is the new revelation," and Julian himself stands "on the threshold" of a similar revelation. To the horror of Gregory and Basil, Julian now conceives of himself as a messiah who is destined to found a Third Empire, an "empire of the spirit" which will restore man's "lost likeness to the deity." He sees himself as destined to stand in a line that stretches from Adam through Moses and Alexander to Christ: "In each successive generation there has been *one* soul in which Adam has been reborn in all his purity; he was strong in Moses the lawgiver; in the Macedonian Alexander he had the power to conquer

82

the earth; he was almost perfect in Jesus of Nazareth. But you see, Basil, *grasping his arm* they all lacked what is promised to *me,* . . . the pure woman!"

The final confirmation of this vision is to come this evening; "the last veil will fall" in a seance that Maximus will hold. Basil and Gregory retreat, appalled by what they take to be Julian's madness, and Julian is left alone with Maximus for the great revelation. In an orgiastic, Dionysian rite, Maximus summons up spirits. The first, a face hovering in a blue flame, tells Julian that he is to "establish the empire" and that this will be done "by way of freedom."

JULIAN. Tell me all! What is the way of freedom?

VOICE. The way of necessity.

JULIAN. And by what power?

VOICE. By *willing*.

JULIAN. *What* shall I will?

VOICE. What you *must*.

When the spirit vanishes, Maximus interprets the message to Julian:

MAXIMUS. There are three empires.

JULIAN. Three?

MAXIMUS. First, that empire which was founded on the tree of knowledge; then that empire which was founded on the tree of the cross . . .

JULIAN. And the third?

MAXIMUS. The third is the empire of the great mystery, the empire which shall be founded on the tree of knowledge and the tree of the cross together, because it hates and loves them both, and because it has its living springs under Adam's grave and Golgotha.

Maximus now summons up three other spirits, the "three cornerstones under the wrath of necessity" and the "three great helpers in denial." The first is Cain, who tells Julian that he willed what he had to, because "I was *myself!*" The second is Judas, who describes himself as the "twelfth wheel" who sent the chariot "into glory." But he, too, has willed what he had to will. The third spirit cannot appear because, Maximus discovers, it is still among the living. Julian, if he is this third spirit, thus stands not in the succession of Moses and Christ but in that of the "helpers in denial," Cain and Judas. He violently rejects this possibility:

JULIAN. No; a thousand times no! Away from me, evil man! I repudiate you and all your works. . . .

MAXIMUS. And necessity?

JULIAN. I defy necessity! I will not serve it. I am free, free, free!

The experience presented in this bizarre scene provides Julian's motivation for the rest of the action, but its meaning is clouded with paradoxes and unanswered questions. As Maximus insists, "The signs conflict." Is Julian doomed to be the third "cornerstone under the wrath of necessity"? Or is he, as he insists, "free," as Moses and Christ were free? Indeed, is the great vision of a Third Empire an authentic one, or is Maximus a charlatan and Julian a madman, as Basil and Gregory believe?

Julian has no time to ponder these questions, for the seance is broken off by the arrival of the Emperor's emissary, Leontes, who comes to proclaim Julian the new Caesar, heir to the imperial throne. Gallus has been "executed" by the jealous Constantius, who now orders Julian to take his place and go to take charge of the campaign against the barbarians in Gaul. Julian wavers, knowing that a fate like Gallus's may await him, but then impulsively agrees when a series of coincidences persuades him that this new development has been prophesied as the beginning of the chain of events that will lead to the Third Empire. The last and most decisive of these is Constantius's offer of his sister Helena as Julian's bride. "The pure woman!" Julian cries. "Everything is miraculously fulfilled! Robe me in the purple!" He departs for Gaul as Maximus murmurs, Brand-like, "Victory and light to the man who *wills*."

This decision of Julian's to set his feet upon the path to the imperial throne in the belief that he is advancing toward the Third Kingdom is the major turning point in the play. The rest of the play is a series of events which demonstrate the fatal error of his decision and prove Julian to be not a Christ-like leader but a Judas-like pawn of the "world-will."

The disillusionment begins with Act IV. In Gaul, Julian has
fallen, as he feared he would, into the coils of the Emperor's
jealousy and hatred. He has triumphed against the Alemanni and
won the love and respect of his army, but he fears that his successes
will arouse the Emperor's jealousy even more. He is surrounded
by spies, and every detail of his life, even his menus, is dictated
from afar by the Emperor. He is particularly worried by an incident
in his recent campaign; King Chnodomar, a captured German
chieftain, has hailed him as "mighty Emperor." Julian fears that
Constantius will seize upon this as a pretext for having him murdered, as he did Gallus. He proposes to Helena that he relinquish
the rank of Caesar and retire with her to solitude and study. But
Helena lusts after the throne and tries to persuade him to seize it
from Constantius. Again, the pressure of events forces him into
an impulsive decision. A tribune, Decentius, arrives to place Julian
under arrest and escort him to Rome. Helena is poisoned by a gift
of fruit sent by the Emperor and she dies, revealing in her hysterical
babbling that she has been the mistress of Gallus and that she is
now pregnant by a priest commissioned by Constantius to seduce
her. Julian refuses to submit to arrest, summons his army around
him, and has them proclaim him Emperor.

Julian's apostasy is completed in Act V. In hiding in the catacombs beneath the church in Vienne, he ponders the choices open
to him. He can submit to Constantius and renounce his soldiers'
acclamations of him as Emperor or he can push forward toward
the throne. To submit to Constantius means almost certain death;
to oppose him is for Julian to set himself against Christianity itself.
Maximus urges him to renounce finally the paralyzing, life-hating
faith of the Christians and seize power, to choose between "life"
and "the lie." The choice is made when Julian hears the Christians
in the church above singing hymns to Helena, whom they have
elevated to sainthood and to whose body they are bringing their
sick to be healed. Julian descends into the depths below and sacrifices to the old gods, renouncing his last ties with Christianity.
Stained with the sacrificial blood, he throws open the door of the
church and emerges into the light as the soldiers cry "Long live
the Emperor Julian," and he himself proclaims that he is "Free,

85

free! Mine is the kingdom!" But counterpointed against his cry is the monotonous chanting of the Christians: "Thine is the kingdom, and the power, and the glory, for ever and ever, amen!"

The Emperor Julian follows Julian through the tragic train of events growing out of his decision at the end of the first part. This second play is marred by a certain falling-off of dramatic tension and by some strained effects, perhaps the inevitable consequences of the fact that the outcome of Julian's career is so clearly foreshadowed in Part I.

Act I of *The Emperor Julian*, which begins with the funeral procession of Constantius, shows Julian already enmeshed in the deceit and corruption of the court. His own behavior is hypocritical: "I am filled with the utmost apprehension at the thought of taking the helm after such a great and virtuous and dearly beloved Emperor," he tells Caesarius. But he is surrounded by egregious flatterers, to whose blatant lies he seems curiously vulnerable. Over the coffin of Constantius he proclaims his allegiance to the pagan gods and announces a policy of religious tolerance, the first step toward a Third Empire that will unite "the tree of knowledge and the tree of the cross." He assumes the office of Chief Priest and openly sacrifices to Fortuna before the silent crowd.

From the beginning of his reign, Julian combines a hysterical megalomania with an utter inability to administer the empire. Already he is haunted by visions of divine power: "I esteem the gods too highly to wish to usurp an unwarrantable seat among them, although I am fully aware that often, particularly in olden times, there were heroes and rulers so distinguished by the grace and favor of the gods that it was difficult to say whether they were rightly to be reckoned as mortals or immortals." He is completely unable to understand the attitudes of his subjects or the effects of his actions, however, and he is shielded from any real knowledge of public reaction by the constant lies of his toadies and flatterers, whom, with predictable ineptness, he immediately appoints to positions of power. The only truthful man at court, Ursulus, he has arrested and prosecuted for carrying out the commands of Constantius.

Julian meanwhile pursues his veneration of the pagan gods, and appears in Dionysian rites in the role of Dionysus himself, dressed in a panther-skin and with vine-leaves in his hair. His quest for pagan beauty is no more successful now, however, than it was in the old days in Athens:

> JULIAN. Was there any beauty in that? . . .
>
> Where were the elders with their white beards? Where were the pure maidens with bands on their brow, modest of bearing, and chaste amid the joys of the dance?
>
> For shame, you whores! . . . *He tears off the panther-skin, and throws it to one side.*
>
> Where has beauty gone? Will she not return at the Emperor's bidding?
>
> Ugh, this foul debauchery! . . .
>
> Those faces! Those distorted features screaming with every kind of vice. Cankers of body and soul. . . .

Faced with disappointments and disillusionment in Constantinople, he flees to Antioch to "be nearer Helios, as he rises."

In Act II, Julian's hatred of Christianity, which he has tried to veil behind his public policy of tolerance, comes to the surface, and systematic persecutions begin. Julian's place among the "helpers in denial" now becomes clear. Sunshine Christians flock out of the churches to worship the pagan gods of their emperor. But Julian's persecutions only strengthen the faith of the genuine Christians. The first of his unwitting converts is his old school friend Gregory. In Athens he was only a nominal Christian; but now, faced with Julian's persecutions, Gregory's congregation at Nazianzus has ordained him priest: "Me, a priest! I wanted it, and I didn't. I had to, and I didn't dare. I wrestled with the Lord God as the patriarch wrestled with Him in the days of the Old Covenant. What went on inside me during the night that followed I do not know. But I *do* know that before the cock crow I spoke face to face with our Crucified Lord. . . . Then I was his."

Similarly, Agathon, Julian's childhood friend in Cappadocia, becomes a martyr, with his brother Hilarion, to Julian. There has always been a note of fanaticism in his faith; at the beginning of *Caesar's Apostasy* he has exulted with Julian in the razing of a temple to Cybele and the slaughter of the worshippers. But now he has attacked the temple of Venus and Julian has him tortured

87

mercilessly. He is released, crazed by his suffering, and is preserved to be Julian's nemesis.

In Act III, signs multiply that Julian is fated to lose in his struggle with the Galilean. Frantic with confusion and dismay over the triumphs of the Christians, he retreats even further into a maniacal pedantry, attempting to prove by his writing the truth of his position. He appears at the beginning of Act III as a low-comedy pedant, "wearing a ragged coat, fastened with a piece of rope; hair and beard are unkempt, and his fingers are stained with ink; in both hands, under his arms, and tucked in his belt, he is carrying piles of parchment rolls and papers."

Most damaging of all his failures is his failure to carry out his attempt to defy Christian prophecy by rebuilding the temple at Jerusalem. Under Jovian, the Emperor's servants have attempted the task, but miraculous earthquakes have leveled not only the new structure but the old ruins as well. Thus Julian has unwittingly carried out the prophecy that "there shall not be left one stone upon another."

It is at this low point in his fortunes that Julian embarks upon his project to conquer the world. He seeks the advice of Maximus, who tells him that he has gone astray in his mission:

> MAXIMUS. You know that I have never approved what you have done as Emperor. You wanted to make the youth into a child again. The empire of the flesh has been swallowed up by the empire of the spirit. But the empire of the spirit is not the final stage, any more than the youth is. You wanted to prevent the youth from growing, . . . to prevent him from becoming a man. O you fool, drawing your sword against what shall be, . . . against the third empire, where he who is two in one shall rule.

This double "Emperor-God" will be "Logos in Pan . . . Pan in Logos," and he will be bodied forth "in him who wills himself."

Julian has erred in turning aside from the quest for the Third Empire, trying to revive the "first empire" of paganism, and identifying his opponent as the "second empire" of the Galilean. His interpretation of Maximus's words—and Maximus does not object —is that he should launch forth into a campaign to conquer the world.

Ibsen presents Julian as teetering on the edge of insanity through the two final acts of the play. His campaign against the Persians is dogged by misfortune and portents of doom, but as his fortunes decline, Julian's megalomania breaks all bounds. With a niggling pedantry, he attempts to prove that, despite his reverses, he belongs among the immortals of human history:

> I will not speak of the fact that the Galileans consider the Jew, Jesus of Nazareth, to have been thus chosen; because these people are wrong, . . . as my treatise against them will show in detail. But I will mention Prometheus of ancient times, an outstanding hero, who conferred even greater benefits on mankind than the immortals apparently wished . . . for which he had to suffer much pain and scorn, before he was finally admitted to the company of the gods, . . . where he had essentially always belonged.
>
> And may not the same be said of Heracles and of Achilles, and finally of the Macedonian Alexander, with whose exploits some have compared my achievements in Gaul, and more particularly, my aims on this campaign?

He has dreamed that Minerva and Apollo have led him to the summit of a mountain and promised him that he will become a god. And by the end of the act, he has ordered his bust set up on all the army paytables and commanded all the soldiers to sacrifice to him as to a god.

In the line of march, he meets Basil of Caesarea and his sister Macrina, whose letters to Basil he has read when they were together in Athens. Basil shrewdly perceives that Julian's campaign against the Persians is no new departure but a continuation of his struggle against Christ: "Who is he leading his armies against? Not so much against the King of Persia as against Christ. . . . It is becoming clearer and clearer to me that it is *us* the blow is aimed at. All the defeats he suffered in Antioch, all the resistance he has encountered, all the humiliations and disappointments he has had to endure because of his ungodly conduct . . . all that he intends shall be buried in oblivion by a victorious campaign." Maximus continues to reassure Julian that he is the prophet of the Third Empire, not a "helper in denial," but he tells him that he must truly seek the Third Empire, not merely try to revive paganism. "The world's vine has grown old, and yet you think that you can go on offering fresh grapes to those who are thirsting for the new wine."

As Julian's end approaches, in Act V, his obsession with Christ becomes more and more overt. His army is trapped on a desert plain, their ships burned, total defeat apparently near, and Julian broods on the riddle of Christ. He has finally learned that his persecutions only increase the Christians' power. "Can you explain this riddle to me?" he asks Oribases. "With twelve humble men, fishermen, unlettered folk, he founded this."

In the depths of his depression, he yearns to "lay waste the world" with poison, fire, or the sword that Caligula dreamed of, mighty enough to slaughter the whole world at one blow. As the Persians attack, he desperately cries that he will sacrifice to the gods.

> MAXIMUS. Which gods, you fool? Where are they . . . and what are they?
>
> JULIAN. I will sacrifice to one or other of them. I will sacrifice to many. One of them must surely hear me. I will call upon something outside me and above me. . . .

He falls, not at the hands of the attacking Persians but at the hand of the crazed Agathon, who hurls a spear at him crying "With Christ for Christ!" The spear, Agathon says before he is struck down by the Persians, is "The Roman's spear from Golgotha." "Thou hast conquered, Galilean," Julian cries out as he falls.

Dying amid the ruins of his empire, Julian regrets nothing: "I have nothing to repent of. I know in my own mind that I used to the best of my ability the power which circumstances placed in my hands, and which emanates from the divine. I have never deliberately wronged anyone. There were good and valid reasons for this campaign; and if some think I have not lived up to expectations they should in fairness remember that there is a mysterious power outside us which essentially determines the outcome of human endeavour." He cries out to the sun as he dies: "Oh sun, sun, why didst thou deceive me?"

Maximus, standing over Julian's body, at last acknowledges his error in interpreting the message of the spirit symposium:

90

Led astray like Cain. Led astray like Judas. . . . Your God is a wasteful god, Galileans! He is lavish with souls. Were you, Julian, not the right one, this time either . . . sacrificed on the altar of necessity? Is life worth while? All is a game and a jest. . . . To *will* is to *have to will*. Oh my beloved . . . all the signs deceived me, all the omens spoke with a double tongue, so that I saw in you the mediator between the two empires. The third empire shall come! The spirit of man shall reclaim its heritage . . . and burnt offerings shall be made for you and your two guests in the symposium.

The final words are Basil's and Macrina's. Julian, they say, was a "glorious shattered instrument of the Lord," a "rod of correction . . . not for our death, but for our resurrection."

MACRINA. Fearful is the mystery of election. What do we know. . . ?

BASIL. Is it not written: one vessel is made unto dishonour and another unto honour?

MACRINA. Oh brother, let us not seek to the bottom of this abyss. *She bends over the body, and covers the face.* Erring human souls . . . if you were *forced* to err, allowance will indeed be made on that great day when the Mighty One shall come in a cloud to judge the living dead and the dead who live! . . .

The "positive philosophy" of *Emperor and Galilean* postulates a World-Will which moves toward an ultimate reconciliation of all the antithetical forces in the play: pagan beauty and Christian goodness, the tree of knowledge and the tree of the cross, freedom and necessity, love and will. A few great supermen of history— Moses, Alexander, Jesus—have, in their freedom and wholeness of being, recalled Adam's state before the Fall and anticipated man's future state. By their individual wills, they have advanced the World-Will. But others—Cain, Judas, Julian—have been false Adams. They have not willed the progress of the World-Will in true freedom, but have been its unwitting instruments, as "helpers in denial."

This rather murky philosophy, aside from its borrowings from various bodies of nineteenth-century Hegelian thought, is a projection, on a "world-historical" scale, of the character of Julian, who is tormented throughout his life by a haunting sense of self-division and who hopelessly yearns for wholeness and security of being, a "third empire" of the self.

Julian's general psychological position is powerfully presented in the fantasy he reports to Gregory and Basil in the third act of *Caesar's Apostasy:*

> It happened one night as I prayed and fasted. I felt myself being transported far away . . . far into space and beyond time; around me was bright shimmering sunlight, and I was standing alone on a ship with slackened sails in the glassy sparkling Aegean sea. Islands towered up in the distance like airy banks of cloud at anchor, and the ship lay heavy and drowsy on the wine-dark surface. . . .
>
> Then see! The surface grew more and more transparent, lighter, thinner; at last it was no longer there, and my ship was poised over a terrible empty abyss. No vegetation, no sun down there, . . . only the lifeless black slimy sea-bed in all its horrible nakedness. . .

This dream is the setting for Julian's "great redemptive revelation": "That which is, is not, and that which is not, is." But it is also a schizoid anxiety fantasy, in which the dreamer's fears of ego-loss are represented as the sense of being poised over "a terrible empty abyss" and his perception of the world as dead is represented as the vision of "the lifeless black slimy sea-bed." The fantasy is thus parallel to Brand's journey over a thin shell of ice covering an abyss and to Peer Gynt's lie of riding a buck down a narrow ridge.

The paralyzing and pervasive sense of a threatened self constantly in danger of being engulfed, which is indicated by Julian's dream, helps to bring into focus a number of his other characteristics. Although Julian's inner world is a "lifeless black slimy sea-bed," he finds the external world even more threatening, and he withdraws into a habitual morbid introspection. In this inner world he alternates between exaggerated feelings of guilt and self-hatred and an equally exaggerated sense of power approaching omnipotence. In the first scene of the play, he demonstrates both poles of his self-estimation. He tells Agathon, "Here the anguish of my soul grows worse every day. Evil thoughts crowd in on me. . . . Alas, Agathon, it's nothing short of sin and blasphemy to kneel to me. If you knew how heavy my burden of guilt is now." He wears a hair shirt and whips himself with scourges. And yet in the same scene he confesses his feeling that he is an extraordinary being, perhaps a god:

JULIAN. Did I ever tell you what my mother dreamt the night before I was born?

AGATHON. Not that I remember.

JULIAN. No, no, that's true, . . . I only heard it later.

AGATHON. What did she dream?

JULIAN. My mother dreamt she was giving birth to Achilles.

This alternation continues through the play and becomes even more extreme, until Julian, near the end of his life, mingles moments of abysmal despair with the megalomania that leads him to have himself proclaimed a god.

Julian, in his relationships with others, demonstrates the characteristic strategy of approaching intimacy and then fleeing from it. He genuinely loves Helena and confesses to her that he has never loved anyone else:

JULIAN. How irresistibly, how divinely beautiful you are!

HELENA, *clinging to him.* Am I, Julian?

JULIAN, *embracing her.* You are the only woman I have ever loved, . . . the only one who has ever loved me.

But after his disillusionment with her and her death, he never establishes an intimate relationship with a woman again. He is overcome with revulsion at the sight of the half-naked women in the procession of Dionysus, and Phocion comments in Act II of Part II: "He is a modest man, you may be sure. He doesn't notice women. I'll swear that since his wife died he hasn't often . . . ; I tell you, he spends the whole night writing."

This avoidance of intimate relationships with women extends to other people in general. His scorn and contempt for those around him and for his subjects is a way of holding them at a distance and thus avoiding the ego-threat of being "invaded" by another person. "The ignorant mob never knows what to make of the unexpected," he tells his subjects. "Laugh, if you want! Cross yourselves! I can see you would jeer at me; you would stone me, if you dared. . . . Oh, how ashamed I am of this city, which has sunk lower than the barbarians, and which knows no better than to cling to the crazy notions of an ignorant Jew! . . . Forward! Stand aside, . . . don't get in our way!"

93

His intellectualism, too, is a manifestation of his preoccupation with the inner world into which he has retreated. He is a brilliant scholar when the play opens, but the defensive nature of his bookishness becomes clear later, in Part II, when he incongruously retreats into an absurd pedantry as events turn against him.

Julian's character, then, is very similar to Brand's, and the general course of the action in this play is much like that of *Brand*. Brand's defensive fanaticism might have had results much like those of Julian's if they had not been confined to a narrow valley but had been worked out upon the stage of an empire. If we "stand back" from the busy and confused surface action of *Emperor and Galilean*, the sequence of crises and decisions in the spiritual development of Julian assumes a shape much like that of *Brand* and like those of Ibsen's other plays.

The action of *Caesar's Apostasy* constitutes a mythic ascent to the heights. The play begins in the "polluted valley" of Constantinople. The origins of Julian's neurosis are evident in the picture we get of his frightful childhood. He spent his first six years in Cappadocia, in the company of Gallus and Agathon. This time seems like a happy dream to him later, as a man. But the bliss of early childhood has been ended by Constantius, who has murdered eleven of Julian's family and brought Julian and Gallus to the court of Constantinople.

In the last act of *Caesar's Apostasy*, Julian describes what life was like under the supervision of Constantius: "In all his dealings with me has he not been like a shipwrecked boat without a rudder, . . . drifting now to the left on the current of distrust, now driven to the right by gusts of remorse? Did he not stagger on to the imperial throne, terror-stricken, his purple mantle dripping with my father's blood? And perhaps with my mother's too. . . . Every night I have lain sweating with terror, lest the day just past should be my last."

Constantius is psychotically suspicious of everyone. At his first entrance with Julian he catches him up on every word and every movement:

> CONSTANTIUS *stops suddenly, turns round to Prince* JULIAN *and asks sharply,* Where is Gallus?

JULIAN, *turning pale*. Gallus? Why do you want Gallus?

CONSTANTIUS. I caught you that time?

JULIAN. My lord . . . !

EUSEBIA, *seizing the* EMPEROR *by the hand*. Come on, come on!

CONSTANTIUS. That was the voice of conscience. What are you up to, the two of you?

But Julian has also been terrorized in youth by priests, as he tells Maximus in Act V:

MAXIMUS. Were Constantius and death your worst terrors? Think!

JULIAN. Yes, I suppose you are right. The priest . . . ! My whole youth has been a perpetual dread of the Emperor and Christ. Oh, he is terrible, this mysterious . . . this merciless god-man! Wherever I wanted to go, he loomed up large and forbidding in my path, adamant and pitiless in his demands.

MAXIMUS. And these demands . . . were they *within* you?

JULIAN. Always imposed from without. Always "thou shalt." When my soul curled up inside me, consumed with a piercing hatred for the murder of my family, the commandment said, "Love thine enemy!" When my spirit, bemused by beauty, thirsted for the traditions and images of the lost world of the Greeks, I was paralyzed by the Christian command: "Seek only the one thing needful!" When I felt sweet desires and longings of the flesh, the Prince of Self-denial would strike terror into me with his: "Die unto this life, and live in the life beyond!"

This speech suggests a secondary interpretation of the title of the play; "Emperor" and "Galilean" are not only Julian and his enemy, they also stand for the two forces which terrified him as a child. And as the ambiguity of his reference to the "merciless god-man" suggests, they are emotionally identified in his mind. The political terrorism of Constantius and the religious terrorism of the priests have had identical effects; they have turned Julian into an anxiety-ridden fanatic.

Julian even feels that the air in Constantinople is poisonous and he yearns for the fresh heights of his innocent childhood:

JULIAN. I can't stand the Palace air. I think it's unhealthy here. . . . This is not like Macellum. Macellum lies high up. Not another town is as high in the whole of Cappadocia; ah, how the fresh wind sweeps over from the Taurus snows . . . !

Julian's flight from this stifling tomb world to the sunny freedom of Athens is the first stage in his ascent to the heights. The rest of Part I is devoted to his adoption of a project of the will as a defense against the anxieties internalized from both Emperor and Galilean. This project of the will is the dream of the Third Empire, conceived in the seance scene in Ephesus and finally adopted in the last scene of Part I in the Vienne catacombs. In the course of events which lead to this decision, Julian encounters a fascinating woman, Helena, and a gentle woman, Basil's sister Macrina. Julian is bemused by the prophecy that he has been promised "the pure woman." At first he believes Helena to be this pure woman and becomes Caesar on the strength of Constantius's promise of her hand. But Helena turns out to be corrupt almost beyond belief.

The figure of Macrina, although she does not appear until Act IV of Part II, is a shadowy presence throughout the play. We first hear of her in Act II of Part I, when Basil reads Julian a letter from her. Julian is immediately strangely drawn to her: "When you tell me of the things she writes, I have the impression of listening to something fully rounded and whole, which I had long been yearning for." She is similarly attracted to him, even without meeting him: " 'Whenever you write about your friend, the Emperor's young cousin, my soul is filled with great and radiant joy. . . .' " They finally meet only late in Julian's life, when the march to Persia takes him past the hermits' cells of Basil and Macrina. In her letters to Athens, she had called Julian a great servant of God, a "David born again, who shall slay the champions of the pagans." Now she sees him still as God's instrument, though an unwitting one. She boldly tells him that he is "no more than a scourge in God's hand." But his very hatred testifies to his belief: "What is it you hate and persecute? Not him, but your belief in him. And isn't he alive in your hate and persecution, just as he is alive in our love?" Julian is strangely moved by her words. "Basil," he says, "I wish I had known this woman before." The last lines of the play and the final judgment upon Julian are given to Macrina.

The antithetical figures of Macrina and Helena represent the choice Julian makes at this point in his life between love and will. Julian's ambition of establishing a Third Empire is rooted in his childhood fears of both Emperor and Galilean; he adopts it as a way of avoiding the acceptance of love that Macrina personifies. The death of Helena's unborn child is a "first child-death" which underscores Julian's rejection of his own potentialities.

Julian's final step in adopting his project of the will—his decision to accept the imperial purple—is presented in a remarkable scene full of imagery of regression and rebirth. The scene is the catacombs beneath the church in Vienne. Steps lead to passages even lower, and the vault, like Furia's tomb and Brand's parsonage, is "dimly lit" by a flickering lamp. The vault, like the bottom of the sea, is full of "gliding, clammy shadows" and "slimy things," but Julian descends even deeper into the winding, lower passages for the sacrifice that will climax his apostasy. When the sacrifice is finished he emerges like one reborn, climbing up from the lower depths, with "blood on his forehead, breast, and hands."

Acts I to III of *Emperor Julian* present the middle stage of the myth of the self: the pursuit of the project of the will and its gradual degeneration. Julian returns to the polluted valley of his primary home, Constantinople, armed with his defensive project of the will. But his pursuit of his project drives him to greater and greater extremes. His reign becomes a nightmare of terrorism and he himself comes near to madness until, at the end of Act III, he adopts his megalomaniacal ambition to "possess the world."

Acts IV and V, Julian's final campaign against the Persians, are full of muted suggestions of an abortive ascent to the peaks. Julian's march to Persia takes him into a "wild mountainous country" on the eastern frontier of the empire. His strategy is to march straight east along the Tigris—which will carry his supply ships—cross a desert and a ridge of high mountains, and attack King Sapor at Ctesiphon. He is moving at once toward "Helios, as he rises," and the mountain heights. But his wandering path ends short of the mountains, on "a stony desert plain, without trees or grass." In the distance, between the army and the mountains, the Persians have set fire to the grass and the army is immobilized until the ground cools. The scene is Dantesque in its reflection of spiritual aridity.

97

Julian's death scene takes place on the plain at the foot of the mountains. It is *"Daybreak. Mist."* The battle begins and Julian rushes in, without helmet and armor, carrying only sword and shield, convinced that he cannot die except in Phrygia, where his death has been prophesied. As the dawn breaks, he sees in the morning clouds "the Galilean's hosts" gathering, the women plaiting bow-strings from their hair, like the Viking Hjordis in *The Vikings at Helgeland.* As he falls, struck down by Agathon's spear from Golgotha, it is *"Sunrise."* He is carried to his tent and dies crying out to Helios: "Oh, sun, sun, why didst thou deceive me?" But there is no spiritual enlightenment, no integrating vision for Julian as there was for Brand and for Peer Gynt. He goes to his death convinced that his way of life has been correct: "I have nothing to repent of. I know in my own mind that I used to the best of my ability the power which circumstances placed in my hands." He never attains the psychological "third empire" of wholeness and security.

There is no doubt that Ibsen believed Julian's dream of a Third Empire to be a valid vision of world history. Fourteen years after the publication of *Emperor and Galilean,* he told the guests at a banquet in Stockholm,

> I believe that the time is not far off when political and social concep-
> tions will cease to exist in their present forms, and from both of them
> will arise a unity, which for a while will contain within itself the con-
> ditions for the happiness of mankind. I believe that poetry, philosophy,
> and religion will be merged in a new category and become a new vital
> force, of which we who are living now can have no conception. It has
> been said of me on different occasions that I am a pessimist. And so I
> am insofar as I do not believe in the everlastingness of human ideals.
> But I am also an optimist insofar as I firmly believe in the capacity for
> the propagation and development of ideals. Especially, to be more
> definite, I believe that the ideals of our time, while disintegrating, are
> tending toward what in my play *Emperor and Galilean* I designated
> "the third kingdom."

Behind the social and cultural criticism of the rest of the plays of Ibsen's career runs the tacit belief that a "third empire" is possible in which the tensions and conflicts he presents in his characters' worlds will be reconciled. Indeed, he perhaps presents this "third empire" better and more subtly in these later plays than in the great double-drama he hoped would be his masterpiece. From our perspective, *Emperor and Galilean* is chiefly interesting as a herculean effort to translate a myth of the individual self into a general interpretation of human history.

6. The Realistic Plays I

When I read the news from home, when I think of all that respectable, all that estimable narrow-mindedness and materialism, I feel like an insane man hopelessly staring at one single spot of deepest blackness.

IBSEN TO BJOERNSON (1866)

IT IS HARD to think of a parallel in the history of drama to Ibsen's abrupt change in style between *Emperor and Galilean* (1873) and *The Pillars of Society* (1877). He had written fourteen plays over a period of twenty-five years, culminating in *Brand, Peer Gynt,* and the great double-drama he considered his masterpiece. Now, suddenly, he turned his back on the dramatic technique he had slowly mastered through a long apprenticeship and began to learn a new one. The result was the "naturalistic cycle" of twelve spare, economical, polemic, "modern" plays, from *The Pillars of Society* to *When We Dead Awaken* (1899).

There seem to have been many reasons for this radical shift of style, but a major one was the influence of Georg Brandes. Although Ibsen did not meet Brandes until 1871, he had corresponded with him since 1866. He had an enormous respect for Brandes's judgment; for close to forty years it was Brandes's opinion that he awaited most eagerly each time he published a play. In 1871 Brandes had applied for a position at the University of Copenhagen. His radicalism and his Jewish ancestry eventually kept him from appointment to a position, but he was invited to demonstrate his qualifications by giving a series of lectures, for which he chose the subject "Main Currents in Nineteenth-Century Literature." The opening lecture, delivered on November 3, 1871, was a courageous and sweeping attack upon the outdated abstract idealism of Danish literature and culture. He called instead for the examination of contemporary problems in literature. "What keeps a literature alive in our days is that it submits problems to debate. Thus, for example, George Sand debates the problem of the relations between the sexes, Byron and Feuerbach religion, John Stuart Mill and Proudhon property, Turgenev, Spielhagen and Emile Augier social conditions. A literature that does not submit problems to debate loses all meaning." [1]

When the lecture was published Brandes sent a copy to Ibsen. Ibsen read it and wrote to Brandes,

> I must turn to what has been continually in my thoughts and has even disturbed my sleep. I have read your lectures. No more dangerous book could fall into the hands of a pregnant writer. It is one of those works that place a yawning gulf between yesterday and today. . . . It reminds me of the gold fields of California when they were first discovered. They either made millionaires of men or ruined them. Is the spiritual constitution in the North robust enough? I don't know; but it makes no difference. Whoever cannot sustain the new ideas must fall.

His next play was *The Pillars of Society;* in this and in the half-dozen plays that followed he "submitted problems to debate" in a form designed to "make the spectator feel as if he were actually sitting, listening, and looking at events happening in real life" (as he told a prospective producer of *Ghosts*). It was not until the last decade of his career that he began to abandon this intention and deal more directly with his characters' inner lives.

Ibsen's spectacular shift in style, however, should not blind us to the continuity in his work. In the realistic plays the characters and settings are modern, the obvious conflicts turn around contemporary social problems, and the style is calculated to make us feel that we are "looking at events happening in real life." But the characters are psychologically similar to those in the earlier plays and their fundamental conflicts remain much the same. Even the style is much less objective than it is often taken to be; in the realistic plays, as in the earlier ones, the settings, the characters, and the action are often presented subjectively, as they appear to the protagonists.

In the realistic plays, furthermore, Ibsen's myth of the self con-

1. Georg Brandes, "Inaugural Lecture, 1871," trans. Evert Sprinchorn, in *The Theory of the Modern Stage,* ed. Eric Bentley (Baltimore, 1968), p. 388.

tinues to shape the underlying action. At the heart of each play is a protagonist's struggle to achieve self-realization, and his struggle invariably assumes the shape of the myth that appeared earlier in *Brand* and *Peer Gynt:* an ascent out of a polluted valley up to the heights, a return to the valley armed with a project of the will, and a final ascent to the peaks for an ecstatic death and rebirth. In the earlier plays this pattern is presented fairly directly; in the realistic plays it is concealed by the techniques of realistic verisimilitude. But it is constantly at work, providing the emotional center of the character development, supplying the basis for the recurring imagery of light and darkness—rooms, buildings, geographical locations, and the like—and lending the sense that every detail in the plays is part of a large, coherent whole.

I

A Doll's House established the formal model for the modern drama Brandes had called for which would "submit questions to debate." Its immediate predecessor, *The Pillars of Society,* was an experimental piece which betrayed, in its stiffness of construction, Ibsen's initial awkwardness in working toward the new form he had in mind. But the construction of *A Doll's House* was polished and confident. In its economy and concentration, its cool, ironic tone, and its unsentimental treatment of contemporary problems, it laid down the principles not only for the plays that were to follow in Ibsen's career but also for the dominant tradition in modern drama since Ibsen.

The play also finally established Ibsen as a major international dramatist. *Brand* and *Peer Gynt* had made him famous in Scandinavia, but it was not until *A Doll's House* that he became well known through the rest of Europe and America. When the play was published, in December of 1879, it immediately became a sensational success and the focal point for the worldwide controversy over women's rights. The large first printing was sold out within a month and two more printings were needed within three months. The fame that had been denied Ibsen as author of *Emperor and Galilean* now came to him as the creator of Nora.

Considering the tumultuous reception of *A Doll's House* as a major feminist document, Ibsen's words at a banquet given in his honor twenty years later by the Norwegian League for Women's Rights are rather surprising: "I am not a member of the Women's Rights League. Whatever I have written has been without any conscious thought of making propaganda. I have been more the poet and less the social philosopher than people generally seem inclined to believe. I thank you for the toast, but must disclaim the honor of having consciously worked for the women's rights movement. I am not even quite clear as to just what this women's rights movement really is. To me it has seemed a problem of mankind in general."

In *A Doll's House,* as in the other realistic plays, the "problem submitted to debate" is less fundamental to the action than the "problem of mankind in general" which underlies it: the struggle of the individual for liberation from the forces in his own character that hold him captive. Ibsen once wrote to Brandes that the fact that Brand was a priest was not important, he could equally well have been a sculptor or a politician. *A Doll's House* demonstrates that he could also have been a woman, for Nora's struggle with herself is fundamentally very much like Brand's self-conflict.

Such an interpretation is implicit in the opening scene of the play. No gloss on Norwegian marriage laws or nineteenth-century family life can explain why an apparently high-spirited young woman like Nora would submit to Helmer's repellent combination of bullying and baby-talk. Yet she humiliates herself by sneaking forbidden macaroons, begging for money, and playing "larks and squirrels" for the benefit of her insufferable husband. We very soon suspect what is later confirmed in the play: that Nora's childish behavior as a doll in a doll's house is not merely a role forced on her from without, but one which she herself has adopted to present to the outside world, including Helmer, while she lives a secret, inner life of her own.

We learn something of the origins of Nora's personality in her last-act conversation with Helmer, when she recalls her childhood:

NORA. A great wrong has been done to me, Torvald. First by Papa, and then by you. . . . When I lived with Papa, he used to tell me what he thought about everything, so that I never had any opinions but his. And if I did have any of my own, I kept them quiet, because he wouldn't have liked them. He called me his little doll, and he played with me just the way I played with my dolls. Then I came here to live in your house—

TORVALD. What kind of a way is that to describe our marriage?

NORA, *undisturbed.* I mean, then I passed from Papa's hands into yours. You arranged everything the way you wanted it, so that I simply took over your taste in everything—or pretended I did—I don't really know—I think it was a little of both—first one and then the other. Now I look back on it, it's as if I've been living here like a pauper, from hand to mouth. I performed tricks for you, and you gave me food and drink. But that was how you wanted it. You and Papa have done me a great wrong. It's your fault that I have done nothing with my life.

Nora emphasizes in this speech the stifling of her intellectual development in her childhood home and in Helmer's home, but as she half-realizes, the psychological damage has been much greater than this. The undercurrent of unconscious sexuality in Nora's descriptions here and elsewhere of her relationship with her father is reminiscent of the combination of playfulness and flirtatiousness in the relationship between Peer Gynt and Aase. Like Peer, Nora has found refuge from "troublesome thoughts" in compulsive fantasizing and role-playing. A surrogate for her dead mother in her father's household, she felt deeply inadequate; in a parallel situation, Peer Gynt dreams of being an emperor, Nora has tried to remain a child.

Nora's primary home with her father became a tomb world for her; the metaphor she chooses for it, "a doll's house," sums up its psychic threat of turning her into an inanimate object, a "doll" without an identity of its own. The home she found with Helmer during the early days of their marriage was simply a continuation of this tomb world; she passed from being a doll-child into being a doll-wife.

The first crisis in this situation was the trip to Italy, a year after their marriage, and the circumstances surrounding it. Torvald became ill from overwork and the doctor told Nora that he had to go to a warmer climate; his condition had to be kept a secret from

she betrays the strain of her life in a number of ways, including the slightly hysterical edge to her "playful" relationship with Torvald.

That her secondary home has become a tomb world is visually suggested by the setting and lighting. The Helmer doll's house is actually an apartment on the lower floor of an apartment building. The Stenborg apartment, where the fancy-dress ball is held, is on an upper floor. It is Christmas time and bitterly cold outside; the Helmer doors and windows are kept tightly shut and the continually burning fire in the stove keeps the room overheated, as Nora, and even Helmer, complain several times. The first two acts take place in the early evening, the third late at night, and the room is dimly lighted by lamps throughout. During Act II, as Nora's possible avenues of escape are cut off, one by one, leaving her only the prospect of suicide, as she thinks, the room "begins to grow dark." When Nora realizes that Dr. Rank is in love with her and that she cannot borrow money from him, she quietly calls, "Helen, bring the lamp." Through the rest of this act and the following act, the lamp stands on the table, a small pool of light in the otherwise shadowy room. Nora and Helmer alternately approach this focal point and withdraw from it, as they work out their relationship. Helmer tends to turn lights out—he shouts to the maid to "put out the light on the staircase" just before he launches into his denunciation of Nora after reading Krogstad's letter—but Nora forces him to sit down with her by the lamp for their final confrontation. The dark, claustrophobic "doll's house" thus comes to suggest Nora's frightening inner world, as Brand's similarly stifling parsonage comes to suggest his, and in *A Doll's House,* as in *Brand,* the dim flame of the lamp suggests the threatened self.

The final collapse of Nora's project of the will comes with Torvald's reaction to Krogstad's letter revealing her forgery. She has built up an elaborate private fantasy of what would happen when Torvald learned the truth; in their final conversation she reveals it to Torvald:

NORA. I've waited so patiently, for eight whole years—well, good heavens, I'm not such a fool as to suppose that miracles occur every day. Then this dreadful thing happened to me, and then I *knew:*

"Now the miracle will take place!" When Krogstad's letter was lying out there, it never occurred to me for a moment that you would let that man trample over you. I *knew* that you would say to him: "Publish the facts to the world." And when he had done this—

HELMER. Yes, what then? When I'd exposed my wife's name to shame and scandal—

NORA. Then I was certain that you would step forward and take all the blame on yourself, and say: "I am the one who is guilty!"

Helmer's reaction, of course, is totally different; he flies into a fury and wildly attacks Nora for "condemning him to humiliation and ruin simply for the weakness of a woman."

Nora's transformation at this point is parallel to Brand's when he decides to "march under my own flag, even if none will follow" and begins his ascent to the peaks. And the end of the play contains many muted reminiscences of Brand's ascent to the peaks. Nora at first "is silent and stares unblinkingly at him." Then she quietly goes out and changes into her everyday clothes from her party costume. "What's this? Not in bed?" cries Torvald when she re-enters. "Have you changed?" She answers, "Yes, Torvald. I've changed." The conversation that follows is full of suggestions of death and rebirth. Nora renounces the whole previous course of her life—as Brand does before the Ice Church—strips herself of all ties to Torvald including his ring, and declares her intention of beginning her life over as a mature human being. The death of the old Nora is suggested in the mythic "child-death" of the threat to her three children whom she is abandoning. And her spectacular final exit, with its famous slamming door, is out of the stifling tomb world of the doll's house into the December snow that recalls Brand's mountain peaks. Dawn is breaking as Nora renounces "upon the peaks" not merely the social pressures that have kept her a captive in her marriage but the psychological division that has made her a willing collaborator in her own imprisonment.

A Doll's House is representative of Ibsen's realistic plays not only in its focus upon a "problem for debate" and in its tight, closed construction, but also in the interplay it sets up between its social and psychological levels. The plot is logical and credible and the characters are provided with explicit, conscious motivations for all their actions, but there is more to the play than the brilliance of its surface structure. It gains depth and power from the myth of the self which underlies the overt plot and which gives Nora, unpretentious as she is, the stature of a mythic figure.

II

It is generally recognized that *Ghosts* is closely related to *A Doll's House*. Mrs. Alving is Ibsen's reply to those who thought Nora should not have left her husband—a Nora who stayed home, twenty years later. Ibsen's preliminary notes about Mrs. Alving echo Nora's third-act realization that her father and her husband have done her "a great wrong" and that she is not qualified to rear her own children: "These modern women, misused as daughters, as sisters, as wives, not educated according to their talents, barred from their vocation, robbed of their inheritance, their minds embittered—these are the women who are to provide the mothers for the new generation. What will be the consequence?"

The relationship between Nora Helmer and Helen Alving goes far beyond the general parallelism of their situations, however. Ibsen once wrote, to a defender of *Ghosts*, "*Ghosts* had to be written. After Nora, Mrs. Alving had to come." Nora and Mrs. Alving are as closely related as Brand and Peer Gynt. Although they make opposite choices at the crucial turning points in their lives, they are so similar psychologically and their inner experiences follow so parallel a course that they can best be understood together.

We discover few details about Mrs. Alving's childhood home in the course of the play but it is clear that, as much as Nora, she has been "misused as a daughter." She tells her son in Act III: "They had taught me about duty and things like that, and I sat here for too long believing in them. In the end everything became a matter of duty—*my* duty, and *his* duty, and—I'm afraid I made his home intolerable for your poor father, Oswald." Her marriage itself has been a matter of duty, involving none of the joy of life. Parson Manders commends her, in Act II, for having followed the advice of her mother and her two aunts, "as was your duty." "The three of them worked out a balance-sheet for me," Mrs. Alving recalls.

As she comes to see, her early married life was merely a con-

109

tinuation of her life at home with her mother and aunts. Captain Alving was not a depraved man when she met him:

> MRS. ALVING. You should have known your father when he was a young lieutenant. He was full of the joy of life, Oswald.
>
> OSWALD. Yes, I know.
>
> MRS. ALVING. It was like a sunny morning just to see him. And the untamed power and the vitality he had!

He was imprisoned by his post, however, in a stagnant small town where there was no wholesome "outlet for the excess of vitality in him," and his bride "didn't bring any sunshine into his home." Nora's reaction to her childhood with her father was retreat into childish role-playing; Mrs. Alving's reaction to her rearing by her mother and aunts was adoption of their grim and duty-ridden morality. Both carried these defenses against free and secure love into their marriages.

The first stage in the Alving marriage was brought to a close by a crisis exactly parallel to the crisis of Torvald's illness and Nora's forgery in *A Doll's House:* at the end of one year of marriage. Alving by this time had turned his "excess of vitality" into self-destructive dissipation, and Helen had fled the house to take refuge with Parson Manders, with whom she had fallen in love. It is clear that Manders returned her love, although he refuses to admit by the time of the play that he has ever thought of her "except as another man's wedded wife." He regards his refusal of her as his "life's greatest victory": "You may thank God," he tells her, "that I possessed the necessary firmness—that I was able to dissuade you from your frenzied intentions and that it was granted to me to lead you back on to the path of duty and home to your lawful husband."

Mrs. Alving's reaction to this episode makes her situation closely parallel to Nora's. Her flight to Manders was an ascent to the heights, like Nora's decision to forge the note, and like Nora she made it the occasion for the adoption of a project of the will. She not only returned to Captain Alving, she conceived a fierce determination to preserve the facade of a successful marriage and to hide her husband's true character from everyone, including their son. (Oswald was born shortly after her flight from Alving to Manders.) Her first step was to persuade Alving to move out of town to the isolated and gloomy Rosenvald estate. Here she kept him company in his dissipations so he would not drink in public: "To keep him at home in the evenings—and at night—I had to make myself his companion in his secret dissipations up in his room. There I had to sit alone with him, had to clink my glass with his and drink with him, listen to his obscene and senseless drivelling, had to fight him with my fists to haul him into bed—." She gained a weapon against him when he fathered an illegitimate child on the maid Joanna. She held this over his head, took over the management of the estate, and sent Oswald, by this time almost seven years old, away to school so he could not see what his father was like. This state of affairs lasted for eighteen years; at the time of the play Alving has been dead for ten years.

Aside from its social and moral implications, this domestic arrangement (which Strindberg savagely parodied as the story of Julie's family in *Miss Julie*) is very revealing psychologically. As Mrs. Alving comes to realize in the course of the play, it has not only been a means of preserving Alving's reputation and his son's respect for him, but it has also, perhaps more significantly, been a way for Mrs. Alving to protect herself against the threat of loving intimacy, the "joy of life." Its emphasis upon secrecy is also revealing; Mrs. Alving's exaggerated fear of public opinion leads her to adopt a strategy by which she lives a secret life totally unlike the image she presents to the world. We may suspect that she has found this secrecy satisfying in some way, despite her sufferings with her husband, as Nora seems to have taken some pleasure in her secret life, repaying the debt.

As Mrs. Alving herself comes to acknowledge, in other words, her decision after her flight to Manders has been neurotic, a self-divisive and defensive "decision on the heights." She has retreated from the threatening "joy of life" into an exaggerated project of the will. The mythic character of the action is suggested by the contrast between the two men in her life, Manders and Alving, who are parallel to Helmer and Rank in *A Doll's House* as "gentle" and "fascinating" figures. Manders and Helmer are ostensibly unthreatening and paternal, while Alving and Rank are disturbingly sexually fascinating and secretly diseased. The birth of the con-

111

genitally doomed Oswald soon after the decision, in addition to its overt functions in the play, constitutes a first child-death and thus signals Mrs. Alving's renunciation of one side of her nature.

This background of *Ghosts,* gradually divulged during the course of the play, helps us understand the implications of the stage setting and lighting, which constitute one of Ibsen's most effective representations in the realistic plays of a character's psychological tomb world. The play, which covers only about eighteen hours of dramatic time, opens just before the final collapse of Mrs. Alving's project of the will. The general shape of the action would be clear if we only watched a good production of the play, not hearing the dialogue but watching the visual effects carefully. Although it is about noon when the play opens, the Alving home is murky, and at the back, "through the glass wall a gloomy fjord landscape is discernible, veiled by heavy rain. . . . The mist lies heavily over the landscape." The Alving garden-room is described in the text only as "spacious," t Ibsen laid particular stress upon its darkness in his letter to Duke of Meiningen concerning the Meiningen Players' 1886 roduction of the play: "The interiors of Norwegian country houses usually show no specially marked national characteristics nowadays. The living rooms of the oldest family houses of this type are sometimes covered with colored, dark wallpaper. . . . The furniture is kept to the style of the First Empire; however, the colors are consistently darker. This is roughly the way I have imagined the living room in Mrs. Alving's house."

Act II takes place in the late afternoon, Act III during the night, of the day on which the play begins. During Act II, as in the second act of *A Doll's House,* "dusk begins to gather slowly." As the shadows gather, Oswald confesses to his mother his deep sense of guilt over his disease. Mrs. Alving decides to tell her son the truth about his father, in order to free him of this guilt; she calls for Regina to "bring in the lamp." This lamp—the recurring representation in Ibsen of the threatened self—is "still burning on the table" during Act III, and Oswald, Mrs. Alving, and Regina all sit around this pool of light in the otherwise dark room, as they explore the truth of their past relationships.

The stage space thus comes to be equated with Mrs. Alving's

112

mind, dark and constricted, a dim lamp suggesting the fragile ego, with the present action going on in the foreground and partially repressed or half-forgotten memories pushed into the "inner rooms," such as the adjoining dining room in which, at the end of Act I, she glimpses through a half-open door Oswald's ghostly reenactment of his father's philandering.

The present action of the play covers the final collapse of Mrs. Alving's project of the will and her attempt at an ascent to the peaks. To put it in terms of the title metaphor, the fundamental action is "to free oneself of ghosts," as the fundamental action of *A Doll's House* is "to walk out of the doll's house." Mrs. Alving has already achieved some degree of intellectual freedom when the play begins, as we see from her Act I discussion of the progressive books which so scandalize Parson Manders. She has changed her opinions about many of the intellectual and moral ghosts in her culture: "I almost think we are all ghosts—all of us, Pastor Manders. It isn't just what we have inherited from our father and mother that walks in us. It is all kinds of dead ideas and all sorts of old and obsolete beliefs. They are not alive in us; but they remain in us none the less, and we can never rid ourselves of them. I only have to take a newspaper and read it, and I see ghosts between the lines. There must be ghosts all over the country. They lie as thick as grains of sand. And we're all so horribly afraid of the light."

The surface action and themes of the play directly illustrate this speech, of course; Oswald's syphilis, Mrs. Alving's devotion to duty, the moral injunctions for wives to stay with their husbands and for sons to honor their fathers, and the taboo against incest are all "ghosts" of the kind Mrs. Alving mentions. But the speech is also emotionally "right" for Mrs. Alving in a way that has nothing to do with the explicit themes of the play. The feelings that one is an insubstantial "ghost," that one is in danger of being controlled by outside forces, and that one has "dead" things within, all reveal the fundamental ego-insecurity that has led Mrs. Alving to adopt her life strategy.

Despite Mrs. Alving's partial intellectual liberation at the beginning of the play, she remains emotionally imprisoned by her own "cowardice," to use her own term. She demonstrates in the

course of the play her intellectual liberation from certain "ghosts":
the exaggerated emphasis upon duty, the injunction to stay with one's
husband no matter what the circumstances, the commandment to
honor one's father, and the ban against incest. She has renounced
inviolable "ideals" and has begun to make judgments on the basis
of particular cases. When Manders asks, "Have you forgotten that
a child shall love and honour its father and mother?" she replies,
"Let us not generalize so. Let us ask: 'Shall Oswald love and
honour Captain Alving?'"

Despite this progress toward intellectual freedom, however, Mrs.
Alving, at the end of the play, cannot free herself of the last
"ghost" which controls her: she cannot renounce the injunction
against killing one's child and thus cannot perform the mercy-killing
Oswald has begged for.

The reasons for this final failure to achieve intellectual and moral
freedom lie in Mrs. Alving's failure, despite her advanced ideas, to
achieve psychic freedom. In the first two acts of the play she reveals
the degree to which she has renounced the ideals she was taught as
a girl and by which she has lived. She still apparently believes that
her decision at the time of her flight to Parson Manders was right,
however. She sees herself as a victim of her rearing, of Manders,
and of her husband. It is not until the end of Act II, when Oswald
talks about the "joy of life" he has experienced in Paris, that she
begins to see the degree to which she has imprisoned herself by her
renunciation of love and the choice of will as the ruling force in her
life. This realization is parallel to Brand's renunciation of his mission
and his decision to "march under his own flag" and to Nora's sudden
insight after Helmer's attack on her in Act III of *A Doll's House*.
Oswald has told her of life in Paris.

OSWALD. I'm afraid that everything in me will degenerate into ugliness
here.

MRS. ALVING *looks hard at him.* You think that would happen?

OSWALD. I know it. Live the same life here as down there, and it
wouldn't be the same life.

MRS. ALVING, *who has listened intently, rises, her eyes large and
thoughtful.* Now I see.

OSWALD. What do you see?

MRS. ALVING. Now I understand for the first time. And now I can speak.

The renunciation of the "decision on the heights" implied by this scene, however, is not followed by the kind of transcending reintegration of the self upon the peaks that Nora achieves. It is too late for Mrs. Alving; she remains the prisoner of her ghosts. She has not attained psychological freedom, and the symbolism of the end of the play is thus bitterly ironic. Oswald is sitting in an armchair as "day breaks." Mrs. Alving puts out the lamp, just as Oswald reveals his final disintegration: "Mother, give me the sun." The stage direction reads, *"The sun rises. The glacier and the snow-capped peaks in the background glitter in the morning light."* The stage, which has been dark throughout the play, is suddenly flooded with blinding white light, associated throughout Ibsen's plays with transcendence and spiritual unity. But Mrs. Alving stands, back to the peaks, staring at Oswald: "I can't bear this! I can't bear it! No! Where did he put them? Here! No; no; no! Yes! No; no!" The last we heard of Nora was the door slamming on her way out; Mrs. Alving, another "woman of the modern age," has stayed and her last word is "no."

III

An Enemy of the People is at once the most high-spirited and the most overtly didactic of Ibsen's major plays. Dr. Stockmann is a major comic creation, a courageous spokesman for Ibsen's ideas, which are presented explicitly by means of the public speech in Act IV. He is made even more attractive by his minor failings—his naiveté, his impetuousness, and his touches of vanity and self-indulgence. Ranged around him is a rogues' gallery of caricatures of Norwegian small-town types, from the tea-drinking Mayor down through representatives of the "free press" and the "compact majority" to the timid proletarian radical, Hovstad.

Ibsen wrote *An Enemy of the People* very quickly; he began it in March of 1882, at the height of the controversy over *Ghosts,* and completed it in June, less than three months later. It is true that he had been planning the play two years earlier and had laid his plans aside to write *Ghosts*. Nevertheless, the final version of the play seems to have been influenced by the reception of *Ghosts,* especially the attacks from the liberal press in Norway, which particularly infuriated Ibsen. In January, just before beginning the play, for example, he had written to Brandes, using language very much like Stockmann's:

> And what can be said of the attitude assumed by the so-called liberal press—of those leaders of the people who speak and write of freedom of action and thought but who at the same time make themselves the slaves of the supposed opinions of their subscribers? I receive more and more proof that there is something demoralizing in engaging in politics and in joining parties. It will never, in any case, be possible to me to join a party that has the majority on its side. Bjoernson says, "The majority is always right." And as a practical politician he is bound, I suppose, to say so. I, on the contrary, must of necessity say, "The minority is always right." Naturally I am not thinking of that minority of standpatters who are left behind by the great middle party that we call liberal; I mean that minority which leads the van and pushes on to points the majority has not yet reached. I mean: that man is right who has allied himself most closely with the future.

These sentiments, and a number of similar ones from the letters written about this time, are repeated almost verbatim by Stockmann in his Act IV speech to the public meeting. Stockmann, like Ibsen, is anything but a democrat; he is a thoroughgoing aristocrat, though the aristocracy he calls for is one of the mind and spirit. Audiences, probably rightly, have generally chosen to emphasize less Stockmann's radical individualism than his courageous defiance of established authority, and have made *An Enemy of the People* into a "revolutionary" play in ways very far from Ibsen's intention.

Despite the similarity of Ibsen's and Stockmann's views, however, the doctor is much more than a mouthpiece for Ibsen, a portrait of the artist as a village radical. The comic irony with which Ibsen portrayed Stockmann is suggested in his comments in the letter he sent to his publisher along with the manuscript:

> I have the pleasure of sending you herewith the remainder of the manuscript of my new play. I have enjoyed writing this play, and I feel quite lost and lonely now that it is out of my hands. Dr. Stockmann

and I got on so very well together; we agree on so many subjects. But the doctor is more muddle-headed than I am; and moreover he has other peculiarities that permit him to say things which would not be taken so well if I myself said them. I think you will agree with me when you have read the manuscript.

There is something of Hjalmar Ekdal as well as of Gregers Werle in Dr. Stockmann's character. Like Hjalmar, he leaves the household to his quiet, competent wife, whom he often dismays with his habit of having guests in for meals they can ill afford. "Catherine says I earn almost as much as we spend," he proudly tells his brother. And like Hjalmar with his bread and butter, Stockmann is an inveterate snacker although, unlike Hjalmar, Stockmann enjoys seeing others eat, too. He is incredibly naive; as late as Act III he is still convinced that his discovery that the Baths are polluted will earn him the love and gratitude of his fellow citizens, and he modestly tells Hovstad that he must discourage any proposals for "a torchlight procession or a banquet or—a subscription for some little token of thanks." A comic irony envelops even the final tableau. "I've made a great discovery," he announces. "The strongest man in the world is he who stands most alone." But as he speaks, he is standing in the middle of an admiring group made up of his wife, his daughter, his two sons, and Captain Horster, who has donated his house to Stockmann. The actual last lines of the play are Mrs. Stockmann's loving, "Oh, Thomas—!" and Petra's "Father!" as she "warmly clasps his hands."

Much of the richness and complexity of character that make Stockmann more than a two-dimensional mouthpiece comes from the presence in the play of Ibsen's myth of the self. Stockmann— gregarious, outgoing, and impulsive—seems at the opposite pole from such lonely, introspective, and self-conscious characters as Brand and Mrs. Alving. And yet his inner experiences and his spiritual development have much in common with theirs. This psychological background also helps to account for the strange combination of traits in his character: his gullibility, his quick temper, his fierce individualism, his egotism, and his obstinacy. It helps to explain the psychological roots of his final slogan: "The strongest man in the world is he who stands most alone."

The original plan for the Baths came from Dr. Stockmann himself, although his brother Peter tries to claim equal credit for it. He has thought of the plan while working as a rural doctor in the north. He describes the circumstances in his fourth-act speech:

> DR. STOCKMANN. For years I lived far up in the north. As I wandered among those people who lived scattered over the mountains, I often thought it would have been better for those poor degraded creatures if they'd had a vet instead of a man like me! . . . I sat there brooding like a duck on an egg; and the chick I hatched was—the plan for these Baths.

Once conceived, the idea has possessed Stockmann. At first it has met with indifference in the town, but he has persisted. "For years I fought alone for this idea! I wrote, and wrote—" he reminds his brother.

The plan for the Baths thus takes on the character of an obsessive project of the will, and the setting in which it is conceived is appropriate for such a project. Although the dominant settings for the myth of the self are "the valley," "the heights," and "the peaks," the cardinal compass points are sometimes subsumed into the pattern. The north is associated with the will and with projects of the will. Brand is a northerner, and he tells Ejnar that he was never "at home among you southerners." Gregers Werle, Rebecca West, and Ellida Wangel all conceive projects of the will in the isolated north. The south is associated with wholeness and the "joy of life." Nora has had a glimpse of these qualities on her trip to Italy and Oswald yearns for the sunlight and joy of Paris. Erhart Borkman's flight from the externally imposed duties of his northern home is toward the sunlight of Italy. The west, more rarely, is associated with freedom, as in *The Pillars of Society,* and the east, because the sun rises there, sometimes symbolizes transcendence and integration, as in *Emperor and Galilean.*

The plan for the Baths, desirable as it is for its own sake, is sufficiently ambiguous in its psychological meaning for Stockmann to explain his otherwise incredible blindness to reality at the beginning of the play. Obsessed by his project, he has built up a ludicrously idealistic conception of his fellow citizens. He believes that his self-centered and cynical brother will only regret that he

118

was not the one to discover the pollution of the Baths, he takes the representatives of the "free press" and the "compact majority" at their own evaluation, and he believes that the mass of his fellow townspeople will spontaneously offer him a torchlight procession for having revealed the truth, even though it is against their own interests. Most telling of all, he has a naive conception of his own motivations; he does not realize until the last scene how much of his own courage has been based on his presumed financial security.

Stockmann's project of the will, like all projects of the will in Ibsen, has led its creator into a position farther and farther removed from reality. The action of the play covers its gradual collapse, as one support after another is taken away from Stockmann: first his idealistic conception of his brother, then his illusions about the free press, the property owners, and the mass of citizens, and finally his illusions about his own motivations.

Stockmann's reaction to the loss of his defensive project is psychologically consistent with this interpretation of the project itself. Many of his attitudes and actions seem like distant echoes of Brand's lonely withdrawal into an inner world. Stockmann's ebullient self-confidence sometimes verges on messianism, as when he compares himself to Christ after the disastrous public meeting ("I'm not so forgiving as a certain person. I don't say, 'I forgive ye, for ye know not what ye do!'") and when he chooses twelve for the number of his pupil-disciples at the end of the play. His exaggerated respect for scientific facts to the neglect of any sympathetic understanding of their implications for his fellow citizens also indicates something of a defensive withdrawal into the world of his own mind. And most telling of all, the doctrine he enunciates at the public meeting can be read not only as a heroic battle-cry of individualism but also, in its celebration of the lonely, self-sufficient individual and its savage contempt for the "masses," as a defensive, schizoid "rising above" the threat of other people. There is a certain hysterical quality in Dr. Stockmann's cry for the whole town to be wiped out—"Let the whole land be laid waste! Let the whole people be exterminated!"—and in his scathing attacks on the "majority" as "vermin," "short-winded sheep," and "filthy, ragged, common curs."

This ambiguous undercurrent in the public meeting scene continues through the last act of the play, which is full of muted suggestions of the kind of mystic integration and rebirth associated with an "ascent to the peaks." When the act begins it appears that Stockmann has reached the lowest point in his fortunes. It is the morning after the tumultuous public meeting at which he was branded an "enemy of the people," Captain Horster has had to escort him and his family home in order to prevent their being physically assaulted, and the mob has broken out all the windows in the house. Stockmann has decided to emigrate to America with his family. A series of visitors—"the Devil's messengers"—however, disillusion him even more. First he learns that Horster has been fired by his shipowner. Then the Mayor arrives to deliver Stockmann's own letter of dismissal, tells him that his father-in-law's will leaves all his money to Stockmann, and accuses him of creating a scandal merely to please his embittered father-in-law. The father-in-law himself, Morten Kiil, is next; his pride has been hurt by the suggestion that his tanneries have poisoned the Baths, he has bought up most of the shares in the Baths, and he tells Stockmann that his wife will lose her inheritance if he does not recant. At this temptation, Stockmann wavers: "I must talk to Catherine. She knows about these things."

When Kiil leaves, Hovstad and Aslaksen arrive. They have heard of Morten Kiil's purchases of stock and assume that Stockmann has merely been trying to drive down the value of the stocks for personal profit. They threaten to expose him if he does not share his profits with them.

At this final straw, Stockmann loses his last illusion about his fellow townspeople that survived from his project of the will. He chases Hovstad and Aslaksen off with an umbrella and sends a note to Kiil refusing to recant. In a scene reminiscent of Brand's decision to "march under his own flag," he decides to remain in the town and start a school to build a new society of "free men and aristocrats." A hint of the mythic mountain peaks survives in the "glorious fresh spring air" blowing in through the shattered windows of Stockmann's study, as he gathers his family and friends around him and announces the birth of the new Stockmann—the "strongest man in the world" because he "stands alone."

IV

In the letter that accompanied the manuscript of *The Wild Duck,* Ibsen told his publisher that "this new play occupies a position by itself among my dramatic works, its plan and method differing in several respects from my former ones." It is not clear what Ibsen regarded as especially innovative in the play, but a passage earlier in the letter suggests that he was particularly conscious of the complexity of the characters: "Long, daily association with the characters in this play has endeared them to me, in spite of their manifold failings. And I hope that they may find good and kind friends among the great reading public, and more particularly among the actor tribe—for all of them, without exception, are rewarding roles. But the study and representation of these characters will not be an easy task; and therefore the book should be offered to the theaters as early as possible in the season."

August Lindberg, who directed the historic first Swedish production of the play, wrote to Ibsen, while he was preparing the production, "With Doctor Ibsen's newest play we have entered virgin territory where we have to make our way with pick and shovel. The people in the play are completely new, and where would we get by relying on old theatrical cliches?"

In most of Ibsen's earlier plays the action had clearly revolved around one central character. At the center of *The Wild Duck* stand two figures with approximately equal claims to our attention—Gregers Werle and Hjalmar Ekdal—and ranged around them is an extraordinary gallery of well-developed characters: Haakon Werle, Old Ekdal, Gina, Mrs. Soerby, Hedvig, Relling, and Molvik. Even the tiny roles of the servants Pettersen and Jensen are well worked out and Ibsen gave particular instructions for casting them, in his correspondence regarding the first production.

A corollary of this richness of characterization is a considerable ambiguity, of which Ibsen was also highly conscious. The critics, he told his publisher, "will find several things to squabble about and several things to interpret." No character in the play is trustworthy enough to serve as a point of reference; all are treated with an irony more pervasive and more sardonic than that in any other of Ibsen's plays. And the play's ending leaves its ambiguities unresolved. A child is dead, but none of the characters seems to have learned anything. Hjalmar is already busily at work, turning his grief into a sentimental pose of self-pity and self-congratulation, and Gregers seems determined to continue to pursue his "destiny" to "present the claim of the ideal."

Apparently most perplexing of all to early readers was the way in which *The Wild Duck* seemed to reverse the implications of *An Enemy of the People*. Gregers Werle seemed to be a grotesque parody of Thomas Stockmann, and the theme, "Deprive the average human being of his life-lie, and you rob him of his happiness," seemed a perverse reversal of the ringing cry in *An Enemy of the People* to face the truth, no matter what the price. Actually, Thomas Stockmann's character is more ambiguous than it first appears to be, and aspects of his personality appear not only in Gregers Werle but in Hjalmar Ekdal as well. It is as if Stockmann's character had been split into two figures: Gregers embodying Stockmann's stubborn, though myopic idealism, and Hjalmar embodying his naiveté, his self-indulgence, and his capacity for self-delusion.

Gregers Werle is Ibsen's most unsympathetic study in the character type he treated most often: the schizoid who makes his personal insecurity the basis of a fanatical pursuit of a project of the will. Gregers loathes himself; he is highly conscious of his physical ugliness and hates even his name:

> GREGERS. When one has the misfortune to be called Gregers—with Werle on top of it—Hjalmar, have you ever heard anything so awful?
>
> HJALMAR. Oh, I don't think it's awful at all.
>
> GREGERS. Oh, nonsense. Ugh! I'd want to spit on anyone who had a name like that.

Unable to establish secure and unself-conscious relationships with others, he alternates between a lonely withdrawal and an obsessive probing into others' lives. He has spent much of his adult life in self-imposed isolation at the "Hoydal works" and thinks of himself as a perpetual outsider—the "thirteenth at table." Yet even at Hoydal he cannot keep from meddling with the cottagers' lives, and there is a compulsive quality in his tampering with the lives of the Ekdal family that cannot be explained by any abstract sense of family responsibility. He is tormented by a pervasive sense of guilt. "It's you," he tells his father, "I have to thank for the fact that I'm continually haunted by a guilty conscience." But he himself half-realizes that his sense of guilt is too deep-seated to be explained merely by a feeling of responsibility for his father's misdeeds. His conscience is "sick," he tells Werle, and many of his actions stem from a desperate attempt to escape the torture of nameless guilt. Gregers's self-hatred and sense of guilt, however, are accompanied by an irrational megalomania. He thinks of himself as having a high, though painful, destiny and compares himself to Christ, who was also "thirteenth at table."

Behind these particular traits lies a fundamental weakness of the ego. Terrified by an external world he finds threatening, Gregers has withdrawn into an inner world with ambiguous threats of its own. This world is suggested by his fascination with "the bottom of the deep blue sea." He first uses the phrase casually while discussing with Hedvig the wild duck's loneliness and strangeness: "And she's been down to the bottom of the deep blue sea." Hedvig finds the phrase unusual and says that when he says it, "I always think of it all as being 'the deep blue sea.'" Gregers returns to the expression through the rest of the play, fascinated in a way that suggests a personal meaning beyond its literal application to the Ekdals' attic. His general manner of living may be seen as a kind of panic-stricken alternation between retreat into his own "deep blue sea," with its ambiguous combination of secure isolation and the threat of regression, and flight out of the "sea" into rigid and defensive relationships with others.

The origins of Gregers's personal insecurity are made fairly explicit. He grew up in a tense and unhappy household. Werle, like Brand's mother, married for money and then found that there was none. Mrs. Werle, like Mrs. Alving, inflicted upon her husband a grim and duty-ridden morality. Mrs. Soerby says, and Gina agrees, that he had to "spend all his youth and the best years of his life listening to sermons—very often occasioned by quite imaginary offences, from what I've heard." The result was that Werle turned to a series of sordid seductions, culminating, like Captain Alving's, in his fathering a child upon the housemaid. Mrs. Werle, for her part, became an alcoholic and died of the effects of drink at about the time of Hedvig's birth.

Gregers has emerged from this environment with a quite irrational hatred of his father and an equally unrealistic, idealized memory of his mother. He resembles his mother physically, and bitterly resents what he regards as his father's maltreatment of her. When he accuses Werle of having an affair with Gina, Werle asks,

WERLE. Who has said such a thing to you?

GREGERS. My unhappy mother told me. The last time I saw her.

WERLE. Your mother! I might have known it. She and you always clung together. She turned you against me from the first.

GREGERS. No. It was all the suffering and humiliation she had to endure before she finally succumbed and came to such a pitiful end.

WERLE. Oh, she didn't have to suffer. Not more than most people, anyway. But one can't do anything with people who are oversensitive and romantic. I've learned that much.

Gregers's escape from this tormented household to his lonely exile at the Hoydal works has been a defensive withdrawal "to the heights." At Hoydal, an isolated place in the north like the setting in which Stockmann conceives his plan for the Baths, he has had time to brood. "Oh, I've been wonderfully lonely," he tells Hjalmar, "I've had plenty of time to brood over things." The result of his brooding has been the conception of his "project of the will," his self-imposed mission to "present the claim of the ideal" to all those with whom he comes in contact. Relling, who has known Gregers at Hoydal, recalls his behavior there:

RELLING. He went round all the workmen's cottages, shoving something in their faces which he called the "claim of the ideal."

GREGERS. I was young then.

RELLING. You're right there. You were very young. And as for that claim of the ideal—you never got anyone to honour it before I left.

Gregers has not moderated his demands, however. "I've a strong suspicion you're still carrying that 'claim of the ideal' unabridged in your back pocket," Relling tells him, and Gregers answers, "I carry it in my heart." Gregers's withdrawal to Hoydal and his adoption of a defensive project of the will has been marked by a first child-death in the form of the birth of Hedvig, with her congenital defect of the eyes.

Gregers's return to his childhood home and the action of the play is thus a mythic return to the childhood "valley" and a pursuit of the project of the will. The neurotic basis of his idealistically rationalized but irresponsible meddling in the Ekdals' lives is obvious not only from the extravagance of his actions but from hints he himself drops from time to time about his tormented state of mind. "If I am to go on living," he tells his father, "I must try to find some cure for my sick conscience." And when Relling tells him, at the end of the play, that he has not brought about any permanent change in Hjalmar, Gregers replies, "If you are right, and I am wrong, life is not worth living." Like Brand, he cannot afford to admit even to himself that his ideal, with all the suffering it has caused, may be suspect.

The mythic pattern that underlies Gregers's behavior is a "maimed rite," however. His project of the will collapses with the death of Hedvig and the reversion of Hjalmar back to his customary self-delusion. But, unlike Brand, Gregers does not renounce his project or ascend to any transforming experience "on the peaks." The play ends abruptly after the death of Hedvig (a "second child-death"), with Gregers still insisting that "Hedvig has not died in vain" and declaring his intention to continue pursuing his "destiny." The bitterly ironic tone of the ending and its sense of unresolved tensions stems in large part from this truncation of the mythic pattern implied by the earlier part of the play.

Like most of the realistic plays, *The Wild Duck* takes place in the tomb world projected by the protagonist as the correlative of his own guilt and anxiety. And as in the other plays, the darkness and claustrophobia of the environment are not assigned specifically to the perceptions of the protagonist but pervade the entire world of the play. "I lay much stress in this play on the lighting," Ibsen wrote to Lindberg, "I have wanted it to correspond to the basic mood prevailing in each of the five acts." Both settings of the play call for complex arrangements of light and darkness. The foreground in

Act I is the study of Haakon Werle's house, where "lighted lamps with green shades throw a soft light." Through folding doors at the back of the room can be seen "a large and elegant room, brilliantly lit by lamps and candelabra." During the action this brilliant inner room becomes the focal point for the party which is going on, attended by court officials and wealthy businessmen. It is into the dim study, however, that the major characters retreat for a series of confrontations revolving around their past relationships. Gregers and Hjalmar explore here the circumstances of Hjalmar's marriage with Gina, Old Ekdal slips like a ghost across the room, unacknowledged by his own son, and Gregers bitterly recalls his childhood in a confrontation with his father. The effect is as if we were looking out on the public life of society *through* the private situations of the protagonists in the foreground.

A second double set serves for the other four acts of the play. In the Ekdal apartment the spatial relationships of the Werle home are echoed by the studio in the foreground, the attic in the background. But now, as if we had moved around the scene, it is the foreground which is the more brilliantly lighted. Although in Act II the studio is lighted only by a shaded lamp, the attic is murkier yet. A few shafts of moonlight shine through small skylights, "while the rest lies in shadow." As Hjalmar, Old Ekdal, and Hedvig move in and out of this attic room, each seeing different things in it, the double set becomes a kind of model of their minds.

The dim, multi-dimensional settings of *The Wild Duck* are also an integral part of the imagery of sight which constitutes a basic metaphor in the play. The theme of the contrast between art as vision and photography as reflection recalls some remarks Ibsen had made ten years before to a group of Norwegian students: "Now what does it mean to be a poet? It was a long time before I realized that to be a poet means essentially to see; but mark well, to see in such a way that whatever is seen is perceived by his audience just as the poet saw it." Journalists, on the other hand, are literary photographers: they reflect rather than see, and Ibsen contrasted the two in his many attacks on newspapermen through the middle plays, including Hovstad and Billing in *An Enemy of the People* and Mortensgaard in *Rosmersholm*. Says Hovstad, "Well, I ask you, gentlemen,

126

what is the primary duty of an editor? Is it not to reflect the opinions of his readers? Has he not been entrusted with what might be described as an unspoken mandate to advance the cause of those who hold the same views as himself, with all the eloquence of which he is capable? Or am I mistaken?" The photographer and the journalist arrange reality so as to reflect already existing opinions; they do not "see" reality in all its ambiguity.

The character of Hjalmar Ekdal seems to have been based upon that of Edvard Larsen, a photographer with whom Ibsen had once lodged, and in the earliest notes for the play he is referred to as "E.L." or simply "the photographer." Hjalmar's photography thus seems to be fundamental, perhaps the kernel from which Ibsen developed his character. It is Haakon Werle who has advised Hjalmar, after his father's disgrace, to take up photography and who has paid for setting up his studio. This has been a convenient way to bring together Hjalmar and Gina, who has studied retouching. Now, however, it is Gina who does most of the actual photography, while Hjalmar does the retouching. By the time Act III opens with Hjalmar sitting at the table retouching a photograph, we have seen several examples of his retouching, including his account to Gina and Hedvig in Act II of the party at Werle's, in which he comes off considerably better than he did at the actual party. This is Hjalmar's characteristic strategy for dealing with reality—to retouch it to fit some roughly appropriate cliché, preferably flattering to himself. He is unable to see even simple things clearly; he regularly calls his father "that silver-haired old man," though, as Relling sardonically observes, he is bald and wears a brown wig. At the end of the play, Relling predicts that within nine months Hjalmar will have been able to retouch even Hedvig's death into a "theme for a recitation," all about "the child untimely ripped from her father's bosom."

Hjalmar is not alone in his difficulty in seeing beyond poses and stereotypes. In the dim light of the Werle study and the Ekdal studio, the intricate relationships of the two families are constantly shifting and rearranging themselves according to the perspective at any given moment. Much remains ambiguous at the end of the play, even to the audience: the paternity of Hedvig, the relative guilt of Werle and his wife for their poisoned relationship, the degree of criminal involvement of Werle in the timber fraud. Werle and Hedvig are losing their sight, but the others have so much difficulty in seeing that a metaphor for the whole play might be the game of blind man's buff that Mrs. Soerby and the guests are playing at the end of Act I.

Gregers angrily tells his father in Act I that he knows the only reason he has been called down from Hoydal is so the elder Werle could present a suitable picture to the public: "Father and son— *tableau!*" He tells his father he hates him because he has "seen him at close quarters," but Werle points out that Gregers has seen with his mother's "blurred vision." And indeed Gregers's efforts to arrange the Ekdal family into a pose that fits his own ideal are more disastrous than his father's arrangements. Old Ekdal is no seer either; his job is "copying," and his attic-forest is no more like the real forest than is the photographer's backdrop it so much resembles. Even the realistic Gina is deceived by the poses others have arranged. "Hjalmar isn't just an ordinary photographer," she tells Gregers. And during the third and fourth acts, as her own marriage is collapsing around her, she occupies herself with arranging and taking a posed portrait of an engaged couple.

Almost all of the characters in *The Wild Duck* are photographers who have been deceived by their own tableaus. And in the Ekdal studio, it is as destructive to pose others as to allow oneself to be reduced to a figure in a tableau. Werle is usually considered to be a relatively clear-sighted character in the play, despite his impending blindness. And indeed his prospective marriage to Mrs. Soerby seems to hold out the promise of a genuine marriage built on truth and openness. But in his first marriage, in spite of the misery of the relationship, he has preserved a facade of marital happiness, like the one Mrs. Alving carefully constructed for her similar marriage. The results of such manipulations appear in his son, as pathetic a victim as Oswald, if a less obvious one. Relling, too, is generally regarded as a kind of seer, with his ability to "see through" the folly of Gregers. But he, too, is a photographer, who goes about arranging poses and offering them as therapeutic "life-lies." The difference between him and Hjalmar is that he is not taken in by his own tableaus, but he has nothing to put in their place in his own life.

128

Unable to deceive himself with a life-lie of his own and never having risen to an integrating perception of himself upon the peaks, he buries himself in his room "on a lower floor," and wastes his life in debauchery and impotence.

Of all the characters in the play, only Hedvig is potentially a seer, who could attain a "higher view of things," rather than a photographer, manipulating appearances in a dim studio. She likes to draw and tells Gregers that she would like to stop retouching photographs and become an engraver, so she could make pictures like the ones in the English books the "Flying Dutchman" left in the attic. The point is even clearer in the manuscript notes to the play, in which Ibsen planned to have Hedvig give up her drawing when she realized that her drawings were "not her own creation." Her fate is even more affecting because of her potentiality for the kind of vision the others in the play lack.

The world of *The Wild Duck,* with its murky shadows through which the characters grope, unable to see, is a tomb world, a "single spot of deepest blackness." None of its characters ever rises to the integrating transcendence of the peaks, and the curtain falls upon a scene as dark as the one upon which it rose.

7. The Realistic Plays II

To express oneself in one's life is, I feel, something of the finest that man can achieve. We all try to do this, but most of us make a mess of it.

IBSEN TO BJOERNSON (1882)

I

Rosmersholm is one of the most baffling and enigmatic of Ibsen's plays. The action of the play is very simple but the characters are so complex and their motivations so subtle and indirect that the effect of the play is likely to be bewildering.

At the time the play opens, John Rosmer, a pastor who has retired from the active ministry, has been a widower for a little over a year. His wife, Beata, has drowned herself in a millrace. He is living in his family's ancestral home, Rosmersholm, with his housekeeper, Rebecca West, who came to Rosmersholm about a year before Beata's suicide. The play itself consists of a series of conversations in which the motivations that lie behind this situation are explored. Rosmer first reveals to his brother-in-law Kroll, headmaster of the local school, that he has come to hold liberal social beliefs and that he has renounced the teachings of the church. He now intends to devote his efforts to the goal of "creating a responsible public opinion in this country." He intends to "make all the people in this country noblemen" by "emancipating their minds and purifying their wills."

Kroll and Mortensgaard, publisher of the local radical newspaper, despite their opposite social and political views, both feel threatened by Rosmer's plan and separately they try to gain control over him by

130

raising disturbing questions about the circumstances of Beata's suicide and the nature of his relationship with Rebecca West. Kroll tells Rosmer that Beata had visited him shortly before her death and told him things that later led him to believe that she had killed herself in order to leave Rosmer free to marry Rebecca. Mortensgaard independently confirms this by reporting a letter he received from Beata at about the same time.

Rosmer is deeply troubled by these reports, but he tries to free himself from the burden of the past by "confronting it with something new, and living, and real": he asks Rebecca to marry him. Oddly, however, since she is clearly in love with him, she vehemently refuses and says that if he ever asks her again she will "go the way Beata went."

Kroll now confronts Rebecca with suspicions about her past. She has nursed the invalid Dr. West until his death shortly before she came to Rosmersholm. Kroll presents some ambiguous evidence that suggests that Rebecca is actually the illegitimate daughter of Dr. West. Rebecca reacts strongly to this suggestion, telling Kroll that she doesn't want people to think of her as illegitimate. Immediately after this interview she attempts to free Rosmer of his sense of guilt for Beata's death by confessing that she was responsible for implanting in Beata's mind the idea that she was a barrier to Rosmer's happiness. Rebecca then prepares to leave Rosmersholm permanently.

In a long, last-act scene, however, Rosmer and Rebecca continue to explore their relationship. Rosmer, under the influence of Kroll and his friends and of his own guilt and depression, has abandoned his ideal of ennobling his fellow countrymen. Rebecca, for her part, confesses what she had omitted before: that she was motivated in her behavior toward Beata by a "blinding, uncontrollable passion" for Rosmer. After Beata's death this passion has been gradually transformed to a "great and selfless love that asks nothing more than companionship." She cannot marry Rosmer now, even though she would otherwise be free to, "because Rosmersholm has drained my strength. It has broken my courage and paralysed my will. The time is past when I was afraid of nothing. I have lost the power to take action, John." She also says she cannot marry Rosmer because she had been another man's mistress before she came to Rosmersholm.

Rosmer pleads with Rebecca to give him back his faith in her love and suggests that she could do this by "going the way that Beata went." She consents; Rosmer says he is "no longer afraid" and will join her. They join themselves in marriage, go down to the millrace, and drown themselves.

This plot is full of motifs and situations that are familiar from a number of earlier Ibsen plays. The theme of the power of the past over the present is reminiscent of *Ghosts,* the anatomy of small-town politics recalls both *The Pillars of Society* and *An Enemy of the People,* and Rosmer's ambition to "make all the people in this country noblemen" is very much like Stockmann's aim in setting up his school. The sources and the circumstances of composition of the play also throw some light upon it. The character of Rosmer was based upon that of a Swedish poet, Count Carl Snoilsky, whose career Ibsen had followed for over twenty years. Five years before Ibsen wrote the play Snoilsky had divorced his wife and remarried. About the same time, he had come to believe that poetry should not concern itself with the merely beautiful, but should deal with contemporary problems. He felt, however, that his aristocratic background prevented him from dealing effectively with these problems. Ibsen had spent four days with Snoilsky and his second wife at the time he was planning the play and had been deeply impressed by his ideas and his self-analysis. The picture the play presents of the depth and bitterness of the divisions in Norwegian political life apparently stems from Ibsen's observations during a trip to Norway during the summer of 1885. The country had just survived a bitter battle between Conservatives and Liberals over the composition of the Storthing, the legislative body, and Ibsen was deeply disturbed by the fanaticism and bitterness he encountered. These feelings are recorded in Rosmer's reactions to the conservative Kroll and the liberal Mortensgaard in the play.

Neither the reminiscences of other plays nor the historical sources of the play help to resolve the difficult questions of motivation that *Rosmersholm* presents, however. Despite the fact that virtually the whole play consists of introspective dissections of the past and confessions of motives and intentions, the explanations the characters offer of their actions are often unconvincing, and we have a strong sense of quite different motivations which underlie the action but which remain concealed at the end of the play. Rosmer, for example, attributes his failure to pursue his plan to educate and elevate his fellow citizens to the paralyzing sense of guilt he feels after Kroll's revelations of Beata's state of mind just before her suicide. Yet, even before these revelations, he has made no move to pursue his plans; in the year or more since Beata's death he has remained completely secluded and withdrawn from active life. Rebecca's vehement refusal to marry Rosmer similarly seems inadequately explained. Her explanation that her passion has changed to a love that "asks nothing more than companionship" explains nothing, and her second explanation that she has had a previous affair is even more feeble, since this fact does not seem to have deterred her in her original pursuit of Rosmer. Most troubling of all is the logic behind the double suicide at the end. Rosmer tells Rebecca that if she commits suicide he will "regain his faith" in his life's work. Yet he joins her in the suicide, apparently as a demonstration of the faith and courage she has given him by her decision.

Some of these problems may be resolved by exploring the appearances in the play of Ibsen's myth of the self and the way he uses it to illuminate the minds of Rosmer and Rebecca. One possibly fruitful way to look at the play is as Ibsen's fullest exploration of the "fascinating woman" figure in the myth that underlies all his plays. Rosmer himself is closely related psychologically to a number of earlier Ibsen protagonists, including Brand, Peer Gynt, Mrs. Alving, and Gregers Werle, while Rebecca's parallels, as a woman who presents an ambiguous challenge to both aspiration and sexuality, include Furia, Gerd, and Hilde Wangel. In most of Ibsen's plays, however, the fascinating woman figure appears briefly and remains a shadowy figure of interest only in relation to the protagonist. In *Rosmersholm* (as also in *Little Eyolf* and *When We Dead Awaken*) she is a fully characterized individual who commands our attention equally with the protagonist.

Rosmersholm is Ibsen's "endgame," a complex set of moves pointed from the opening lines toward death. The roar of the millrace is heard in the background throughout the play, and Mrs. Helseth, from the first scene, expects the appearance of "the white horses of Rosmersholm," which presage death. As the curtain goes up on the first act, Rebecca is sitting in an armchair, "crocheting a large white woolen shawl, which is almost completed." The shawl remains on stage for much of the play, with Rebecca working on it from time to time. It is finished by the final scene, and Rebecca puts it on for her final walk to her death with Rosmer, saying, "I must retire from the game, John." The white shawl is her shroud; it becomes also her wedding veil as she puts it over her head for Rosmer's strange ceremony: "Rebecca, now I place my hand on your head. . . . And take you in marriage as my lawful wife."

The sense of doom that hangs over the play comes, in large part, from the fact that Rosmer and Rebecca are almost mathematically balanced against each other in a deadly symmetry; their relationship can only end in death. In many ways they are antithetical—Rebecca is, or has been, free, active, and pagan; Rosmer is bound by his "white horses," contemplative, Christian—but in more fundamental ways they are fatally similar. The pattern of Rosmer's spiritual life is partially reduplicated in Rebecca's; the result is a mutually destructive complementarity.

Rosmer's personality and the influences that have formed it are vividly suggested by the setting of the play. *Rosmersholm* is, with *A Doll's House,* one of the two Ibsen plays named after their settings, and the house itself is the major symbol in the play. Like Brand's parsonage, the Helmer doll's house, and Mrs. Alving's Rosenvold, it is a powerful symbol of the spiritual "ghosts" of heredity, childhood experiences, and decaying social conventions. Around the wall of the morning room at Rosmersholm hang portraits of the Rosmer ancestors, who have been soldiers and priests in alternate generations. "It's the dead who cling to Rosmersholm," Mrs. Helseth tells Rebecca, "almost as though they couldn't free themselves from the ones left behind." The house is the embodiment of the "Rosmer view of life," a body of rigid and high-minded moral traditions, like the ghosts that walk the Alving home. As Mrs. Helseth tells Rebecca, it is a place where "little children never cry," and when they grow up, "they never laugh until the day they die."

Morally the house represents the "Rosmer view of life"; psychologically it is a tomb world which reflects the gloomy inner world of John Rosmer. Rosmer has apparently always been aloof, introspective, and passive. Although he has become a minister in accordance with Rosmer tradition, he has given up the active ministry, in order, he says, "to read, to bury myself in those fields of thought that had hitherto been closed to me." He follows events in town only indirectly by report; he takes no active part in them. He tends to think of himself as a potential savior with the power to "emancipate" and "purify" his fellowmen, though he takes no active steps to do so. He also tends toward lack of affect. "Have you ever heard or seen the Pastor laugh?" Mrs. Helseth asks Rebecca, and Rebecca acknowledges that she has not. He seems indifferent to sex or perhaps even repelled by it. He has made no move to make Rebecca his mistress during the time they have been together, giving as his reason his belief that their love is "above" sensuality: "With you I found a happiness that was calm and joyful and not merely based on sensuality. When you really think about it, Rebecca—we were like two children falling sweetly and secretly in love. We made no demands, we dreamed no dreams." One of his reasons for believing that Beata was insane was her "sensuality": "Those uncontrollable, sick fits of sensuality—and the way she expected me to reciprocate them. She—frightened me."

Despite this fear of sensuality and intimacy and his tendency to defend himself by "rising above" such feelings into a lofty idealism, Rosmer sometimes swings to the other pole of yielding himself completely to the influence of another person. Rebecca has been preceded by Ulrik Brendel and Kroll as such influences upon him. Rosmer's gloom comes in large part from a pervasive and vague sense of guilt, for which he can hardly assign a cause. Rosmer's behavior before the conversation with Kroll and the ease with which he assumes responsibility for Beata's death suggest that his guilt is more deep-seated than he is willing to admit and that Beata's death merely provides a pretext for expressing it. "Oh, can't you ever stop thinking about guilt?" asks Rebecca, and Rosmer answers, "You don't know how it feels."

All these characteristics indicate a person with a weak sense of self, who has withdrawn from threatening personal contacts into an inner world of lonely introspection, which he finds only slightly less threatening than the outer one.

The arrival of Rebecca West in the Rosmer household has initiated the first serious challenge to Rosmer's life-strategy. Rebecca has been something "new, and living, and real." She has offered not only the possibility of a free sensuality he has never had the courage to achieve, but also a spiritual challenge to move into active life and help "ennoble" his fellow citizens. The division in Rosmer's self which this challenge exposes is reflected in the opposing figures of Beata and Rebecca at this point upon the psychological "heights."

Rosmer thinks he has taken up Rebecca's challenge and moved toward freedom and love. In fact, however, he has continued his old strategy by choosing to regard their feeling for each other as "a happiness that was calm and joyful and not merely based on sensuality." It is not until after he learns of his possible unconscious complicity in Beata's death that he finds this relationship inadequate and asks Rebecca to be his wife.

This view of Rosmer's personality helps to explain his strange passivity, his exaggerated sense of responsibility for Beata's death, and his failure to take action either in pursuing his education project or in making Rebecca his mistress or his wife. Rosmer's paralysis is explained in the play in moral terms, as the result of the "Rosmer view of life"; in psychological terms, it can be explained as the result of his insecurity of self which leads him to withdraw from the personal relationships which he finds threatening in the outer world.

Rebecca presents a similar problem of interpretation. She, too, is affected by a kind of paralysis which prevents her from accepting Rosmer's offer of marriage, despite the fact that this is the goal she has sought for over two years. She offers a number of explanations for this: the fact that her passion has been transformed in a "great and selfless love" beyond sensuality, the fact that the Rosmer view of life has "infected and poisoned" her will, and the fact that she has had a previous lover.

Freud deals with the ambiguity of these explicit motives in his brilliant essay on *Rosmersholm* in "Some Character Types Met With

136

in Psychoanalytic Work" (1915).[1] He argues that Rebecca's explanation of her refusal to Rosmer "only exposes one motive in order to conceal another." The concealed motive is her sense of oedipal guilt over her relationship with Dr. West. This whole relationship is clouded with ambiguity in the play. Dr. West was a friend of her mother, and after her death Rebecca cared for him until his death. Kroll explores this relationship in his puzzling scene wth Rebecca in Act III:

> KROLL. Your mother's occupation must of course have brought her into frequent contact with the district physician.
>
> REBECCA. It did.
>
> KROLL. And as soon as your mother dies, he takes you into his own home. He treats you harshly. Yet you stay with him. You know he won't leave you a penny—all you got was a case of books. Yet you stay with him. Put up with his tantrums—look after him until the day he dies.

Kroll tells Rebecca that Dr. West was her father and that her behavior was due to "an unconscious filial instinct." Rebecca reacts very violently to this:

> REBECCA *walks around, twisting and untwisting her hands.* It isn't possible. It's only something you're trying to make me imagine. It can't be true. It can't! Not possibly—!

She quickly composes herself and tells Kroll that she is disturbed merely because "I just don't want people to think of me as illegitimate." Freud, however, believes that Rebecca has not known that Dr. West was her father until Kroll tells her. Her agitation comes from her realization that she has committed incest, since Dr. West is the lover whose existence she hints at to Rosmer in Act IV.

Rebecca's refusal of Rosmer in Act II, which precedes the scene with Kroll, Freud believes to be motivated by a vague sense of oedipal guilt which has been with her throughout her time at Rosmersholm. Although she does not yet know that Dr. West was her father, she must have at least suspected that he was her mother's lover and the fact that she had taken her mother's place must have strongly impressed her. Her life in the Rosmer household—the

---

1. *Collected Papers,* trans. Joan Riviere (New York, 1959), pp. 318–344.

passion for Rosmer and the enmity toward his wife—has been a compulsive replica of her relations with her mother and with Dr. West. Her vague guilt becomes specific when Kroll unwittingly shows her that fantasy is fact, that she has literally committed incest with Dr. West. This accounts for the peculiar fact that the affair she mentions to Rosmer, carried on when she was free and unattached, carries more weight than her guilty involvement in Beata's death; it is conclusive because it carries with it the shame of incest.

Rebecca, of course, has not consciously made the connection between Dr. West and Rosmer, and so she is honest in her statement of her reasons why she cannot marry Rosmer: "Just as under the influence of Dr. West she had become a freethinker and contemner of religious morality, so she is transformed by her love for Rosmer into a being with a conscience and an ideal. This much of the mental processes within her she does herself understand, and so she is justified in describing Rosmer's influence as the motive of the change in her—the only one of which she could be aware."

Freud's analysis of Rebecca's motivations seems obviously correct, and it illuminates the fundamental similarity between Rosmer and Rebecca which underlies their contrasting superficial characteristics. Rebecca is wrong when she tells Rosmer that she was completely free when she came to Rosmersholm and that she has lost her courage, freedom, and will as a result of the Rosmer view of life. Actually, she has been as much enslaved by her past as Rosmer, and her idealistic ambition to liberate Rosmer has been exactly parallel to Rosmer's high-minded plan to liberate his fellow countrymen. Both ideals have been defensive strategies against "troublesome thoughts" and both have inevitably failed. Both Rebecca and Rosmer have tried to free others without first freeing themselves.

In the course of the play, both Rebecca's and Rosmer's projects of the will collapse and they arrive at the final scene stripped of these idealistic defenses. They undergo a profound spiritual transformation, and a "great calm" comes over them, "the kind of calm you find on a bird-cliff up in the far north, under the midnight sun." Rosmer is "no longer afraid," and at last they can become man and wife, in his brief symbolic ceremony. But the reborn Rebecca and Rosmer can find no way of living for the future. The consequences of their actions are inescapable; they cannot erase the past:

REBECCA. Are you so completely sure—that this way is the best one for you?

ROSMER. I know that it is the only one.

REBECCA. Suppose you are wrong? Suppose it is only an illusion? One of the white horses of Rosmersholm?

ROSMER. That may be. We shall never escape them—we who live in this house.

Like Brand, Rosmer and Rebecca are reborn "on the peaks," but their rebirth is almost immediately followed by death. But it is a death freely chosen; to this extent they have escaped the burden of the past.

There is a strong temptation in reading *Rosmersholm* to accept Rebecca's own evaluation of herself and to view her as the victim of Rosmer and the Rosmer view of life. Shaw, for example, thought Rosmer was motivated to commit suicide by "the superstition of expiation by sacrifice," while Rebecca has a "higher light" and goes to her death out of fellowship with the man she loves. In the final scene, as throughout this difficult play, however, explicit motives are seldom the true ones. Rebecca and Rosmer stand in a much more complex relationship than that of victim and victimizer, and the richness and depth of the play comes from the way their destinies, so closely parallel, are fatally intertwined.

II

The Lady from the Sea is very closely linked to *Rosmersholm.* In one of the earliest reviews of the play, Edmund Gosse pointed out how it seems to be antithetically balanced against *Rosmersholm:* "It is in some respects the reverse of *Rosmersholm;* the bitterness of restrained and baulked individuality, which ends in death, being contrasted with the sweetness of emancipated and gratified individuality, which leads to health and peace."

The contrast is sharpened by the many similarities of plot and characters. Both are plays about second wives in which the shadow of the first wife hangs heavily over the action. (In one of the preliminary drafts of *Rosmersholm,* Rebecca was actually married to Rosmer.) Rebecca, like Ellida, comes from the north and is fascinated by the sea; at one point Ulrik Brendel even addresses her as "bewitching lady from the sea." Both women feel their present freedom of action limited by the past and try to fight their way free of its influence. Their close identification in Ibsen's mind may even be indicated in the fact that Bolette and Hilde were originally intended to be Rebecca's stepdaughters, but were dropped from *Rosmersholm* and later incorporated as Ellida's stepdaughters in *The Lady from the Sea.* Rosmer and Wangel themselves have some points of similarity, in their contemplative, melancholy natures. Perhaps Wangel was originally intended to be even more like Rosmer; in the earliest notes he is a lawyer, "refined, superior, bitter," with a past he cannot overcome.

In the final version of *The Lady from the Sea,* however, Wangel is clearly a secondary character, and the chief emphasis falls upon Ellida and her struggle to attain the inner freedom that will make a "true marriage" with Wangel possible. The forces in her character that hold her captive and the form her struggle for self-liberation takes are similar to Rebecca's. The outcome, of course, is different, but the situations are so similar it is almost as if Ellida's history constituted a kind of "second chance" for Rebecca.

The Lady from the Sea is an experimental play, not only in its exploration of alternate possibilities inherent in the materials of its predecessor, but also in its unusual blending of the subjective and the objective. In the six plays that preceded it, from *The Pillars of Society* through *Rosmersholm,* the settings, characters, and action had been highly colored by the perceptions of the protagonists, but it had always been possible also to accept the play as objective reality. In *The Lady from the Sea,* however, it is impossible to accept the Stranger and his behavior literally; we see him through Ellida's eyes. In this respect *The Lady from the Sea* anticipates the blending of the realistic and the mythic in the last four plays, from *The Master Builder* on.

At the point where *The Lady from the Sea* opens, Ellida is in a dangerously depressed mental state. As she confesses to Wangel, with whom she has had no sexual relations in three years, she is obsessed with a yearning homesickness for the sea. Although they live in a pleasant home on a fjord, she feels oppressed and stifled and thinks of the water in the fjord as "sick" and "poisonous." She expresses her yearning for the sea in long, daily baths in the sea. She is alienated from her stepdaughters Bolette and Hilde, whom she ignores and who in return exclude her from the family group. The situation is aggravated by the fact that Wangel himself is worried and preoccupied with Ellida's mental state and consequently also neglects his daughters. This only intensifies their resentment of their stepmother.

The sequence of events that has brought Ellida to this tomb world is gradually divulged during the course of the play. She was born in the far north, at Skjoldviken, where her father was a lighthouse keeper. Her mother became insane and died in an asylum, apparently while Ellida was still very young. She therefore spent her childhood alone with her father in the isolated lighthouse. Ellida thus belongs in the long line of Ibsen protagonists who have been reared in isolation by single parents of the opposite sex.

Ten years before the time of the play, Ellida's lonely life with her father was interrupted by the entrance of two men into her life. Arnholm, the village schoolmaster, who made frequent calls upon her father, became her "best and truest friend," and at last proposed marriage. She refused him, however, because she had already fallen in love with the second man, a sailor on an American ship which had come into Skjoldviken for repairs. This was a strange affair. She saw him only a few times and knew almost nothing about him, only that he was from Finmark, in the far north, and that he had spent most of his life at sea. She didn't even know his name; he called himself both Freeman and Alfred Johnston, but acknowledged that neither was his true name. Even at this time she felt that he had a strange power over her; in describing the relationship to Wangel, she says that she "had no will of her own" when he was with her.

Their brief affair was abruptly ended when he asked her to meet him early one morning and told her that he had killed the captain of his ship during the night, "because it was right." He put Ellida's ring and his on a key-chain, threw them into the sea, saying that now they were "married to the sea," and fled. Ellida received six letters from him, and although she replied, telling him that she never

141

wanted to hear from him again, he continued to write her that someday he would call her and that she was to come at once.

About four years after her affair with the Stranger, Ellida quite suddenly married Dr. Wangel, the local doctor who came to Skjoldviken after the Stranger's departure. Looking back on the circumstances of her marriage, she feels that she has sold herself. She had spoken to Dr. Wangel only two or three times and then one day he came out to the lighthouse, talked to her at length about the happiness of his first marriage, and asked her to be his wife. She agreed, but in retrospect she sees that she did not marry Wangel "of her own free will." She felt helpless and alone and was tempted by the prospect of money and security. They married and moved south to the little resort town in which the action of the play takes place. A little over a year after their marriage a baby was born, but died when he was four or five months old.

This cluster of events, considered as a whole, throws considerable light on Ellida's personality and motivations. She has retreated from her sinister childhood home, with her mother insane and Ellida isolated with her father in the phallic lighthouse, up to an experience "on the heights." The split in her self is indicated by the almost simultaneous appearance of Arnholm and the Stranger. Arnholm, a schoolmaster and about ten years older than Ellida, is a gentle, paternal figure, while the Stranger is an exotic and fascinating man who "paralyzes her will." She ostensibly rejects both and returns to life with her father in the lighthouse, but she carries the memory of the experience with her as a defense against threats of intimacy. When Wangel appears on the scene she is able to accept his offer of marriage without committing herself emotionally, by telling herself that she is marrying for security but that her "true life" lies elsewhere. She has preserved this attitude through the five or six years of their marriage. In Act I, when Arnholm tries to comfort her because of the birthday party which indicates her exclusion from Wangel's and his daughters' "life of memories," she tells him that she herself lives a secret life from which they are excluded. The death of the child is a first child-death which signals Ellida's self-division.

Ellida's marriage to Wangel thus constitutes a project of the will. She has resolved to fulfill her side of the "bargain" by being a good wife to Wangel and a good mother to his daughters without fully committing herself to them emotionally. Her project is in danger of collapsing at the point where the play opens, because she has come to love Wangel. Her secret life is "so dreadful," she tells Arnholm, because "I have grown so very fond of him," and she is unequivocal throughout the play in telling Wangel that she loves no one but him. The neurotic symptoms she displays are a result of the tension between her defensive inner life and the free, loving outer life her love for Wangel now makes possible.

This situation is symbolized most fully in Ellida's ambivalent feelings for the sea. Even as a child she has been strongly attracted to the sea, but now it has become "a kind of passion with her," Wangel says. She identifies the Stranger with the sea, and feels that his power over her is like the power of the tide. Her dead child had the Stranger's eyes: strange, staring eyes that "changed with the sea." The Stranger, like the sea itself, simultaneously attracts and terrifies her. "Oh, Wangel! Save me from myself!" she cries when she feels the Stranger's pull.

The strength and ambivalence of Ellida's feelings for the sea indicate its unconscious meaning for her as a symbol of regression. Terrified by the outer world of experience, she yearns to retreat into the safety of an inner world. Yet such a retreat has its own threat of ultimate regression and thus total ego-loss. She therefore adopts the characteristic schizoid strategy of alternately withdrawing into the inner world and escaping from it, of regularly venturing to the brink of annihilation, with its mingled attraction and threat. This is the same impulse that lies behind Brand's fascination with the "avalanche" and the "abyss."

Ellida's situation at the beginning of the play is thus similar to Rebecca's at the beginning of *Rosmersholm*. Both have come out of the north, from childhoods shadowed by incest guilt. Both have met men who hold the possibility of deep and fulfilling love and both have adopted projects of the will as defenses against the threat they feel is inherent in this kind of love. Both face the collapse of their projects and try to fight their way free of their pasts, to achieve a sense of self-unity, and to move into "free and responsible" relationships.

The fact that Rebecca fails and Ellida succeeds is due to the difference in the characters of Rosmer and Wangel. Rosmer is fatally similar to Rebecca in his psychological makeup, but in the course of writing *The Lady from the Sea,* Ibsen changed Wangel from a Rosmer-like, "refined, superior, and bitter" lawyer, haunted by his own past, into a gentle, humane, and well-integrated doctor, ready to minister to Ellida in her confrontation with her self and her rebirth as a new person.

The impending collapse of Ellida's schizoid strategy is signaled by the reappearance of the Stranger, a figure straight out of the myth of the self, hardly rationalized at all in realistic terms. It is barely credible that "Alfred Johnston" would return and ask Ellida to abandon her husband and go away with him, but the way in which he alternates between speaking as Ellida's inner voice and as a real sailor cannot be explained at all in realistic terms. Dr. Wangel points up the subjective character of the Stranger's appearance when he points out to Ellida that, although the Stranger now looks very different from her memory of him as she described it to Wangel, Ellida has apparently noticed no difference at all. Ibsen was very concerned that the ambiguity in the Stranger's status be preserved. Not only did he not give him a name, but he also objected strongly when the director of an early German production wanted to list him in the program as "Ein Seemann," "Ein fremder Seemann," or "Ein Steuermann":

> Actually he is none of these. When Ellida met him ten years ago, he was second mate. Seven years later he signed on as a simple boatswain, that is, in a decidedly lower position. And now he appears as a passenger on a tourist ship. He does not belong to the ship's crew. He is dressed as a casual tourist, not in traveling clothes. No one is supposed to know what he is, just as no one is supposed to know *who* he is or what his real name is. This uncertainty about him is the essential element in the method I have deliberately chosen.

With a doctor's insight, Wangel sees that Ellida's confrontation with the Stranger is really a confrontation with herself: "I begin to understand you, little by little. You think and feel in pictures and visual

144

images. Your restless yearning for the sea—your yearning for this stranger—all that was nothing more than an expression of your longing for freedom. Nothing more."

Wangel still interprets Ellida's triumph over herself in moral terms, however; she gains control over her past when she is allowed to "choose freely." Psychologically her renunciation of the Stranger and her free and loving acceptance of Wangel is a regenerative and ecstatic experience, parallel to other such experiences "on the peaks" in Ibsen, though it is here represented in terms of a descent to the underworld of the unconscious and a return to light and freedom.

In Act III, the Stranger first appears to Ellida in the darkest, most sinister part of the tomb world of the play, which has come to suggest Ellida's own inner world. It is "a corner of Dr. Wangel's garden . . . damp and marshy, and overshadowed by large and old trees." Nearby is a stagnant carp-pond in which ancient, overgrown, monsterlike carp move slowly under the water. At the Stranger's first appearance, Ellida is "staring down into the pond."

It is to this shadowy and sinister setting that Ellida must deliberately return in Act V for her final confrontation with the Stranger. When the scene begins, Wangel is still determined to "help" Ellida by repelling the Stranger himself, but the Stranger insists that the choice be Ellida's. Wangel senses the psychological danger Ellida is in:

> WANGEL, *quietly, in pain.* I see it, Ellida! Little by little you are slipping away from me. Your longing for the boundless, the infinite, will end by driving your mind into darkness.
>
> ELLIDA. Oh, yes, yes! I feel it! Like—black soundless wings—beating over me.

Wangel desperately arrests this slipping back into loss of self by giving Ellida the responsibility of making the choice herself, "in freedom." He tells her that he loves her: "You have become a part of me, Ellida. Through the years we have lived together." For a moment Wangel and the Stranger confront each other, with Ellida wavering between the two—Wangel representing the outer world of love and freedom, the Stranger the inner world of retreat and regression. Ellida then turns to the Stranger and says, "I cannot go

145

with you. . . . I no longer fear you. I no longer want you." The Stranger easily accepts the choice, tells her "Henceforth you are no more to me than a lost ship," vaults over the fence, and is gone.

At a similar point, Rebecca West also makes a "free and responsible" decision and gains a long-withheld sense of security and freedom from fear, as John Rosmer does also. But the burden of the past is too heavy for them and they cannot face a life in the future. Ellida, with the support of her wise and loving husband, moves beyond her regenerative experience into a future of love and peace.

III

Hedda Gabler is the most savage of Ibsen's studies in the personality type which, tormented by insecurity of self, seeks to defend itself against the threats of life by pursuing fanatical and destructive projects of the will. The anxiety which drives Rebecca West to adopt the goal of "liberating" Rosmer and which drives Ellida Wangel into a cold and loveless marriage impels Hedda into a maniacal attempt to "shape a man's destiny," which ends in the destruction of Eilert Loevborg and finally of herself. Hedda's extremism makes her closely kin to Catiline, Brand, and Gregers Werle, but she is perhaps most closely related to the Emperor Julian; in many ways, Hedda Gabler is a portrait of Julian the Apostate as a suburban housewife.

The central fact about Hedda Gabler is that she is constantly in the grip of a terrible, inescapable, paralyzing anxiety, despite her pose of easy negligence and boredom. She is "bored" by Aunt Juliana, by the prospect of domesticity in her new house, and most of all by her new husband. "There's only one thing for which I have any natural talent," she tells Judge Brack, "boring myself to death." If we take Hedda's statement at face value, we can interpret her actions as those of a woman casually and irresponsibly seeking some excitement to relieve the tedium of her life. Hedda, however, is not merely suffering from boredom, unless we use that word to refer to a state of desperation bordering on panic. We are given a hint of

146

the intensity of Hedda's suffering early in the play, when, after adopting an air of casual indifference throughout her first scene with Tesman and Aunt Juliana, Hedda is left alone for a moment and she "walks up and down the room raising her arms and clenching her fists as though in desperation."

The source of this desperation provides the key to the interpretation of Hedda's character. What Hedda fears, above all, is the intimacy of close human relationships, because she unconsciously feels that such intimacy implies being "invaded" or "possessed" by another person and consequently having one's ego drowned or smothered. Paradoxically, however, Hedda also seeks out close relationships of a certain kind. Complete withdrawal from others presents another ego-threat: that of complete regression into one's inner world. She therefore cultivates certain close relationships, provided they are heavily surrounded by restrictions and limitations that keep them from becoming too intimate and thus too threatening.

Hedda's early relationship with Eilert Loevborg is an illuminating example of this strategy. They recall it together in Act II. Loevborg would visit Hedda in the afternoons and they would sit together on the sofa, ostensibly looking at an illustrated paper, while Hedda's father sat across the room, reading. Behind the paper, however, Hedda would have Loevborg give her detailed accounts of his debaucheries—"days and nights of drinking and————." Loevborg was puzzled by her passionate curiosity, but complied with her desire to know the secrets of his life. He also joined her in regarding their relationship as a kind of "comradeship," until finally one day he tried to make love to her. Hedda responded by drawing one of her father's pistols and threatening to shoot him.

This episode illustrates Hedda's characteristic "in and out" strategy of human relationships. She has complementary needs to cultivate human relationships that preserve her contact with the outer world and to control them when they threaten to "invade" her inner world.

The same strategy underlies her marriage. She insists to Judge Brack—and perhaps believes herself—that she married strictly for prestige and security. She had "danced herself tired," she tells Brack. She believed that Tesman was a distinguished scholar and

147

would some day be a famous and wealthy man. Her very vehemence in insisting upon her cynical motives for marriage betrays her fear, not only of sexuality, but of any kind of intimacy related to marriage. When Brack uses the word "love," she replies, "Oh, don't use that sickly, stupid word!" Although the marriage has obviously been consummated, Hedda reacts violently to any suggestion of sexuality; when Tesman naively says that he has "good reason to know" about Hedda's figure, she says impatiently, "You haven't good reason to know anything." The marriage with Tesman offers not only financial security, but the opportunity to maintain a controlled relationship of highly guarded and limited intimacy, a chance to "rest" from the threats of her many admirers before her marriage.

Terrified by relationships that would be satisfying to most people but that seem to present the threat of engulfment for her, Hedda has withdrawn from the outer world into a world of her own, in which she can carefully preserve her fragile sense of self. This inner world is like a dark cave, from which Hedda looks out upon the outside world with mingled feelings of fear and yearning. Ibsen suggested Hedda's attitude toward even the dull and innocuous Tesman family in a letter to Kristina Steen, an actress involved in one of the first productions of the play: "Joergen Tesman, his old aunts, and the faithful servant Berte together form a picture of complete unity. They think alike, they share the same memories and have the same outlook on life. To Hedda they appear like a strange and hostile power, aimed at her very being."

This inner world is suggested by the setting of the play, which mirrors Hedda's mind as closely as Rosmersholm mirrors the tomb worlds of Rosmer and Rebecca West. Like so many of Ibsen's characters, Hedda likes shadowy, dimly lighted places away from the sunlight of authentic experience. On her first entrance, she immediately makes Tesman close the curtains that Aunt Juliana has opened to let in the morning sun. She also hates flowers in the house, and quickly removes the bouquets that are in the room in Act I in honor of her homecoming. (The life-hating Beata, in *Rosmersholm*, has had the same antipathy.) Already the portrait of her father hangs over the sofa, a correlative of the self-perception that makes her think of herself still as Hedda Gabler rather than Hedda

148

Tesman. The two rooms that might be nurseries stand empty, in an image of sterility that is to reappear in Aline's empty nurseries in *The Master Builder*.

Within her comparatively "safe" inner world, Hedda adopts characteristic schizoid strategies of defense. She delights in secrecy. The pretended misunderstanding over Aunt Juliana's bonnet offers not only the opportunity to demonstrate her superiority over another person but a certain delight in deception for its own sake. She smiles when she tells Judge Brack about how she pretended to think the hat was the servant's, but when Brack asks her why she played such a cruel trick, she replies, "nervously, walking across the room": "Sometimes a mood like that hits me. And I can't stop myself. Oh, I don't know how to explain it." The incident recalls her pleasure in the secrecy of her peculiar relationship with Loevborg when she was a girl, when she delighted in exploring a forbidden world, "especially if it could be done in secrecy."

The need to feel superior which Hedda's love of secrets implies appears also in her extreme contempt for others. Tesman, his aunts, and the servant seem to be "a strange and hostile power, aimed at her very being," as Ibsen said, but she counters their threat by belittling and ridiculing them. She defends herself against Thea Elvsted, whose intimacy with Loevborg she hopelessly envies, in the same way: by making fun of her behind her back and by openly bullying and terrifying her. "I think I'll burn your hair off after all. . . . you little idiot!" she tells her.

Despite Hedda's contempt for others and her own sense of secret power, however, she is also tormented by self-contempt. She partially understands the sources of her anxiety and helplessly yearns to escape from her inner world into warm and anxiety-free relationships. She thinks of her inability to do so as "cowardice." In discussing with Loevborg the evening when he tried to make love to her and she threatened him with the pistol, she confesses, "My failure to shoot you wasn't my worst act of cowardice that evening," and later she thinks that if only she had "courage," then "one might be able to live. In spite of everything."

Hedda's principal defense against the threat she feels of being invaded and controlled by others is to invade and control them. Her yearning for "the power to shape a human destiny" which leads her to destroy Loevborg has already manifested itself in other situations, including her early relationship with Loevborg and her relationship with her husband. An important element in the secretive, controlled intimacy with Loevborg was the fact that she was in absolute command of the situation; when he rebelled, she threatened his life. Although she doesn't think Tesman is "worth bothering about," she has established complete control of his career, their living arrangements, and every aspect of their life, and she tells Brack that she is toying with the idea of making Tesman go into politics.

> BRACK. What satisfaction would that give you? If he turned out to be no good? Why do you want to make him do that?
> HEDDA. Because I'm bored.

The threat that Judge Brack presents to Hedda is the fact that he is driven by similar compulsions to exercise secret control over others. He is strong enough to present a challenge to her and she delights in thinking that she can control him in the "triangular friendship" they plan. When his knowledge of Hedda's involvement in Loevborg's death makes him "the only cock on the dunghill," however, she cannot face the terror of being in the power of another and shoots herself.

Hedda, then, is a thoroughly schizoid personality, driven by the terror of ego-loss back into an inner world. From this inner world, she tries to defend herself against the engulfment threats that others represent to her by anxiety-ridden strategies of secrecy, contempt for others, and attempts to control other people's lives.

The progress of the action which grows out of these strategies closely follows the pattern of Ibsen's myth of the self. Hedda is like Julian and Gregers Werle in that she never attains release on the peaks from the torment of her self-division, but her psychological progress otherwise incorporates the full myth, compressed into the two days the play covers.

The roots of Hedda's warped psychological make-up lie in the valley of her childhood. Like Nora Helmer and Ellida Wangel, she has been reared alone by her father. No mention is ever made of her dead mother, but the sinister presence of General Gabler hangs over the entire play, by means of his portrait, which Hedda has already hung in the drawing room, and his pistols. These pistols, with their combined paternal and phallic associations, are intimately related to Hedda's hysterical and aggressive strategies of living. When she is frustrated by the prospect of financial difficulty, at the end of Act I, she immediately turns to the pistols:

HEDDA. Oh, well. I still have one thing left to amuse myself with.

TESMAN, *joyfully.* Thank goodness for that. What's that, Hedda? What?

HEDDA *looks at him with concealed scorn.* My pistols, George darling.

TESMAN, *alarmed.* Pistols!

HEDDA, *her eyes cold.* General Gabler's pistols.

TESMAN. For heaven's sake, Hedda dear, don't touch those things. They're dangerous. Hedda—please—for my sake! What?

Later in the play she uses the pistols to intimidate Judge Brack, to drive Loevborg to suicide, and finally to kill herself. The pistols thus come to symbolize the defensiveness and the self-destructiveness implanted in Hedda by her relationship with her father.

Like Nora and Mrs. Alving, Hedda has passed into marriage without altering in the least her values and attitudes. Like theirs, her marriage has been a loveless marriage of convenience; the love that helped bring about Ellida's long-delayed transformation has been missing in her life. Thus she still thinks of herself as Hedda Gabler rather than Hedda Tesman.

At the point where the play opens, however, Hedda's rigid strategy of defense has begun to show signs of cracking. She finds herself dangerously threatened by the unavoidable intimacies of married life, and her control over George's life is threatened by the unexpected prospect of competition by Loevborg for the academic appointment. The most terrifying threat of all, however, is the fact that she is unexpectedly pregnant. She knows that motherhood will make it impossible to maintain the cold and defensive manner of living she finds necessary.

These combined circumstances precipitate a crisis in Hedda's emotional life and propel her into a "decision on the heights." The reappearance of Loevborg brings together the two men in her life, the gentle, paternal Tesman and the fascinating, Dionysian Loevborg, thus recapitulating the choice she has made earlier and symbolizing the deep division in her self. Terrified by the many threats she feels to her precarious style of life—her pregnancy, the enforced intimacy with George and Juliana, the overt sexuality of Loevborg —she retreats into a "project of the will": to shape a human destiny by driving Loevborg to embrace "Dionysian beauty." This complex of events merely recapitulates dramatically a "decision on the heights" which Hedda has gradually made earlier. Tesman and Loevborg have already presented themselves to her as choices, and the project to control the lives of other people is a long-standing ambition. The events of the play compress and epitomize what has already taken place slowly and over a long period of time.

Hedda's fantasy of seeing Loevborg with "vine leaves in his hair" and her unrealistic demands for "beauty" and "nobility" suggest the way in which Hedda, from within the dark cave of her inner world, imagines the world of freedom and sensuality from which she is forever barred. The imagery recalls *Emperor and Galilean,* in which the similarly tormented Julian fantasizes about the joy of life in the same terms. Neither Julian nor Hedda can face the concrete reality of the sensual life: the actual Dionysian rites or the sordid details of Loevborg's debauchery.

The burning of Loevborg's manuscript at the end of Act III is a first child-death which symbolizes Hedda's attempt to kill one side of her nature. Loevborg and Thea Elvsted have already referred to the book as their "child," and as Hedda feeds the pages into the fire, she whispers that she is burning the child:

> HEDDA. I'm burning your child, Thea! You with your beautiful wavy hair! The child Eilert Loevborg gave you. I'm burning it! I am burning your child!

Hedda is obviously expressing her hatred and envy of Thea for the intimacy she has attained with Loevborg. But even more fundamentally, she is expressing the underlying motive for her incredibly cruel treatment of Loevborg: her desperate need to "kill" in herself the yearning for the freedom and sensuality she associates with Loevborg.

As this account of Hedda's psychological state suggests, the mo-

152

tives for her suicide are rather complex. The immediate, overt reason for shooting herself is that Judge Brack has managed to get control over her. Her last words are a reply to Judge Brack's subtly threatening promise to stop by "every evening" from now on: "Yes, that'll suit you, won't it, Judge? The only cock on the dunghill." But behind this immediate threat lies the total collapse of Hedda's long-standing life strategy. Faced with the prospect of motherhood and a lifetime of enforced intimacy with George and his family, and threatened by Judge Brack and the dangerous attraction of Eilert Loevborg, Hedda has staked everything upon her power to "shape another human destiny." Her project has inevitably failed when it encountered living reality; Loevborg has died a sordid death, Judge Brack has a new hold over her, and Thea Elvsted is an even more infuriating object of envy than before, as she begins to cultivate the kind of relationship with George that she had with Loevborg. Hedda can see no way out but death.

It is difficult to see any redeeming qualities in the circumstances of Hedda's suicide. It is true that by this act she finally does something courageous and attains that degree of freedom. She thus separates herself from Judge Brack, who cannot imagine such an act: "People don't *do* such things!" She also manages to shoot herself in the temple, thus achieving the kind of death she had failed to achieve for Loevborg, who died of an accidental shot in the bowels. But to regard her act as "courageous" in any real sense or her death as "beautiful" would be to accept the same demented set of values Hedda has lived by. The ending of *Hedda Gabler* is, with those of *Ghosts* and *The Wild Duck,* among the bleakest in Ibsen's works. Hedda never rises to the peaks, but instead withdraws into an "inner room," draws the curtains around her, and meets her death deep within the inner world in which she has been imprisoned throughout her life.

8. The Last Plays

THE DESIGN of Solness's new house in *The Master Builder* suggests the design of the play itself and of the three plays that followed it. Solness has begun his career, he tells Hilde, as a builder of churches. After his mystical experience atop the tower at Lysanger, he has abandoned church-building and has started building "houses for people to live in." Now, at the end of his career, he has built a house for himself that juxtaposes elements from the earlier stages of his life; it is a house to live in, but it has a high spire, like a church.

Ibsen's own dramatic churches—*Brand* and *Peer Gynt*—are overtly mythic in their structure. Brand's odyssey from the valley up onto the heights, back into the valley and finally up into the Ice Church on the peaks, and Peer's wandering path from Aase's hut up onto the heights with Ingrid, around the world, and finally up onto the peaks for the final encounter with Solveig are both clearly spiritual odysseys; the controlling, shaping force of the plots is the myth they embody. In the plays from *The Pillars of Society* through *Hedda Gabler,* the balance shifts. The mythic pattern is still present, lending depth and power to the action, but it is deeply buried. The course of development of the overt plots is governed by the conventions of "realism," which displace the mythic pattern and create a surface structure obedient to canons of credibility and logic. In the realistic plays, as in the "dramatic poems," however, a subtle tension is always preserved between the surface structure and the mythic structure, despite the shift in emphasis between the two.

154

Occasionally in the realistic plays this tension is severely strained and the mythic structure comes close to the surface, threatening to take over the course of the play, as in the figure of the Stranger in *The Lady from the Sea,* but the dominance of the realistic surface is always preserved.

The most striking aspect of the dramatic method of *The Master Builder* and the plays that follow it is a new balance between these two structural principles, one in which neither is dominant but in which both function equally in the structural development of the play. In *The Lady from the Sea* and *Hedda Gabler* it is possible to deal with the Stranger and with Loevborg's vine leaves in terms of realistic conventions. "Your restless yearning for the sea—your yearning for this stranger—all that was nothing but an expression of your longing for freedom," says Dr. Wangel, desperately trying to suppress the forces that threaten to engulf the cool, rational surface of the play. But no such suppression is possible in *The Master Builder* and its successors. The mythic structure of these plays emerges to assume an equal position with the realistic surface structure. Nor is there any attempt to mediate between the two. Hilde is inexplicable in terms of realistic characterization, but she walks into Solness's solidly real office, and the effect is as if the Greenclad Woman had suddenly appeared in the Helmer drawing room in *A Doll's House,* or as if Gerd had suddenly knocked at Mrs. Alving's door in *Ghosts.*

This radical juxtaposition of two complementary but clearly distinct structural principles has an effect almost as unsettling to modern audiences as it was to Ibsen's contemporary audience. The characteristic reaction is to try to fit the discordant elements into some single mode. If the mode selected is "realism," elaborate attempts are made to explain disturbing characters as studies in neurosis. Thus Hilde becomes a bizarre example of adolescent neurosis and the Rat Wife in *Little Eyolf* merely a crazy old woman. Or the critic may choose instead to regard the play as allegorical. Solness and Hilde become Age and Youth, Art and Life, or some other pair of antithetical values.

Both kinds of reduction do violence to the plays, for they force us to subordinate elements that Ibsen deliberately set up as dramatically equal to the elements the critic chooses to emphasize. Any satisfactory account of these four plays must start with the recognition that they fit into no preexisting category and that their double emphasis upon mythic structure and realistic structure cannot be reduced to a single principle. The plays suffer from any such reductions and appear to be either very muddle-headed realistic plays or perversely clouded allegories, rather than juxtapositions of different, though complementary, structures in which each structure constitutes a continual, complex commentary upon the other. It may be that the reader will ultimately find these juxtapositions unpalatable and agree with Solness's neighbors that a house should not have so high a spire, but at least he will have rejected the plays on the grounds of what they are rather than what they are not.

I

The first scene of *The Master Builder* presents a configuration of characters already familiar from a number of earlier Ibsen plays: in the center, a powerful man burdened with a crushing sense of guilt, and ranged around him, the victims of his attempts to impose his will upon the world. The Broviks, father and son, Kaja Fosli, and Aline Solness are all, in various ways, victims of Solness's will. The relationship between Solness and old Knut Brovik is reminiscent of that between Haakon Werle and Old Ekdal in *The Wild Duck;* Solness has ruined Brovik and now employs him in a spirit of mingled charity and contempt, though he finds his ability to "work out stresses and cubic content and all that bloody nonsense" useful. He exercises a power over Kaja Fosli that surprises and frightens even him:

> SOLNESS. One day this girl, Kaja Fosli, came to see them on some errand or other. She'd never been here before. Well, when I saw how infatuated they were with each other, the idea struck me that if I could get her to come and work here in the office, Ragnar might stay too.
>
> HERDAL. A reasonable supposition.
>
> SOLNESS. Yes, but I didn't mention a word of all this. I just stood and looked at her—and kept wishing from the bottom of my heart that

156

I had her here. Well, I chatted to her in a friendly way about one thing and another. And then she went.

HERDAL. Well?

SOLNESS. But then next day, in the evening, after old Brovik and Ragnar had gone home, she came back and acted just as though we'd come to some kind of agreement.

HERDAL. What kind of agreement?

SOLNESS. The very one I'd been wanting to suggest. But which I hadn't mentioned a word about.

Through his control of Kaja and old Brovik, Solness keeps Ragnar, who is in his thirties, in a subordinate position, though Ragnar yearns to become a builder himself.

It is Aline, however, who is Solness's principal victim, or at least it seems so to him. We are to discover later that Aline is a very ambiguous victim, perhaps less sinned against than sinning, but Solness torments himself with the thought that he is responsible for her wrecked life. He allows Aline to think that he is having an affair with Kaja, when in fact he is not.

HERDAL. And you haven't told your wife all this?

SOLNESS. No.

HERDAL. Why on earth don't you, then?

SOLNESS. Because somehow I feel it does me good to suffer Aline to do me an injustice.

HERDAL *shakes his head.* I'm damned if I understand a word of that.

SOLNESS. Oh, yes—you see it's like paying a minute installment on a great debt—a debt so vast it can never be settled.

HERDAL. A debt to your wife?

SOLNESS. Yes. And that—eases my mind a little. I can breathe more freely—for a while, you understand.

Thus far in the play, the realistic surface of the play is clear and coherent; the Solness household is perhaps a little bizarre, but even Solness's sense of his own dangerous powers is explicable in terms of his mental state. This realistic surface gradually begins to break up, however, with the entrance of Hilde.

SOLNESS. Just you wait, Doctor. One fine day, youth will come and bang on that door—

HERDAL *laughs.* Well, for heaven's sake, what of it?

SOLNESS. What of it? Why that will be the end of master builder Solness.
There is a banging on the door to the left.
SOLNESS *starts.* What was that? Did you hear something?
HERDAL. It's someone banging on the door.
SOLNESS, *loudly.* Come in!
Hilde Wangel comes in through the hall door.

From the point of this spectacular entrance on to the end of the first act, it becomes increasingly difficult to fit Hilde into the realistic surface of the play. At first we may try to regard the circumstances of her appearance as coincidental and her strange behavior as merely hysterical, but by the end of the first act all rational explanations have broken down. It is as if Solness's fantasies and anxieties had escaped the confines of his own mind and assumed a separate life of their own on the stage.

A number of peculiarly insistent details are used in this first scene of Hilde's to establish her double status in the play: as a plausible casual visitor and simultaneously as a mythic projection of a submerged side of Solness's nature. Solness does not recognize her, but oddly both Dr. Herdal and Aline recognize her immediately.

HERDAL *goes closer to her.* But I recognize you, Miss—
HILDE, *delighted.* Oh, no! Is it you—?
HERDAL. Indeed it's me.
To SOLNESS.
We met up in one of the mountain huts this summer.
To HILDE.
What happened to the other ladies?
HILDE. Oh, they went on to the west coast.
HERDAL. They didn't like all that noise in the evenings.
HILDE. No, they didn't.
HERDAL *wags his finger.* And you must confess you flirted a little with us!

Aline, too, has met Hilde in the mountains and has invited her to visit them if she were ever nearby.

Although Hilde is obviously the same Hilde Wangel who appears as Ellida's stepdaughter in *The Lady from the Sea,* she brings with

158

her none of the details of the earlier play except her name, her general background, and her yearning for the "excitement" of controlling another human life. Her father is now said to be the "district physician up at Lysanger." Hilde must be almost twenty-three years old at the time *The Master Builder* takes place, since she was "nearly thirteen" when she first met Solness, ten years before. This would mean that the action of *The Lady from the Sea* has taken place at least five or six years before that of *The Master Builder;* yet neither Ellida nor Bolette is ever mentioned in the later play. Indeed, it is implied that Hilde has been reared alone by her father. The suggestion of an unusually strong attachment between Dr. Wangel and his daughters, an attachment that excluded Ellida, in *The Lady from the Sea,* becomes, in *The Master Builder,* a perhaps even stronger attachment between Wangel and Hilde. She has apparently left home for good, although she announces no plans for after she leaves the Solnesses, and in Act II, when she tells Solness that she wishes he had a more "robust conscience," the following elusive exchange takes place:

SOLNESS. Indeed? Robust? Well! And have you a robust conscience?

HILDE. Yes, I think so. I haven't noticed anything to the contrary.

SOLNESS. I don't suppose you've had much opportunity to test it, have you?

HILDE, *with a tremble round her mouth.* Oh, it wasn't all that easy to leave Father. I'm frightfully fond of him.

SOLNESS. Oh, just for a month or two—

HILDE. I don't think I shall ever go back.

SOLNESS. What, never? Why did you leave him, then?

Hilde avoids replying to this question by teasingly changing the subject:

HILDE, *half serious, half teasing.* Have you forgotten again? The ten years are up!

The most peculiar part of Hilde's behavior in this first scene, however, is her account of her first meeting with Solness at Lysanger and Solness's reaction to this account. After his ascent of the spire to hang the wreath on the new church, he met Hilde at a party, Hilde tells him. He promised to come back in ten years—like a troll—and

159

carry her off to a kingdom of "Orangia." And then he bent her back and kissed her "many, many times." Solness apparently has no recollection of this incident; he finally gives in and tells her that he remembers, but it is clear that he does not, although Hilde later tells Aline, "The master builder has a quite incredible memory. Every little detail—just like that!" Solness himself tries to find some explanation for his inability to remember the incident: "I must have thought all this. I must have wanted it—wished it—desired it. So that—Couldn't that be an explanation?" He admits that for years he has been torturing himself, "trying to remember something—something that had happened to me and that I must have forgotten. But I could never discover what it was." Now that Hilde has appeared, he thinks that he can make use of her to help him against the threat of youth in the figure of Ragnar: "Yes, now I can use you! For you, too, march under a new banner. Youth against youth—."

By the end of the first act it is clear that Hilde cannot be accounted for completely in any purely realistic view of the play. Her ostensible status as a casual, though flirtatious, visitor to the Solness household is only perfunctorily preserved, and it is balanced against her parallel status as an embodiment of a part of Solness's own past. Once established, this double status is preserved through the second and third acts, and indeed the gap between Hilde's two roles widens as the play progresses.

The heart of the second act is the long scene between Solness and Hilde, the second in the series of three such scenes in which Solness reviews his life and the stages that have led him to his present spiritual crisis. He began his career as a builder of churches, but renounced this work after the fire that destroyed Aline's home and enabled him to cut up her estate into building plots and become a builder of "homes for people to live in." The two Solness babies died as an indirect result of the fire; Aline caught a fever in escaping from the burning house, but continued to nurse the babies out of a sense of "duty" and they died. Solness feels a profound sense of guilt over this sequence of events: "So you see, Hilde, it *is* I who am guilty, and both those little boys had to pay with their lives. And is it not also true that it is my fault that Aline has not become what

160

she should and could have become? And what she so longed to become."

It is difficult to find concrete reasons for this consuming sense of guilt. It is clearly established that he was in no way responsible for the fire. Although he noticed a tiny crack in the chimney and daydreamed about the house someday burning down, the fire started in a linen room on the opposite end of the house. If guilt must be assigned for the death of the children it is Aline who must bear it, because of the distorted sense of duty that led her to continue to nurse them. Although he admits the truth of these facts, he nevertheless desperately tries to assume responsibility in some way, in order to account for the burden of guilt he feels. He feels that he has a "troll" inside him who calls to mysterious "helpers and servants" to come and do his will. And he feels that he is the victim of an inexorable force that has allowed him his success at the price of the happiness of others:

> SOLNESS. Mark my words, Hilde. Everything that I have created— beautiful, secure, and friendly—yes, and magnificent, too!—I must sit here and expiate! Pay for it. Not with money. But with human happiness . . . And not only with my happiness, but with the happiness of others, too. You see, Hilde! That's the price that my success as an artist has cost me—and others. And every day of my life I have to sit here and see that price being paid for me—day after day after day!

Hilde's role in this confession is to draw Solness out, to tell him that he suffers from an "under-developed," "frail," and "over-sensitive" conscience, and finally to lead him to cut himself loose from the Broviks and from Kaja by writing an approving note on Ragnar's drawings and sending them to the dying Knut Brovik. As a result of his long interview with her, he conceives the plan to climb to the top of the spire on his new house and hang a ceremonial wreath, something he has not done since his ascent of the church spire at Lysanger ten years before.

The long scene between Solness and Hilde that dominates the third act spirals even more deeply into Solness's past, especially into the circumstances of his renunciation of church-building. Atop the tower at Lysanger, he shouted to God that he intended to be "free" and that henceforth he would never build churches but rather houses for people to live in. Hilde listens to this account and responds by challenging Solness to shift his career yet again and to build her the castle he promised her. The nature of this castle is described in an intensely sexual interchange:

HILDE. Where's my castle? It's *my* castle! I want it now!

SOLNESS, *more earnestly, leans closer to her, with his arms on the table.* What does it look like, this castle of yours, Hilde?

HILDE, *slowly.* My castle must stand high up. High above everything! Open and free on every side. So that I can see for miles around.

SOLNESS. It's got a tower, I suppose?

HILDE. A frightfully high tower. And right up on the top of the tower there'll be a balcony. And that's where I shall stand—

SOLNESS *involuntarily clutches his head.* How can you want to stand so high? Doesn't it make you giddy?

HILDE. I want to stand up there and look down at the others—the ones who build churches! And homes for mothers and fathers and children. And you can come up there and look down too.

SOLNESS, *humbly.* Has the master builder leave to climb up to the princess?

HILDE. If the master builder wishes.

SOLNESS *whispers.* Then—I think the master builder will come.

HILDE *nods.* The master builder—he will come.

The castle is to be, they agree, a "castle in the air" but one built on "a true foundation."

The resolution of the play comes quickly after this conversation. Solness exits, climbs the tower with the wreath, and falls to his death into a stonepit, as Hilde watches "in quiet, crazed triumph." She waves her white shawl in the air and cries "wildly and ecstatically," "*My—my* master builder!"

If we regard this strange plot as a fundamentally realistic one "heightened" by a heavy use of symbolism, we are forced into one of several possible, but unacceptably reductive, interpretations. Hilde herself obviously must be regarded as a central symbol, but it is very difficult to say what she symbolizes. The circumstances of her entrance seem to establish her as "youth" knocking on the door, but, even by the end of the first act, she has come to mean much more

than this. Her conversations with Solness suggest that she represents sexuality and Solness's recovery from the impotence of his
marriage with Aline. Her challenge to Solness to climb the spire
is not only highly sexual in its implications, but may be taken more
broadly as a challenge to aspiration in general. The other obvious
symbols in the play—Solness's progression from churches to homes
to "castles in the air," the dolls that Aline grieves for and which she
carried under her heart "like little unborn children," the spire itself, and the stonepit—all offer similar difficulties.

The fact is that the "symbolism" of *The Master Builder* cannot
be understood as a series of independent symbols held together only
by the necessities of the plot. It forms a coherent mythic configuration and each element in it can be understood only in relation
to the configuration as a whole. The enigmas of the plot result from
the fact that Ibsen has deliberately left the mythic pattern partially
undisguised. He has made no attempt to conceal the mythic pattern
completely under a wholly credible and consistent plot, but has instead balanced the plot and the myth against each other.

The outlines of this myth and the place of each of its elements
within it emerge gradually throughout the play. Solness, at the time
of the play, is "an oldish man," and during the twenty-four hours or
so of the play's action, in his conversations with Dr. Herdal, with
Aline, and especially with Hilde, he circles obsessively around the
pivotal events in his past. The resulting picture, however, is by no
means as clear as it is sometimes assumed to be. For one thing,
Solness's "past," as it figures in the play, takes in only about the last
fifteen years; we are told almost nothing about the first forty-five or
so years of his life. He tells Hilde that he started as a builder of
churches:

SOLNESS *throws his hat on the table.* As you know, I began by building
churches.

HILDE *nods.* Yes, I know that.

SOLNESS. When I was a boy, you see, my parents were pious, country
people. So I thought building churches was the finest work that a
man could choose to do.

HILDE. Yes, yes.

SOLNESS. And I think I may say that I built these humble little churches with such honesty and tenderness and devotion that—that—

HILDE. That—? Well?

SOLNESS. Yes—that I think He ought to have been pleased with me.

He has apparently married relatively late, but the circumstances of his courtship and marriage are never mentioned. We are given the impression, however, that although he has not married for money, Aline comes from a wealthier and more socially prominent family than he. Before his marriage, he worked on a rather small scale, building "humble little churches." Although the marriage with Aline has apparently not brought him any ready cash, they have moved into her family estate and lived in her family's ancestral home. Aline's brief description of the home recalls Ibsen's other "ancestral homes"—Rosenvold, Rosmersholm, the Falk villa—architectural embodiments of the ghosts of the past:

MRS. SOLNESS. All the old portraits on the walls were burned. And all the old silk dresses that had been in our family for generations. And all Mama's and Grandmama's lace, that was burned too. And think of the jewels!
Sadly.
And all the dolls.

Although we are never told directly, we gather that Aline's home burned within a few years of the marriage. They lived in the old house, Solness tells Hilde, during the "first years" of their marriage. Three weeks after the birth of their twin sons, the house burned down. This was twelve or thirteen years before the time of the play; Solness tells Dr. Herdal: "She has never got over it, to this day. Not in all these twelve—thirteen—years." Although no one was harmed directly by the fire, Aline caught a fever in escaping from it, insisted on continuing to nurse the babies out of a sense of "duty," and thus transmitted the fatal fever to them.

The sequence of events immediately following the fire and the death of the children is rather obscure. We are given two accounts of what happened—one in Act II and one in Act III—and they do not correspond exactly. In Act II, Solness tells Hilde that from the day of his children's death he "lost interest in building churches." He rose to the top "fanned by those flames." He divided the old estate up into building lots and turned to building "homes for

164

people to live in" rather than churches. It was apparently during this period of his sudden success that he drove Knut Brovik out of business and took him into his own employ.

The account of these events in Act III is slightly different. Here Solness is describing to Hilde the spiritual transformation that came over him when he built the church in her own town of Lysanger. This church was completed exactly ten years ago and thus was built two or three years after the burning of Aline's home. In this account it appears that Solness continued to build churches during this two- or three-year period. He at first believed that God allowed the house to be burned down in order to free him to "build greater churches to His glory" by freeing him from the ties and claims of love and happiness. He came to this conclusion during the time at Lysanger, where, he says, "I spent so much time by myself brooding and puzzling."

Atop the tower of the church at Lysanger he rebelled against what he conceived to be God's plan for him.

SOLNESS. First, I examined and tried myself—

HILDE. And then—?

SOLNESS. Then, like Him, I did the impossible.

HILDE. The impossible!

SOLNESS. I could never bear to climb up high before. But that day, I did it.

HILDE *jumps up*. Yes, yes, you did!

SOLNESS. And as I stood high up there, right at the top, and placed the wreath over the weathercock, I said to Him: "Listen to me, mighty One! Henceforth I, too, want to be a free master builder. Free in my field, as You are in Yours. I never want to build churches for You again. Only homes, for people to live in."

He cut Aline's estate up into building lots, and for the last ten years his business has flourished. It appears to have been during this time that he drove Knut Brovik out of business and took him into his own offices. From the time of the fire, he tells Hilde, "things went well for me." But his professional success has been paralleled by a gradual spiritual decline that has left him on the verge of insanity.

SOLNESS. But the price, Hilde. The terrible price I had to pay.

165

HILDE. Is there no way to put all that behind you?

SOLNESS. No. Because—to be able to build homes for other people I had to renounce for ever all hope of having a home of my own. I mean a home with children. And for their father and mother.

He is tormented not only by the memory of his dead sons (the possibility of other children is never mentioned) but by Aline's bitterness and duty-ridden melancholy and by his fear that his very thoughts—his "helpers and servants"—are mysteriously transformed, without his acting at all, into actions that wreck the lives of those around him. He feels that he is possessed by a troll within himself who has "sucked Aline's blood" and turned her into a living corpse to whom he is chained, and who has similarly chained Kaja and Ragnar to him despite their own yearnings for love and freedom.

The events of the play itself are as elusive as the events of the past, despite the brisk, matter-of-fact tone with which they are presented. They cover something less than a twenty-four-hour period, from Hilde's arrival on the evening of September 19 to Solness's fall from the tower in the late afternoon of the following day. The spine of this action is presented in the three successive scenes, one in each act, between Solness and Hilde, in the course of which Solness reexamines his life, rejects much of its course, and attempts to redirect it. The climax of these encounters is Solness's resolution, late in the third act and just before his fall, to abandon the building of homes for people to live in and to join Hilde in building "castles in the air." Solness's career thus assumes a shape already familiar from a number of earlier Ibsen plays. His career as a builder of churches has been a psychological valley. He has built his churches with "honesty and tenderness and devotion," but this satisfaction has been purchased at the price of a certain sense of personal waste, which has found expression in his fear of heights and in his vague feelings of guilt over his secret ambition to turn Aline's estate into building lots.

The cluster of events during the period from the burning of the house to the encounter with Hilde at Lysanger constitutes a mythic ascent out of this "valley" onto "the heights." The fire itself and the death of the children signal the rejection of the earlier stage in his

life, and the culmination of this rejection comes at Lysanger, significantly a lonely place in the north, like the settings in which
Brand, Thomas Stockmann, and Gregers Werle adopt their projects
of the will. After a great deal of lonely "brooding and puzzling," he
has finally dared to climb to the top of his new church spire, and
on this elevation adopt a new mode of life. His project of the will is
to build "homes for people to live in," and the adoption of the
project is marked by the appearance of Hilde, a fascinating woman,
to complement Aline, a gentle woman.

The terms upon which this decision is taken help to account for
its ultimate failure, which Solness himself cannot explain satisfac-
torily. The decision to build homes rather than churches is, like the
projects of the will in Ibsen's other plays, a reasonable and apparently laudable ambition. But it has turned sour, and the only
explanation Solness can offer is his mysterious feeling that in some
way he has sacrificed Aline's happiness to the pursuit of his project.
The reasonable response to this would be to point out that the fire
would have broken out and Aline would have lost her children
even if Solness had continued to build churches. Solness's sense of
retribution and his feeling that in some mysterious way he has
"sucked Aline's blood" are displacements of his half-conscious
sense that his decision to build houses for people to live in has involved an important renunciation of a part of himself. Aline herself,
with her grim obsession with "duty" and her self-pitying withdrawal
from life, represents as much a projection of Solness as Hilde does,
though less obviously so, as Solness reveals in his complex attitude
toward her—a mingling of a sense of guilty responsibility and bitter
hostility.

Solness's new house, with its grotesque combination of nurseries
and a spire, suggests the crisis at which Solness has arrived, the
resurgence of the repressed side of his nature, and the imminence
of the final collapse of his project. The imagery here is remarkably
anticipated in one of Ibsen's earliest poems, "Building Plans,"
written at least thirty-four years before *The Master Builder:*

> I remember, as clearly as if it were last night,
> The evening my first poem appeared in black and white.
> I sat there in my den with the smoke clouds rolling free,

Sat smoking and sat dreaming in blest complacency.

I will build me a cloud castle. Two wings shall shape it forth;
A great one and a small one. It shall shine across the North.
The greater one shall shelter a singer immortal;
The smaller to a maiden shall open its portal.

A noble symmetry methought shewed in my double wing;
But afterward there came a sad confusion in the thing.
The castle went crazy, as the master found his wits;
The great one grew too little, and the small one fell to bits.

The "greater" and "smaller" wings of the cloud castle in the poem explicitly suggest art and love, the will and the instincts, and the "sad confusion" in the two is echoed in Solness's peculiar house.

The day covered by *The Master Builder* presents the circumstances of Solness's final rejection of his project of the will and his ascent to the peaks. The construction of the house has foreshadowed the reappearance of Hilde in Solness's life; she heralds the collapse of his project of the will, as the reappearance of Gerd foreshadows the collapse of Brand's. The decision to renounce the building of homes for people to live in and instead build "a castle in the air on a firm foundation" and the decision to ascend the spire are of course closely related. Their significance is suggested by Hilde's demand that the balcony atop the castle be high enough to look down upon both those who build churches and those who build homes; it is to represent, in other words, a reintegration of the self and a transcendence of the self, like Brand's ascent into the annihilating avalanche. The imagery of whiteness is suggested in Hilde's white shawl which she waves "wildly and ecstatically" as Solness falls; Rebecca West and Irene wear similar shawls to their deaths in *Rosmersholm* and *When We Dead Awaken*.

The central question of *The Master Builder* is the source of Solness's overpowering sense of guilt and impotence, which has come close to madness by the time the play takes place. If we interpret the symbolism of the play too hastily or attempt to gloss each symbol separately, we are likely to arrive at too simple an answer to this question. If we take the implications of Hilde's entrance too literally, for example, we are likely to see the source of Solness's soul sickness only in his advancing age and his fear of youth. Or if we interpret the imagery of wreathes, spires, and cloud castles too narrowly, we may conclude that his trouble is sexual and that the final scene is nothing more than a highly allegorical treatment of the arrangement of a sexual liaison between Solness and Hilde. Solness himself offers us little help; despite the fact that throughout the play he is constantly engaged in an almost masochistically savage introspection and self-dissection, his explanations help us only to understand his present state of mind, not its origins. His belief that he is inhabited by a "troll" and his fear that he has "helpers and servants" who carry out his unconscious will are nothing more than neurotic fantasies, desperate attempts to account for the burden of guilt which he cannot otherwise understand. The same may be said of his theory that some mysterious force demands that each of his successes be paid for through the suffering of others and his feeling that he has "paid for" his career as a builder of homes by giving up the possibility of having a home of his own.

Solness's guilt and anxiety are existential guilt and anxiety, and their sources lie far deeper than his specific problems of career, sex, or age. Atop the tower at Lysanger he has purchased a sense of identity at the price of renouncing a part of his own nature. It is this renunciation that has led to the bitterness of his relationship with Aline, his crippling fears of "youth knocking at the door," and his doubts about the validity of his life's work. The appearance of Hilde signals the reappearance of the instincts which he can no longer repress, and the decision to build "castles in the air on a firm foundation" is a decision to try to regain the wholeness of self which he rejected at Lysanger. The ascent of the spire is thus an ascent to the peaks, and the fall into the stonepit is immediately preceded by a brief but triumphant recovery of wholeness and peace—an ending with something of the same ambiguous meaning as those of *Brand* and *Peer Gynt*.

II

Little Eyolf is by all odds the least known, the most seldom read, and the most seldom produced of Ibsen's last twelve plays. It is not hard to see the reasons for this neglect. No play of Ibsen's more stubbornly resists understanding along the lines of the conventional critical wisdom. The actual events of the play are deceptively simple, but considered as elements in a realistic plot they seem bafflingly disjointed and unrelated to each other. At the beginning of the play, Alfred Allmers, a writer and sometime teacher, has just returned from a six-week walking tour in the mountains to his wealthy wife, Rita, his nine-year-old son, Eyolf, and his half-sister, Asta. Eyolf accidentally drowns in the fjord near their house at the end of the first act. The second and third acts are devoted to the reaction of Alfred, Rita, and Asta to this tragedy. Act II is climaxed by Asta's revelation that she has discovered that she and Alfred are not related after all. In Act III she at first rejects an offer of marriage from Borghejm, a road-builder who has been wooing her, and then leaves with him. In the final scene, Alfred and Rita decide to devote their lives to the service of the poor children of the neighborhood.

This slight sequence of events is presented so elusively and ambiguously that it has an almost hermetic quality. And its meaning is not made more accessible by its being enveloped in an enormous amount of reminiscing over the past on the part of the three main characters and by their almost painfully self-conscious explorations of the meaning of their relationship. Here, as in *The Master Builder,* we begin to feel that the characters themselves do not understand the meaning of their experiences and that their "explanations" are to be regarded more as indications of their present states of mind than as trustworthy interpretations of the past.

Allmers is described as "thirty-six or thirty-seven" years old at the time of the play. The details of his life are presented little by little throughout the play, and although, as always in Ibsen, the order in which the events of the past are revealed is crucial to the stage action, we may reconstruct Allmers's life in chronological order in retrospect. Allmers's mother died when he was apparently about ten years old, and his father remarried. The new marriage was not a happy one; the new wife was considerably younger than Allmers's father and, as either a cause or a result of their incompatibility, she had at least one extramarital affair. Asta was born when Alfred

170

was eleven or twelve years old; we learn late in the play that her father was one of her mother's lovers. She and Alfred, however, grew up believing themselves to be half-sister and half-brother. The hostility between the elder Allmers and Asta's mother created a close bond between Alfred and Asta, a bond that deepened when Alfred's father died and Asta's mother died two years later. The name Eyolf had been selected for Asta if she had been a boy, and a childhood game for Alfred and Asta was for Asta to put on boy's clothing and pretend to be Alfred's brother. His private nickname for her, too, was Eyolf.

Despite rather strained finances, Alfred went to the university, aided by Asta, who remained close to him. At the age of twenty-six or twenty-seven, ten years before the time of the play, Alfred met and married Rita. Rita was an heiress, the owner of "gold and green forests," and Alfred was able to retire from teaching and lead a life of leisure, working only on a "great, thick book on *The Responsibility of Man.*" He confesses in the course of the play that his first feeling for Rita was not love but fear and that he married her because of her "consuming beauty" and her gold and her green forests, partially in order to be able to provide well for Asta. Nevertheless, during the early years of their marriage they carried on a vigorous and passionate sexual life. A baby was born after a year of marriage and they named him Eyolf. While he was still a baby the most crucial event in their marriage, before the time of the play, occurred. Eyolf was sleeping on the table while Allmers and Rita made love; he fell and was crippled. During the love-making, Allmers told Rita that his private name for Asta was Eyolf. The shock of the child's accident apparently made Allmers impotent and he and Rita have had no sexual life from that time on.

During the eight years or so since the accident Alfred, Rita, Asta, and the lamed little Eyolf have been living together on a rural estate near a fjord in western Norway. Relations have gradually worsened between Alfred and Rita during this time. He has been a severe taskmaster, both on himself in his work on his book and on Eyolf, whom he has forced to study all day every day until his eyes ached. Rita has reacted to sexual deprivation by becoming violently jealous of Asta, of Alfred's work, and even of Eyolf.

171

This state of affairs has come to a climax of sorts six weeks before the time of the play, when Alfred for the first time in his married life has gone away alone. He has taken a doctor's advice to go on an extended walking tour in the mountains. On this trip he has undergone a strange transformation. When he returns, he announces that he has decided to abandon work on his book and to devote himself completely henceforth to helping Eyolf develop as a human being. He will thus, instead of writing about human responsibility, fulfill the ideal of human responsibility through his own life. The events in the mountains that have led him to this decision are rather mysterious. At first he merely says, "I climbed up into an infinite solitude. I saw the stars rise above the mountain tops. I felt—nearer the stars—almost as if I understood them, and belonged with them. Then I was—able to do it." But much later, near the very end of the play, he reveals much more fully, though still mysteriously, what happened to him in the mountains:

ALLMERS. I was alone up there. In the heart of the high mountains. Suddenly I came to a large, desolate lake. And I had to cross that lake. But I couldn't, for there was no one there, and no boat.

RITA. What happened then?

ALLMERS. I went all alone, with no one to guide me, into a side valley. I thought that way I might be able to push forward over the heights and between the peaks, and so come down on the other side of the lake.

RITA. And you got lost?

ALLMERS. Yes. I lost all sense of direction, for there was no kind of road nor path there. I walked all day—and all night, too. I began to think I would never find my way back.

RITA. I know your thoughts were with us.

ALLMERS. No; they were not. It was strange. Both you and Eyolf had drifted far, far away from me. And Asta too.

RITA. Then what were you thinking about?

ALLMERS. Nothing. I struggled along the deep crevasses, exulting in the peace and serenity of being in the presence of death.

RITA *jumps to her feet.* It's horrible! How can you use such words about it?

ALLMERS. But that was how I felt. I had no fear. I felt that Death and I walked side by side like two good fellow travellers. It all seemed

172

so natural. So logical. After all, in my family we do not live to be old—. . . . That night resolved me. I turned back and came home. To Eyolf.

RITA, *quietly*. Too late.

ALLMERS. Yes. For my fellow traveller came and claimed him. And then he suddenly seemed loathsome to me—and life too—this damned existence we dare not tear ourselves away from. We are earthbound, Rita, you and I.

This strange experience apparently motivates Allmers's behavior when he returns, as well as his announced decision to give up his book, devote all his time to helping Eyolf "fulfill himself," and then return to the mountains, "to the high peaks and the great wide spaces." Eyolf, he declares, will be the first one of the family to achieve self-fulfillment.

The series of events and discoveries which make up the present action of the play necessarily alter this plan. The first and most crucial of these events is the drowning of Eyolf. The circumstances under which this occurs are very suggestive. The Rat Wife is one of the most extraordinary examples of Ibsen's use of the "rationalized supernatural" in the late plays; she may be rationalized as merely a mad old woman, but even her first line establishes her double status in the play: "Begging your pardon—have your honours any troublesome thing that gnaws here in this house?" Her sinister description of how she lures rats down to the sea deepens this impression:

RAT WIFE. And all the little creatures that crept and crawled, they follow us further and further out to the deep water. They have to.

EYOLF. Why do they have to?

RAT WIFE. Because they don't want to. Because they're so afraid of the deep water—that's why they have to swim out to it.

EYOLF. And then they drown?

RAT WIFE. Every single one.
More softly.
And then they've all the dark and quiet and peace they could wish for, little angels. Down there they sleep so sweet, so long a sleep. All the little creatures men hate and persecute.

Only a dramatist who is very confident of his powers could have created such a figure as the Rat Wife and placed her in so subtle a psychological drama as *Little Eyolf*. She is a radical example of

Ibsen's power to externalize deeply buried psychological forces in striking dramatic images.

Despite the Rat Wife's suggestion of supernatural powers, it is by no means clear that she lured Eyolf to his death. After the event, Allmers convinces himself that she was responsible:

> ALLMERS. . . . The boys saw her row out over the fjord. They saw Eyolf standing alone on the end of the jetty, staring after her. Suddenly he—seemed to become giddy. And then he fell—and disappeared.
> ASTA. I know. But—
> ALLMERS. She dragged him down into the deep. I'm sure of it.

Nevertheless, it is hard to absolve Allmers and Rita of blame for the accident, especially in light of the circumstances of Eyolf's laming. It has been clearly established earlier that Eyolf can't swim, but Allmers has told him to "run down to the beach and play with the other boys," and when the Rat Wife exits, Eyolf slips out "unnoticed" after her. In both cases, Allmers has been preoccupied with his own past and with his decision in the mountains, which he is eager to announce to Rita and Asta. Eyolf is "unnoticed" because Allmers is examining Asta's portfolio of letters containing the truth about her relationship with him. This kind of carelessness is particularly ironic, of course, in a man who has been writing a book on "human responsibility" and who has just announced that he intends to embody the idea of responsibility in his own life.

Rita and Alfred, in their long second-act scene, begin to reexamine their attitudes toward Eyolf and to accept some measure of responsibility not only for his death, but for the degree to which they have used him as an instrument of their own selfishness. Rita is haunted by the memory of Eyolf's eyes looking up at her from the bottom of the fjord. Alfred forces her to admit that she resented Eyolf, as she also resented Asta, as a barrier between herself and Alfred. (This is only one of a number of points in the play at which Eyolf and Asta are closely identified.) Rita, in retaliation, accuses Alfred of never having loved Eyolf and of having decided to give up his book for Eyolf's sake only out of his own "self-distrust."

ALLMERS *looks thoughtfully at her.* If you are right in what you are
thinking, our child never really belonged to us.

RITA. No. We never loved him.

ALLMERS. And yet we sit here bitterly mourning his loss.

RITA, *bitterly.* Yes. Isn't it odd? That we are sitting here mourning a
little stranger boy.

The second act is concluded by Asta's revelation to Alfred that she
is not really his half-sister; she has discovered in her mother's letters
that her real father was her mother's lover, not Alfred's father.

The last act of *Little Eyolf* is devoted to the attempts of Alfred,
Rita, and Asta to adjust their plans for the future in light of the
three crucial events of the recent past: Alfred's experience in the
mountains, the death of Eyolf, and the revelation of the true relationship of Alfred and Asta. Alfred at first suggests to Rita, in a
scene reminiscent of the last act of *Rosmersholm,* that they join
Eyolf in death:

ALLMERS *looks at her closely.* If you were given the choice now—if you
could follow Eyolf to—to where he now is—

RITA. Yes?

ALLMERS. If you could be sure you would find him again. Know him
—understand him—

RITA. Yes, yes?

ALLMERS. Would you leap the gulf to join him? Leave all this? Renounce life? Would you do that, Rita?

Neither Allmers nor Rita, however, is willing to make this sacrifice.
"This is where we belong. Here on earth. Living," Allmers finally
tells Rita, and she agrees.

Allmers then decides to leave Rita and return to the "old peace-
ful, innocent" life with Asta. He tells Asta that living with Rita
makes both him and Rita "evil and detestable" and that he wants to
return to her "to be cleansed and purified from my life with—."
Asta absolutely refuses, however, and at this point tells Allmers
what she has learned of their relationship from her mother's
letters. Allmers at first refuses to accept her refusal and Rita joins
him in begging Asta to stay with them and be their "Eyolf." Asta,
however, in desperation, agrees to leave with the engineer Borghejm,

although she has previously refused his suit, in order to remove herself from the temptation of life with Alfred and Rita:

> ASTA *throws her arms round* RITA's *neck.* Thank you, Rita. For everything.
> *Goes over to* ALLMERS *and clasps his hand.*
> Good-bye, Alfred. Good-bye.
> ALLMERS, *quietly.* What is this, Asta? Are you running away?
> ASTA. Yes, Alfred. I am.
> ALLMERS. From me?
> ASTA *whispers.* From you—and from myself.
> ALLMERS *shrinks.* Ah—!

The ending of the play is a long scene between Allmers and Rita after Asta's departure with Borghejm. Most of the problems in the interpretation of the play lie in this powerful but elusive final scene. Both seem to feel, perhaps for the first time, the full impact of Eyolf's death and to realize that they will never be able to escape from the memory of him. But other forces seem to be at work as well, bringing about a radical transformation in their characters.

> RITA. A change is taking place in me. Oh, God! It hurts me so!
> ALLMERS. Hurts?
> RITA. Yes. Like a birth.
> ALLMERS. That is what it is. A birth. Or a resurrection. A transition. To another way of living.
> RITA *stares sadly ahead of her.* Yes. But it means the wreck of all life's happiness.
> ALLMERS. In that wreck lies our victory.

Allmers still turns over in his mind the possibilities for his future. He rejects Rita's suggestion that he resume work on his book, and tells her that he thinks it would be best for them to part. She immediately assumes that he intends to follow Asta, but he tells her that he will never see Asta again and that he wants to return to the mountains, "up into my solitude." He then tells her the details of his strange experience in the mountains. Rita says that when he is gone, she intends to bring the poor, neglected village children up to the house and rear them. Allmers reacts incredulously at first to this suggestion; he resents the fact that none of the villagers tried to

176

save Eyolf and wants the village "levelled to the ground." After some thought, however, he acknowledges that he and Rita have done nothing to help others and that they may be able to fill their empty lives with this kind of social service. He agrees, then, to stay with Rita and join her in her plan:

ALLMERS. We have a long day ahead of us, Rita.

RITA. You will see. A Sunday calm will fall on us now and then.

ALLMERS, *quietly, moved.* Then, perhaps, we shall sense their spirits beside us.

RITA *whispers.* Spirits?

ALLMERS. Yes. Perhaps they will come to visit us. The ones we have lost.

RITA *nods slowly.* Our little Eyolf. And your big Eyolf, too.

ALLMERS. Perhaps now and then, on our way, we shall catch a glimpse of them.

RITA. Where shall we look, Alfred?

ALLMERS, *his eyes meet hers.* Upwards.

RITA. Yes. Upwards.

ALLMERS. Up towards the mountains. Towards the stars. And the great silence.

RITA *stretches out her hand towards him.* Thank you.

This chronological summary of Allmers's life perhaps suggests the shape of the history which the plot of *Little Eyolf* presents. But it can hardly suggest the effect of the plot itself, in which this history is presented obliquely and elliptically in the course of the painful self-examination each undergoes under the pressure of present events. The summary may be useful, however, in considering a number of rather difficult questions in the interpretation of the play.

Allmers, it is very clear, is suffering from only partially repressed desires for Asta, which both of them believe to be incestuous. These desires have poisoned his relationship with Rita, have blocked him from a wholesome relationship with his son, and have paralyzed him with a generalized feeling of guilt, the origins of which he hardly understands. We can read the play merely as the history of such a relationship, its origins and its consequences, and of Allmers's final conquest of it through the shock of Eyolf's death and Asta's revelation of their true relationship. This view of the play, however, though it contains some truth, is obviously inadequate since it provides little help in answering some of the most troublesome questions the play raises: What is the significance of the recurring identification throughout the play of Asta and Eyolf? Why is the subject of "human responsibility" emphasized so much through the play and how is it related to the incest theme? What is the function of the Rat Wife and why is it suggested that she "lured" Eyolf to his death? What happened to Allmers in the mountains, and how is it related to his feelings toward Eyolf, Rita, and Asta? Why is the revelation of Alfred's and Asta's true relationship presented as so absolute an obstacle to their ever seeing each other again, and why do they not at least consider the possibility of becoming lovers, now that the incest barrier has been removed? If the play is regarded merely as a psychological study of Allmers's struggle with his incestuous desires for his presumed sister, then such important elements in the play as the Rat Wife, the book, and the experience in the mountains would seem only to muddy and obscure the progress of the play.

All these problems culminate, perhaps, in the difficulties of the final scene. It is clear that some kind of basic transformation has taken place in both Allmers and Rita and that as a result of this transformation they make the decision to remain together and try to fill the emptiness of their lives with service to others. But it cannot be determined on the basis of the plot alone what kind of transformation has taken place and what the significance of the final decision is. Specifically, is the ending a "happy" one or not? Does it represent a kind of triumph for Allmers and Rita and a genuine prospect for a meaningful life, or does it represent resignation to a kind of spiritual death and "the wreck of all life's happiness"? These problems can be resolved only by reference to the larger patterns of Allmers's life and the spiritual progress they reveal. Allmers's longings for Asta have been only part of a whole mode of being for him, and the transformation which comes over him at the end is not merely a renunciation of his incestuous desires but the death of his whole previous mode of being and his rebirth into another. It is, as he says, "A birth. Or a resurrection. A transition. To another way of living."

It is possible to describe Allmers's previous "way of living" by examining rather carefully the circumstances of his marriage to Rita and the events surrounding it, up to and including Eyolf's fall from the table. This complex of events makes up a mythic "ascent to the heights" and thus helps to explain the origins of the spiritual crisis Allmers is undergoing at the time of the play. Allmers tells Rita, in one of their frank exchanges in Act II, that his first feeling for her was not love, but fear. He has married her because she was "so consumingly beautiful" and because she was rich; he wanted her gold and her green forests so he could always provide for Asta. This confession of motives seems brutally frank, but Rita almost immediately sees that these motives only covered a deeper and more disturbing motive:

RITA. Oh, yes—Asta! So it was Asta who brought us together!

ALLMERS. She knew nothing. She has no inkling of it even now.

RITA. None the less, it was Asta.
Smiles scornfully.
No. It was little Eyolf. Yes, Alfred. Little Eyolf.

ALLMERS. Eyolf?

RITA. You used to call her Eyolf, didn't you. I seem to remember you telling me so once—in a quiet moment.

Rita is, of course, jealous of Asta, but she intuitively draws a distinction between Asta herself and Asta in the role of "Eyolf." As she divines at this point in the play, Asta was involved in Allmers's decision to marry her, not merely because he wanted to provide for her financially, but because he perceived of the marriage as a means of defense against his troublesome attraction toward Asta as a sexual object. Allmers, at the time of the play, looks back upon his childhood and his life with Asta before his marriage as a time of purity and innocence and of "one long ecstasy of dedication." But it is clear that he has been able to maintain this innocent intimacy with Asta only with the help of the incest taboo, which removes her from consideration as a sexual object. Nevertheless there is an unspoken undercurrent of sexuality in their relationship of which they are both aware and which is a source of guilty anxiety for both of them.

Allmers's marriage to Rita, his book on human responsibility, his

179

withdrawal from active life, the sensuality of his early relationship with Rita, Eyolf's fall from the table, and his ensuing impotence are all thus closely intertwined. Allmers has retreated from the superficially innocent but nevertheless troubling "valley" world of his life with Asta, up onto the "heights" of the marriage with Rita. Asta is a "gentle woman," and Allmers retreats from her lure into union with her mirror-image, Rita, an openly sensual "fascinating woman." His desire for Asta can thus be, for the time being, "safely" displaced into the vigorous sexuality of the early days of his marriage. This apparent renunciation of instinct and triumph of will is signaled by the adoption of a "project of the will"—the book on human responsibility—and the apparent death of the Allmers of the days with Asta is signaled by the "first child-death": Eyolf's fall from the table.

The way in which the name "Eyolf" winds its way through these events is highly suggestive. The recurring identification of Asta with Eyolf merely conceals a deeper identification of Eyolf and Allmers himself. Through all the shifting connections of the name throughout the play, "Eyolf" remains the name for the self, the sense of security of being for which Allmers is searching. It is first to be the name of the brother, the alter-ego who is never born. It is then the name Allmers gives Asta when she is dressed up in his clothes and it becomes the secret name which suggests the sense of security which Allmers temporarily achieves in their life together. But the "law of change" is operating, and this "Eyolf" apparently dies when Allmers renounces Asta and marries Rita. The real nature of his marriage, however, is suggested in his choice of a name for their first child and by his telling Rita of his secret name for Asta during their love-making on the day of Eyolf's fall.

Allmers's impotence after the trauma of Eyolf's crippling is closely related to his increasing inability to make any headway with his book. This impotence has continued for over eight years, despite his refusal to accept responsibility for neglecting Eyolf on that day. There is, of course, a more general underlying reason for his impotence, his inability to finish his book, and his bitterness toward Rita; this is his all-enveloping sense of guilt over the choice he has made upon "the heights" of his marriage to Rita. The crippled little

180

Eyolf is a continual reminder of the defensive nature of his project of the will and an ever-present threat of the revival of the rejected self. Typically, this period of the pursuit of the project of the will has lasted ten years.

The events immediately preceding the time of the play and those of the play itself make up a second closely related nucleus of events. The two principal events of the play itself—the drowning of Eyolf and Asta's revelation of her real parentage—do not, as we have seen, suffice to explain the transformation that comes over Allmers in the last scene. These events are explicable only as parts of a more general action which is epitomized in Allmers's experience in the mountains. If we attempt to interpret the play in strictly realistic terms, we must regard Allmers's state of mind at the end of the play as a response to his experiences during the course of the play, and must regard the episode in the mountains as an irrelevant and perhaps gratuitously mystifying appendage. It is, on the contrary, central to the play, and the "real" events can be understood only as subsidiary to it.

Allmers's renunciation of his book on human responsibility, his decision to alter radically his method of rearing little Eyolf, his desire to try to make the crippled Eyolf "whole" in some sense, the death of Eyolf, the departure of Asta forever, and his final decision to join Rita in rearing the neighborhood children as new "little Eyolfs" and to move with her toward "the mountains, the stars, and the great silence"—all are correlatives on the level of plot to elements in the all-encompassing experience in the mountains on the level of myth. They constitute collectively, in other words, an "ascent to the peaks" which is presented directly in Allmers's description of his walking tour.

On the peaks, Allmers has confronted a series of images which suggest the threat of the engulfment of the self from which he has been fleeing all his life: the "large, desolate lake," the "deep crevasses," and the pathless, formless landscape. During this confrontation, the details of his life up to this point have "drifted far, far away" and he has experienced a feeling of emptiness combined with a kind of "exultation." His encounter with his "fellow traveller," Death, has brought no fear, but rather a feeling of "peace and serenity." Significantly, however, Death literally claims not Allmers himself, but little Eyolf, in his role as Allmers's old self, now finally dead.

The series of decisions that result from the experience in the mountains thus all reflect both spiritual death and rebirth. The abandoning of the book signals the final collapse of the "project of the will" to which the marriage to Rita has been so closely related, and the complete reconstitution of the marriage itself signals the rejection of the terms upon which it was originally contracted. The decision no longer to force Eyolf to study continually, but instead to help him develop fully is a similar rejection of the will and a new acceptance of the self which had been unsuccessfully and painfully repressed. This decision is replaced, after Eyolf's drowning, by the similar decision to befriend the wretched children of the area, who will become new "Eyolfs."

The discovery of Asta's parentage and the problems it raises for Allmers and Asta are less important than the withdrawal of Asta from Allmers's life which is thus effected, a withdrawal reminiscent of a whole sequence of scenes in the last acts of Ibsen plays, from Furia's retreat at the end of *Catiline* through the Button Moulder's withdrawal at the end of *Peer Gynt* and the Stranger's return to the sea in the last act of *The Lady from the Sea*.

The actual plot of *Little Eyolf* is likely to seem baffling and even incoherent because Ibsen deliberately refrains from knitting the events of the plot together in a completely self-sufficient network of motivations and explanations. Instead, he balances a frankly elliptical realistic plot structure against an underlying mythic structure made up of the characteristic elements of spiritual valleys, heights, and peaks. The two structures, as in all of Ibsen's late plays, must be considered together and must be regarded as equally important in the interpretation of the play.

This view of the play helps clarify the meaning of the puzzling last scene. This scene is of the utmost interest not only for its own sake and for its crucial significance in the understanding of *Little Eyolf,* but for the fact that it is one of the few places in Ibsen in which the protagonist is shown after the experience of spiritual death and rebirth upon the peaks. In most of the plays this experience is presented as literal death, as it is for example in *Catiline, Brand,* perhaps *Peer Gynt, Emperor and Galilean, Rosmersholm,* and *The Master Builder,* and in most of the others, the play ends with the peak experience itself, as it does in *The Pillars of Society, A Doll's House,* and *The Lady from the Sea.* But in *Little Eyolf,* Allmers dies and is reborn and is then presented with the task of deciding what course his life is to take after this experience.

One recent critic has reviewed the problem of the ending of the play, from Henry James's judgment of it as "too simple, too immediate" down to more recent opinions that Ibsen must have intended the ending to be interpreted as an "unhappy" one, and has concluded that Ibsen intended to "reveal the interior of what, in *Brand,* thirty years before, he had called 'the Ice Church'—the interior of a human soul in which love has died." This interpretation has much to recommend it and rightly points out the relationship between the ending of *Brand,* the most openly mythic of Ibsen's plays, and that of *Little Eyolf.* But it might also be pointed out that Brand never enters the Ice Church; in the few moments of ecstatic insight before the avalanche comes rushing upon him, he rejects the whole course of his life that has led him to the entrance to the Ice Church and is transformed. Neither does Allmers "enter the Ice Church"; he, too, has been reborn upon the peaks and in the last scene he faces the challenge that Brand does not live to take up, that of building a new life based on wholeness and security of being.

III

John Gabriel Borkman might very appropriately have been called *The Father,* if Strindberg had not already used that title nine years before 1896, when Ibsen sat down to work out this most powerful of his studies in the relationships between fathers and sons. The cold, sinister figure of Borkman himself, flanked by the equally threatening figures of his wife, Gunhild, and his sister-in-law, Ella, and the great, dark Rentheim house, stiflingly heated within and choked with snow without, make up a complex of images of parental threat that have the quality of a nightmare. No wonder the twenty-three-year-old Erhart feels that he is being slowly suffocated at home and that he must escape, in a mad midnight dash in a sleigh, to the coast and a boat for Italy.

The characters of Borkman and Erhart are anticipated in a number of earlier Ibsen plays. Ibsen's memory of his own father, who went bankrupt when Ibsen was seven, perhaps lies behind many of the fathers in his plays, including the flamboyant "rich John Gynt," Peer's father, whose grandiose way of life before his fall is like that of Borkman before his arrest, when everyone in Norway called him by his given names, like a king. Old Werle, in *The Wild Duck*, and General Gabler, in *Hedda Gabler*, have Borkman's sinister hold upon their children, and even Alfred Allmers, in his role as Eyolf's father, has created a tomb home from which Eyolf escapes only through death.

A parallel line of threatened sons leads up to Erhart. Peer Gynt flees, like Erhart, from his Norwegian home out into the world, and Julian escapes from the pollution of Constantinople and the threat of his emperor/father to the sunlight of Athens. Oswald Alving attempts such an escape, but the dead hand of Captain Alving draws him back to Norway, to madness and death. The seeds of Erhart lie also in the long line of dead children in Ibsen's plays, from Ulf in *Brand*, down through Ellida's child in *The Lady from the Sea*, to Solness's dead sons in *The Master Builder*.

But in most of these plays, either the father is subordinated to a remotely threatening presence in the background and the action is centered around the son, or the son is reduced to the role of infant victim and the action is centered around the father. *John Gabriel Borkman* is unique in the directness with which it focuses on the father/son relationship itself. Although the monolithic figure of Borkman himself dominates the play, Erhart is the most important secondary character, and the entire action moves inexorably toward the parallel flights of father and son—Borkman's up the winter slopes to his death, and Erhart's out across the sea to Italy and "the joy of life."

As Borkman and Erhart are in many ways the culmination of Ibsen's portraits of fathers and sons, so the play also brings to a culmination the theme of "the home as tomb" that winds its way

through Ibsen's plays from *Catiline* on. The Rentheim house is the
last in the long series of ancestral homes in Ibsen—from Mrs.
Alving's Rosenvold through Rosmersholm, the Falk villa in *Hedda
Gabler,* and Aline's home in *The Master Builder*—that embody,
with their dark, claustrophobic interiors, their walls hung with ancestral portraits, and their inner rooms haunted by "ghosts," the
power of parents over children. It is inhabited by parents, Erhart's
father and his two "mothers," who have died long before the play
begins. "I have seen to your epitaph," Gunhild Borkman tells her
husband.

> BORKMAN, *with a short, dry laugh.* My epitaph! Listen to her! She
> speaks as though I were dead.
> MRS. BORKMAN. You are.
> BORKMAN, *slowly.* Yes, perhaps you're right.

And in the last scene, as Gunhild and Ella stand over Borkman's
body they acknowledge that they, too, have died long ago:

> ELLA. I think it was the cold that killed him.
> MRS. BORKMAN. The cold? That killed him long ago.
> ELLA. And turned us into shadows.
> MRS. BORKMAN. Yes.
> ELLA. One dead man and two shadows. See what the cold has done.

The tomb home of the Rentheim estate is the secondary home of
Borkman, his own creation, and it becomes in turn the primary
home of Erhart, who must break out of it or be annihilated. This is
the most fundamental of the many parallels between father and
son in the play, which thus comes to suggest an endlessly recurring
process of enslavement—a treatment, in terms of the family, of the
process that is treated, in "world-historical" terms, in *Emperor and
Galilean*—"a struggle," Ibsen said, "that will always repeat itself."
The play, bitter enough as it is, would be almost unbearably pessi-
mistic if it were not for the fact that Erhart does manage to break
out of the circle, and the various ironies that surround his flight do
not appreciably diminish his prospects of escaping his father's fate.

The roots of Borkman's living death lie far in the past, and we do
not understand them fully until late in the play, in Borkman's last
conversation with Ella just before his death. In this scene, Borkman

has left the house in which he has entombed himself for the past eight years and has climbed with Ella up to "the heights," a "small clearing high up in the forest" where he and Ella used to meet and from which they can look down on all the surrounding countryside. Here he recalls the ambition that he adopted on the same spot a quarter of a century before, the ambition to free the buried forces of nature through industrial development.

ELLA. We used to sit on that seat, and stare into the distance.

BORKMAN. It was a country of dreams we gazed into.

ELLA *nods heavily*. The country of our dreams, yes. Now it is covered with snow. And the old tree is dead.

BORKMAN, *not listening to her*. Can you see the smoke from the great steamers out on the fjord?

ELLA. No.

BORKMAN. I can. They come and go. They create a sense of fellowship throughout the world. They bring light and warmth to the hearts of men in many thousands of homes. That is what I dreamed of creating.

Borkman's ambition was a "project of the will"; although it seemed a worthwhile and even benevolent aim, it was adopted as a psychological defense, and it grew to be an obsession:

BORKMAN. Ah, but these are only the outworks surrounding the kingdom.

ELLA. What kingdom?

BORKMAN. My kingdom! The kingdom I was about to take possession of when I died.

ELLA. Oh, John, John!

BORKMAN. And there it lies, defenceless, masterless, abandoned to thieves and robbers. Ella! Do you see those mountains far away? Range beyond range, rising and towering! That is my infinite and inexhaustible kingdom.

ELLA. Ah, but it's a cold wind that blows from that kingdom, John.

BORKMAN. To me it is the breath of life. It is a greeting from the spirits that serve me. I feel them, those buried millions. I see those veins of iron ore, stretching their twisting, branching, enticing arms toward me. I've seen you all before, like shadows brought to life— that night when I stood in the vaults of the bank with the lantern

186

in my hand. You wanted to be freed. And I tried to free you. But I
failed. Your treasure sank back into the darkness.
Stretching out his hands.
But let me whisper this to you now, in the stillness of the night. I
love you where you lie like the dead, deep down in the dark. I love
you, treasures that crave for life, with your bright retinue of power
and glory. I love you, love you, love you.

The "dream" has been pushed beyond the limits of reason into
madness. The reasons for this extremity are inherent in the cluster
of events that surround the adoption of Borkman's ambition. We
are told almost nothing of his early life, but judging from his financial difficulties he appears, like Solness, to have come from humble
origins and to be a "self-made man." Some twenty-five years before
the time of the play, he met twin sisters, Ella and Gunhild Rentheim,
who were comparatively wealthy. He fell in love with Ella and
conceived his ambition to become a great capitalist and developer
of the mineral wealth of the area, apparently near Christiania. He
had a rival, however: an attorney named Hinkel, who approached
him with the offer to arrange that he be named chairman of a bank
if he would give up Ella. He accepted this offer in order to get
control of the money he needed to carry out his ambition, and
turned his attentions to Ella's sister, Gunhild, whom he married
after a very short courtship. Ella did not know of this "bargain"
until the time of the play; she blamed Gunhild for taking Borkman
away from her.

Eight or ten years elapsed between Borkman's marriage and his
fall from power. (Erhart is twenty-three years old at the time of the
play, and Borkman has spent three years in jail before his trial, has
served a five-year term in prison, and has been isolated in his house
for eight years, making a total of sixteen years since his arrest.)
During this time he embezzled large sums of money from the bank
of which he was chairman and used the money to build a large
financial empire. He lived flamboyantly and spectacularly:

MRS. BORKMAN. Oh yes! He always said we had to "put on a show"!
Oh, he put on a show all right! Drove a four-in-hand, as though he
were a king. Made people bow and scrape to him, the way they
would to a king.

187

Laughs.
And they called him by his Christian names—throughout the country—just as though he *was* the King. "John Gabriel." Oh, he was a great man in their eyes, was John Gabriel.

At the height of his career he was offered—and refused—a post as a cabinet minister.

Borkman's fall came at the hands of Hinkel. Borkman had been unwise enough not only to confide every detail of his financial affairs to Hinkel but also to put them in writing in private letters. Ella, however, refused Hinkel's proposal of marriage, and Hinkel chose to revenge himself on Borkman. He waited until the moment when Borkman had embarked on his most ambitious project and withdrawn massive sums from the bank for a speculative venture that would take eight days. At that moment Hinkel reported Borkman to the police.

This sequence of events constitutes a mythic ascent to the heights and the adoption, pursuit, and collapse of a "project of the will." The project was Borkman's ambition to "release the spirits that slumber in the mines." He first announced it to Ella, literally "on the heights," at the clearing in the woods where they met. The ambition required a choice between love and will, the consummation of his love for Ella or its renunciation for the sake of pursuing his project. And characteristically, this choice presented itself as between two women, the "fascinating" Ella and the "gentle" Gunhild. The maniacal drive with which Borkman pursued his goal and the crazed fervor that makes his description of it in the last scene so disturbing come from the role the project played as Borkman's defense against the claims of instinct. Borkman's mania drove him, during the decade in which he pursued his project, to greater and greater extravagance and finally to the overreaching venture that resulted in his fall from power, and to the living death in which he has been trapped for the sixteen years preceding the time of the play.

Erhart's fate during this sequence of events is also very significant. At the time of his father's arrest his aunt Ella took him into her house and became a surrogate mother. The collapse of Borkman's project of the will is thus marked by the loss of a child.

Erhart lived with his aunt from the age of seven until the age of fifteen, when his father was released from prison. Erhart's memory of this period of his life is reminiscent of the "aunt-love" lavished upon a number of other Ibsen characters in their childhood, including Hjalmar Ekdal in *The Wild Duck,* and George Tesman in *Hedda Gabler.*

ERHART. Good God, Mother. I'm young! I'm suffocating in this house! I can't breathe here!

MRS. BORKMAN. Here? Living with me?

ERHART. Yes, living with you, Mother.

ELLA. Oh, Erhart, come with me!

ERHART. No, Aunt Ella, it's no better with you. It's different—but no better. It's roses and lavender—it's airless, the same as here.

MRS. BORKMAN. Airless, did you say?

ERHART, *with rising impatience.* Yes—I don't know what else to call it. Your sickly pampering, and—I don't know how to put it—the way you idolise me—I can't stand it any longer.

Ella has bought the old Rentheim house at the bankruptcy auction and has kept the title in her name so it could not be claimed by Borkman's creditors, but she has allowed the Borkmans to live there during the eight years since Borkman was released. Since that time Erhart has been living with Gunhild, who has been trying to prepare him for a "great mission": to redeem the Borkman name from the disrepute into which his father has brought it. Ella has hopes that Erhart will instead carry out another mission: that he will inherit her fortune and adopt and perpetuate the name of Rentheim, which would otherwise die out. At the point where Erhart announces his rejection of both these externally imposed "missions," his father steps in and tries to impose yet another one upon him.

ERHART. I can't dedicate my life to atoning for what someone else has done. Whoever it may be.

MRS. BORKMAN. Erhart! Who has made you change your mind?

ERHART, *stung.* Who—? Couldn't I have done it myself?

MRS. BORKMAN. No, no, no! You are not under your mother's influence any longer. Nor your foster mother's. There is someone else.

ERHART, *trying to seem confident.* I stand on my own feet now, Mother. I have a will of my own.

189

BORKMAN *takes a step towards* ERHART. Then perhaps my turn has
come at last.

ERHART, *distantly respectful*. What do you mean by that, Father?

MRS. BORKMAN. Yes, that I should like to know.

BORKMAN. Listen, Erhart—will you come with your father? You cannot redeem another man's failure. That is only an empty dream,
which has been instilled into you in this airless room. Even if you
were to live like all the saints put together, it would not help me
one whit.

Borkman wants Erhart to join him in an effort to rebuild his fortune
"through work, untiring work for the ideal that inspired me when I
was young, and inspires me a thousand times more strongly today."

The scene thus presents all three of Erhart's parental figures
urging "claims of the ideal" upon him and competing for possession
of him. He recoils finally from these threats in a passionate out-
burst in which he says that he intends to live not for their "missions"
but for "happiness." Gunhild is right, of course: there is "someone
else" who has given Erhart the courage for this revolt and he introduces her at this point. It is Mrs. Wilton, the worldly and sensual
divorcee whom he has been seeing and whom he now intends to
accompany to Italy, in a final escape from his gloomy home. They
will take with them the fifteen-year-old Frida Foldal, daughter of
old Vilhelm Foldal, the frustrated playwright and a victim of Borkman's fall. She is to study music in Italy, but Mrs. Wilton has
thought of other implications of the girl's presence.

MRS. BORKMAN. Mrs. Wilton—do you think you are being wise in
taking this young girl with you?

MRS. WILTON. Men are so unpredictable, Mrs. Borkman. And women
too. When Erhart is tired of me, and I of him, it will be good for
both of us that he should have someone to fall back on, poor boy.

MRS. BORKMAN. And what will you do?

MRS. WILTON. Oh, I shall manage, I promise you. Goodbye, everybody!

This rather odd arrangement serves to point up the carefully
arranged parallel between Erhart's present situation and that of his
father twenty-five years earlier. He faces, as his father did, a choice
between "will" and "instinct," marked by the presence of two
women, the "pretty, pale" Frida Foldal and Fanny Wilton, who is

190

"a strikingly handsome woman in her thirties, with a fine figure, broad, red smiling lips, playful eyes and rich, dark hair." But "on the heights," Erhart makes the opposite choice from his father. He rejects the projects of the will being thrust upon him and chooses the "happiness" of the instinctual life. This decision is shaded by various ironies: a decision between "Frida" and "Fanny" may still await him, and his impetuous flight may turn out to be only a kind of Gyntish "going round about." But these ironies are not insisted upon, and the possibility remains that Erhart may be able to avoid the paralyzing self-division of his father.

In the last act, the focus returns to the father, with Borkman's long-delayed bursting out of his self-imposed entombment and his strange ascent of the mountain to his death. The son's spiritual crisis precipitates the father's attempt at regeneration; the bells are ringing from Erhart's and Mrs. Wilton's speeding sleigh as Borkman walks out of the Rentheim house for the first time in eight years. His climb up the mountain is a desperate attempt to recover what he has lost, and this time he chooses Ella to accompany him in his attempt:

> BORKMAN. I'm outside the wall now, Ella! They'll never catch me now!
>
> ELLA, *down with him.* But you're free in there too, John. You can come and go as you please.
>
> BORKMAN, *quietly, as though frightened.* I shall never go under a roof again. Out here in the night air, it's good! If I were to go up to that room now, the walls and ceiling would shrink and crush me, crush me like a fly—
>
> ELLA. But where will you go?
>
> BORKMAN. I shall go on, and on, and on. See if I can find my way back to freedom and life and humanity. Will you go with me, Ella?
>
> ELLA. I? Now?
>
> BORKMAN. Yes, yes. At once.
>
> ELLA. But—how far—?
>
> BORKMAN. As far as I can go.

The circumstances of Borkman's strange ascent of the mountain are all reminiscent of Brand's progress up to the Ice Church and his redemptive death: the rejection of the previous mode of life, the hope of "rebirth," and the symbolic choice of a companion.

191

But Borkman's death is not redemptive; it has none of the triumphant overtones that Brand's, Solness's, and Rubek's have. He dies "of the cold":

> ELLA. . . . Your love is still buried down there, John. It always has been. But up here, in the daylight, there was a warm, living heart beating for you, and you broke it. Worse, you sold it—for—
>
> BORKMAN, *a cold shudder seems to go through him.* For the kingdom —and the power—and the glory, you mean?
>
> ELLA. That is what I mean. And therefore I prophesy, John Gabriel Borkman, that you will never get the price you demanded for that murder. You will never ride triumphant into your cold kingdom.
>
> BORKMAN *staggers to the seat and sits down heavily.* I fear you are right, Ella.
>
> ELLA. You must not fear that, John. It will be better for you.
>
> BORKMAN, *clutches his chest with a cry.* Ah!
> *Weakly.*
> Now it let go of me.
>
> ELLA. What was it, John?
>
> BORKMAN *sinks back on the seat.* A hand of ice that gripped my heart.
>
> ELLA. John! *You've* felt that hand of ice now?
>
> BORKMAN *mumbles.* No. Not a hand of ice. A hand of iron.
> *He slides down upon the seat.*

John Gabriel Borkman thus joins the series of Ibsen protagonists who die without undergoing the experience of ecstatic reintegration of the self upon "the peaks." In his flight up the mountains he has not reached "the peaks," but has stopped on "the heights," where the original fatal commitment to will was made. The hand of ice that has gripped his heart relaxes, only to be replaced by a hand of iron. Brand, in the moment before his death, has felt "the crust break" and his life "flow rich and warm," but Borkman, like the Emperor Julian and like Hedda Gabler, dies in "the coldness of the heart."

9. Epilogue: *When We Dead Awaken*

> *Not the smallest fascination of Ibsen is the unity of his work. . . . One thing leads to another in a drama which has* Catiline *for prologue and* When We Dead Awaken *for epilogue, the drama of Ibsen's whole* oeuvre.
>
> ERIC BENTLEY (1957)

When We Dead Awaken has claim to be considered Ibsen's greatest play and indeed as one of the handful of works that stand at the summit of dramatic literature. And yet, paradoxically, it is, with *Little Eyolf,* the least known and the most seldom read and produced of Ibsen's major plays. No other play of Ibsen's more unyieldingly resists interpretation along the standard "realistic" lines. James Joyce, just after the play appeared, wrote that *"When We Dead Awaken* may rank with the greatest of the author's works— if, indeed, it be not the greatest." But he predicted that the play would baffle its readers and that many years would pass before it would be understood and Ibsen would "enter his kingdom in jubilation."

Joyce was right. William Archer, Ibsen's chief advocate in England, read the play in preparation for translating it, and wrote to his brother Charles, "It is scabrous to a degree—if it weren't like deserting the Old Man, 'pon my soul I'd let someone else translate it." He thought the play demonstrated that Ibsen's mind was giving way. Twenty-five years later, Hermann Weigand thought so too, and detailed his reasons in his influential and widely read study, *The Modern Ibsen.*[1] The many inconsistencies and even contradictions of the plot, which Weigand listed in minute detail, to him

1. Hermann J. Weigand, *The Modern Ibsen* (New York, 1925), pp. 378–410.

seemed evidence that Ibsen was "no longer able to muster the necessary degree of concentration when he wrote it."

There is no denying these inconsistencies. Weigand is perfectly right in pointing out that it is impossible to tell from the play whether Rubek married Maja before or after he completed his great sculpture "The Day of Resurrection," whether one year or twenty elapsed between Irene's disappearance and the completion of the statue, or whether he has built his luxurious villa on the Taunitzer See very recently or before he met Maja. He is also right that the fact and fiction in Irene's account of her life since she left Rubek are never completely sorted out and that Ibsen leaves Maja's intentions in regard to Ulfhejm somewhat inexplicit.

A somewhat different view might be taken of these inconsistencies and omissions, however. Instead of taking them to be evidence of Ibsen's senility, we might at least consider the possibility that the inconsistencies and omissions not only are deliberate, but are important devices in Ibsen's technique at the culmination of his career. For ten years Ibsen had been experimenting with plays in which he presented a story with a particular mythic shape by means of a revelatory plot which, because of certain calculated omissions and inconsistencies, was not wholly acceptable in realistic terms. He thus reduced the emphasis upon the realistic surface of the plot and increased the emphasis upon the underlying structure of the myth, in effect balancing the mythic structure and the plot structure against each other.

When We Dead Awaken is the most formal of Ibsen's plays. It suggests a string quartet in its economy of means, its three-part structure, and its elaborate interplay among the four major characters: Rubek, an elderly sculptor; Maja, his young, discontented wife; Irene, the model for his masterpiece "The Day of Resurrection"; and Ulfhejm, a vigorous, sensual hunter. The entire play consists of a series of arrangements of these four characters. The first act opens with a long conversation between Rubek and Maja, then almost simultaneously introduces Irene and Ulfhejm, and ends with an equally long conversation between Rubek and Irene. The second act is almost identical in structure, opening with a scene between Rubek and Maja, continuing with a scene between Rubek

194

and Irene, and ending with a brief scene among all four major characters. Act III begins with a scene between Maja and Ulfhejm, continues with a short scene among all four major characters as the two couples pass on the mountain, and ends with a scene between Rubek and Irene. The basic action of the plot thus consists of a gradual, dancelike changing of partners, moving from the Rubek/Maja pairing of the first scene to the Ulfhejm/Maja and Rubek/Irene pairings of the last act.

The almost schematic formality of the plot structure is reinforced by the progression of settings. The entire play consists of Rubek's mythic "ascent to the peaks" and this pattern is subsumed in the settings, beginning with the coastal resort, in a valley by a fjord, of Act I and moving gradually upward to the "mountain health resort" on a "vast treeless plateau" of Act II, and culminating in the "wild, broken mountain top" of Act III.

The structure which underlies these patterns and gives them meaning is the structure of Rubek's life, the sequence of events and choices that have brought him, Irene, and Maja to the living death in which they find themselves at the time of the play. This history is gradually and painfully bared during the course of the play, and the present action can be understood only as part of the larger pattern of the entire history.

The chronology of Rubek's life is rather obscure, as Weigand pointed out, but the sequence of events is clear enough. Many years before, Irene had been both Rubek's model and his inspiration for the masterpiece that won him fame as a sculptor. This statue was called "The Day of Resurrection" and consisted first of a single figure: Rubek recalls, "I wanted to create woman as she will appear when she wakes, pure and undefiled, on the day of resurrection. Not marvelling at what is new, the unknown, the unimagined, but filled with a holy joy at finding herself unchanged— she, a mortal woman!—in the higher, freer, happier kingdom, after the long and dreamless sleep of death."

Irene, apparently, not only inspired the statue, she committed herself completely to Rubek. Rubek reminds her that she left her family and home for him and promised to "serve him in all things." The period of work on the statue was rather extended and Rubek and Irene were intimately attached to each other during this time. They spent their weekends on the Taunitzer See in a little farm-house, and dreamed together of the future and of Rubek's success. Rubek promised to show her "all the glory of the world":

IRENE. I once saw a miraculously beautiful sunrise.

RUBEK. Did you? Where was that?

IRENE. High, high up on a dizzy mountain top. You enticed me up there and promised you would show me all the glory of the world, if—
Stops sharply.

RUBEK. If—? Well?

IRENE. I did as you told me. Followed you to the mountain top. And there I fell on my knees and—worshipped you. And served you.
Is silent for a moment, then quietly.
Then I saw the sunrise.

Despite this intimacy, however, Rubek never made Irene his mistress. "You wronged my inmost being," she tells Rubek, "I stripped myself naked for you to gaze at me. And you never once touched me." It is true that she also tells him that she would have killed him with a sharp needle that she always kept with her if he had touched her, but nevertheless she feels that Rubek has "taken her soul and left her empty." Rubek's explanation of his failure to consummate his relationship with Irene is that he was an artist, "sick with a longing to create the one great work of my life," and that she could serve as the model for the statue only if she remained untouched: "To me, you were something sacred and untouchable, fit only to be adored. I was still young then, Irene. And I was convinced that if I touched you, if I desired you sensually, my vision would be profaned so that I would never be able to achieve what I was striving for. And I still think there is some truth in that." Irene most bitterly remembers Rubek's dismissal of her after the statue was finished. He told her, "I am deeply grateful to you, Irene. This has been an inspiring episode in my life."

If we add to these events Rubek's marriage to Maja, far sepa-rated from them in time but closely related in meaning, the entire configuration constitutes a mythic ascent to the heights. Rubek, figuratively atop a mountain, has adopted his art as a project of the will and has rejected the instinctual side of his nature in favor of

196

the will. His rejection of Irene has been far more than the ending of a casual love affair; it has amounted to a renunciation of a major part of his own nature and to a kind of spiritual murder of Irene. This rejection of the fascinating woman is balanced by his marriage to the gentle woman Maja, who for all her own frustrated sexuality is regarded by Rubek merely as one more outward sign of his fame and success, like his villa on the Taunitzer See.

The period following Irene's departure, the period of the pursuit of Rubek's project of the will, is crucial to the understanding of the play, particularly its theme of the nature of artistic creation. The details of this period are left somewhat shadowy, like the rest of Rubek's life, but its very obscurity makes it more suggestive. Rubek, left alone to pursue his art, has gradually altered "The Day of Resurrection":

> RUBEK. In the years after you left me, Irene, I gained experience and knowledge. I began to envisage "The Day of Resurrection" as something bigger, something—something more complex. That small, round pedestal on which your statue stood erect and lonely—that was no longer big enough to hold all that I now wanted to express.

He has enlarged the pedestal and made the statue a group composition. Out of fissures in the pedestal swarm a throng of ugly figures, "people, with the faces of beasts beneath their human masks. Women and men, as I knew them, from life." The figure of Irene has been moved back into a subordinate position and the radiant expression on her face subdued "to accord with the changed vision I had of life." He has also added himself to the composition as a seated figure dipping his fingers into a spring, a representation of "remorse for a forfeited life."

A similar spirit has informed the other phase of Rubek's career since Irene left. He has turned to carving portrait busts:

> RUBEK. They are not ordinary portrait busts, Maja.
>
> MAJA. Oh, yes they are. These last two or three years—ever since you got that big group finished and out of the house—
>
> RUBEK. Nevertheless, they are not ordinary portraits. Believe me.
>
> MAJA. What are they, then?
>
> RUBEK. There is something hidden within those faces. A secret meaning which people cannot see.
>
> MAJA. Oh, really?

RUBEK. Only I can see it. And I find it intensely amusing. Superficially, there are these "striking likenesses" as they call them, at which people gape, entranced. But deep within, I have sculpted the righteous and estimable faces of horses, the opinionated muzzles of donkeys, the lop ears and shallow brows of dogs, the overgorged chaps of swine, and the dull and brutalized fronts of oxen.

Rubek's art, adopted like Brand's messianic mission and Gregers Werle's service of "the ideal" as a project of the will, has gradually degenerated into a crude misanthropy. Irene is savage in her condemnation of his posing and self-dramatization:

IRENE, *coldly*. Poet!

RUBEK. Why poet?

IRENE. Because you're soft and self-indulgent, and so ready to forgive all your own sins, everything you've ever done or thought. You killed my soul, and then you model yourself as a figure of penance and remorse.
Smiles.
And in your eyes, that settles your account.

Those who are tempted to interpret *When We Dead Awaken* as a rejection of art should consider this exchange carefully. Rubek's art is a false art, not a means of "seeing" life but a defense against it, a project of the will based upon an untenable rejection of the whole self. It must inevitably degenerate, just as the comparable "missions" of Brand, Peer Gynt, Julian, and the rest of Ibsen's protagonists degenerate, as the repressed side of their natures struggles to reassert itself.

Irene, during this period, has undergone a similar spiritual death, even more horrifying because of the deliberately enigmatic way in which she describes it. She has been a music-hall entertainer and, apparently, a prostitute. She has "stood like a statue, naked on a revolving platform, in music halls" and has "been with men." She has been married twice, first to a South American diplomat who shot himself and then to a Russian named von Satow, whom she says she killed "with a fine, sharp dagger I always take to bed with me." She has finally been confined in a hospital for the insane:

IRENE *rises slowly from her chair, trembling.* I was dead for many years. They came and tied me up, tied my arms together behind

198

my back. Then they lowered me into a tomb, with iron bars across the door, and padded walls so that no one up above could hear the shrieks of the dead. But now, slowly, I am beginning to rise from the dead.

Rubek's project of the will has led him and Irene, and Maja as well, to the living death which constitutes the central metaphor of the play and provides its title. This metaphor, as we have seen, appears first in Ibsen's first play and winds its way throughout his work to culminate in this final play. The play begins at the lowest point in Rubek's spiritual life, at the point of the collapse of his project of the will, just before the reappearance of the fascinating woman and the final ascent of the mountain. He finds himself in a gray tomb world as the play opens: He has returned to Norway after a long exile abroad, but he has been unable to renew his spirit by his return. On the contrary, Norway now seems the most deathly of places to him, a place epitomized in the Beckett-like passage in Act I in which he describes the train trip into Norway:

RUBEK. It reminds me of that night we spent in the train, when we were coming up from the Continent—

MAJA. You were asleep the whole time.

RUBEK. Not the whole time. I noticed how silent it was at all the little places we stopped at. I—heard the silence—like you, Maja—And then I realized we had crossed the frontier. Now we were home. I knew it, because at every one of these little roadside halts, the train stopped, and stood quite still—though nothing ever happened.

MAJA. Why did it stop if there was no one there?

RUBEK. Don't know. No one got off, no one got on—and yet the train stood there, absolutely silent, for minute after minute—as it might have been eternity. And at every station I heard two men walking down the platform—one of them had a lantern in his hand—and they muttered to each other, softly, tonelessly, meaninglessly in the night.

MAJA. Yes, you're right. There are always two men, who walk and talk together—

RUBEK. About nothing.

The truth is that Rubek's vision of a dark world from which meaning has departed is a projection of his own deadness. He is as dead as Irene is, as she herself tells him. She has considered killing him, she says, when he said that she was only an episode in his life, as they sat beside the brook recalling their weekends on the Taunitzer See.

IRENE. I took out my knife. I was going to stick it in your back.

RUBEK. Why didn't you?

IRENE. I suddenly realized you were already dead. You'd been dead for years.

RUBEK. Dead?

IRENE. Dead. Like me. We sat there by the Taunitzer See, two clammy corpses, playing our little game together.

The entire play consists of Rubek's "ascent to the peaks" with Irene, an action culminating in the last scene but beginning with Irene's first appearance in Act I. Irene has already begun to "rise from the dead," and in her first conversation with Rubek she challenges him to leave the lowland and ascend the mountain:

IRENE *looks at him, smiles almost imperceptibly, and whispers.* Go high up into the mountains; as high as you can go. Higher, higher— always higher, Arnold.

RUBEK. Are you going up there?

IRENE. Dare you meet me again?

RUBEK. If only we could! Ah, if only we could!

IRENE. Why shouldn't we? If we want to. Come, come, Arnold! Oh, please come up to me—!

The dramatic action of the play itself consists of Rubek's struggle to understand what he has done, to throw off the past, and to be "reborn." Despite his generalized anxiety and his sense of deadness at the beginning of the play, he still believes that his decision upon the heights was right. "I still think there is some truth in that," he tells Irene when he tries to explain why he never touched her, and he still uses his project of the will, his art, to justify the course of his life. But by the end of the act, under Irene's guidance he has begun to realize the meaning of his decision and to feel the re-awakening of old desires:

IRENE. You've forgotten the most precious gift I gave you.

RUBEK. The most precious—? What gift was that?

IRENE. I gave you my soul—young and alive. And left myself empty;

200

soulless. Don't you see? That's why I died, Arnold.
The nun opens the door wide, and stands aside for her. She goes into the pavilion.
RUBEK *stands staring after her; then he whispers.* Irene!

By Act II, Rubek has come to feel that he can no longer go on living without Irene. He tells Maja that she can never understand "what really goes on in an artist's mind" and that he has grown "intolerably bored and tired" of living with her. Maja is by no means disturbed by these harsh words, and she readily suggests that they part. She has by this time apparently become Ulfhejm's mistress. And when Rubek, still reluctant to commit himself fully, does not immediately agree, she even suggests a *ménage a trois.* "Our town house is very large," she tells Rubek. "With a little give and take, there should be room enough in it for three." But when Rubek hesitantly proposes this to Irene later, she curtly replies that their life together "cannot be resurrected" and that all they can do is "go on with the game." When they decide, at the end of the act, to imitate Maja and Ulfhejm in spending a summer night on the mountain, it is in a spirit of playing a game of thinking of what might have been:

RUBEK. Summer night on the mountain! With you!
His eyes meet hers.
Oh, Irene, that could have been our life. And we have wasted it—
IRENE. We only find what we have lost when—
Stops abruptly.
RUBEK. When—?
IRENE. When we dead awaken.
RUBEK *shakes his head sadly.* What do we find then?
IRENE. We find that we have never lived.

Rubek's slow awakening from the dead culminates in the last scene, atop the mountain, at a point exactly parallel to Brand's renunciation of his creed. When Irene tells him it is too late for them, that both of them are dead, he protests that "both in us and around us life rages as fiercely and joyously as ever" and finally fully confesses his crime against Irene and against himself: "I set that dead figure of clay above life, and happiness, and love."

Rubek's and Irene's final lines are full of the ecstasy of a spiritual resurrection:

IRENE. The woman whom you created, rising from the dead, sees life cold and lying on its bier.

RUBEK *throws his arms tightly around her.* Then let us two dead people live life to the full for one short hour before we go down again into our graves!

IRENE. Arnold!

RUBEK. But not here in this half-darkness. Not here, with this hideous dank shroud flapping around us.

IRENE. No, no. Up into the light, where glory shines. Up to the promised mountain top.

RUBEK. Up there we shall celebrate our wedding feast, Irene, my beloved.

IRENE, *proudly.* The sun may look on us, Arnold.

RUBEK. All the powers of light may look on us. And all the powers of darkness, too.
Grips her hand.
Will you come with me now, my bride of grace?

IRENE, *as though transformed.* Freely and willingly, my lord and master.

RUBEK, *leading her.* First we must pass through the mists, Irene. And then—

IRENE. Yes, through the mists. And then up, up to the top of our tower, where it shines in the sunrise.

They begin to climb upward and disappear in the low clouds. The nun appears, searching for Irene, and as an avalanche sweeps down the mountain, burying Rubek and Irene, the nun cries out "Pax vobiscum!" and Maja's happy song of freedom is heard from further down the mountain.

When We Dead Awaken is a fitting culmination to the series of plays that began with *The Master Builder,* in which an elliptical realistic plot is counterpointed against an underlying mythic structure. Ibsen himself apparently viewed the play as the ultimate development of this technique and realized that if he ever wrote another play he would have to turn to another kind of form. He wrote to Moritz Prozor soon after the play appeared, "I cannot say yet whether or not I shall write another play, but if I continue to retain the vigor of mind and body that I enjoy at present, I do not think I shall be able to keep away from the old battlefields permanently. However, if I do appear there again, I shall appear with new weapons and in new armor. You are quite right when you say that the series which ends with the epilogue really began with *The Master Builder*. However, I am reluctant to say more on this subject."

When We Dead Awaken forms the capstone not only of Ibsen's last quartet of plays but of his entire career. Ibsen might have written with equal justice that the play is an epilogue to the series of twenty-six plays that began half a century earlier with *Catiline*. In that first play—and in *Brand,* in which Ibsen had attained his full, mature powers as a dramatist—he had stated very openly the myth upon which his works were to be based: the myth of a spiritual progress from a polluted valley up onto the heights, down again into a living death in the valley, and finally up to an ecstatic death upon the peaks. This myth had provided the emotional substructure to an extraordinarily rich and varied series of dramatic masterpieces. It had been inverted, projected upon the course of world history, submerged beneath the detailed factuality of the realistic style, and brought to the surface again as a counterpoint to otherwise realistic plots. Now, as an epilogue to his works, Ibsen had stated the myth again directly and openly in a play that recalls *Brand* at every point.

The obsessive persistence with which Ibsen returned again and again to the exploration of the schizoid personality and to the development of the myth of the self would suggest its autobiographical basis, even if we knew nothing of Ibsen's lonely childhood, the strength of will with which he mastered the art of dramatic writing, his cold and unsatisfying marriage, and the obvious disparity between the mask of staid respectability he presented to the public and the turbulent and rebellious inner life he revealed in his writings. He himself insisted many times upon the autobiographical character of his work. He once wrote,

Everything that I have written has the closest possible connection with what I have lived through inwardly—even if I have not experienced it outwardly. In every new poem or play I have aimed at my own spiritual emancipation and purification—for no man can escape the responsibilities and the guilts of the society to which he belongs. Hence I once wrote the following lines by way of a dedication in a copy of one of my books:

> Living is a war with the trolls
>   In the depths of the mind and heart;
> Writing means summoning oneself
>   To court and playing the judge's part.

However, if in one sense Brand, Peer Gynt, Mrs. Alving, Gregers Werle, and Arnold Rubek are all Henrik Ibsen, in another sense none of them are. For none of them could have written those dedicatory lines, nor could any of them have written any one of the plays in which Ibsen warred with his personal trolls and summoned himself to court. If the power and conviction of Ibsen's best plays come from their roots in what he himself had "lived through inwardly," it may be also true that, through his art, Ibsen mastered his trolls and attained the self-liberation denied so many of his protagonists.

The dramatic power that Ibsen generated from the personality pattern and the mythic structure he used so often does not result merely from their subjectivity, however. It results in large part from the connections Ibsen was able to make between his personal stresses and those in his society, for as he wrote, "no man can escape the responsibilities and the guilts of the society to which he belongs." The Ibsen protagonist, terrified by a threatening and bewildering outer world, divided against himself, and retreating into obsessive projects of the will, is a remarkably accurate representation of modern man himself. Julian and his Third Empire are a distant foreboding of Hitler and his Third Reich, and Gregers Werle and Hedda Gabler foreshadow a whole world of insecure, "other-directed" organization men. It may be that Ibsen's permanent contribution to dramatic art is his fifty-year search for and attack upon the trolls of modern man.

Index

DATE			